D1241068

TEST YOURSELF CCNA

Cisco Certified Network Associate

(Exam 640-507)

Second Edition

TEST YOURSELF CCNA

Cisco® Certified Network Associate

(Exam 640-507)

Second Edition

Syngress Media, Inc.

Osborne/McGraw-Hill

Berkeley New York St. Louis San Francisco Auckland Bogotá
Hamburg London Madrid Mexico City Milan Montreal New Delhi
Panama City Paris São Paulo Singapore Sydney Tokyo Toronto

Osborne/**McGraw-Hill**
2600 Tenth Street
Berkeley, California 94710
U.S.A.

For information on translations or book distributors outside the U.S.A., or to arrange bulk
purchase discounts for sales promotions, premiums, or fund-raisers, please contact
Osborne/**McGraw-Hill** at the above address.

Test Yourself CCNA Cisco Certified Network Associate (Exam 640-507) Second Edition

1234567890 AGM AGM 01987654321

ISBN 0-07-212668-X

KEY	SERIAL NUMBER
001	YBR75P9KL2
002	LAUF56E3NQ
003	STEMN889MK
004	23NRDQU8P9
005	CCNN4ESZXW

Publisher
Brandon A. Nordin

**Vice President and
Associate Publisher**
Scott Rogers

Editorial Director
Gareth Hancock

Associate Acquisitions Editor
Timothy Green

Editorial Management
Syngress Media, Inc.

Project Editor
Mark Listewnik

Project Manager
Laurie Stewart

Acquisitions Coordinator
Jessica Wilson

Series Editor
Mark Buchmann

Technical Editor
Bradley Dunsmore

Copy Editors
Kathleen Faughnan,
Nancy Faughnan

Proofreaders
Kari Brooks, Anne Cadigan

Computer Designer
Maureen Forys,
Happenstance Type-O-Rama

Illustrator
Jeff Wilson

Series Design
Maureen Forys,
Happenstance Type-O-Rama

Cover Design
Greg Scott

Cover Image
imagebank

This book was composed with QuarkXPress 4.11 on a Macintosh G4.

About Syngress Media

Syngress Media creates books and software for Information Technology professionals seeking skill enhancement and career advancement. Its products are designed to comply with vendor and industry standard course curricula, and are optimized for certification exam preparation. Visit the Syngress Web site at www.syngress.com.

Contributors

John Bankson (CCNA and MCSE+I) is the Network Manager for a large midwestern law firm in Kansas City, Missouri. He specializes in Microsoft BackOffice products, Compaq Servers, and Cisco equipment. John holds a BS in Computer Science and an MS in Management Information Systems. He recently finished upgrading his MCSE certification on the Windows 2000 track and is currently working on his Compaq ASE and Cisco CCNP certifications. He lives in Lenexa, Kansas, and can be reached at johnbankson@yahoo.com.

Mark Burke (CCNA, MCNE, MCSE, and ASE) is a System's Integrator with GE Capital Information Technology Solutions. In his seventh year as an IT professional, he has implemented several workstation, server, and network solutions. Currently he serves in the Network Operations Department for Great-West Life Insurance Company. Mark and his wife, Teresa, live in Winnipeg, Manitoba, Canada together with their two daughters, Michaela and Tazia.

Mark Carter (CCNA) works for Sprint Canada as a Technical Implementation Manager designing enterprise IP, Frame Relay and ATM networks, and delivering Internet services up to OC-3 speeds. He has several years of experience in LAN/WAN design, as well as experience in routing, switching, TCP/IP, SNA and protocol analysis.

Mark holds a Bachelor's Degree in Electrical and Electronic Engineering, majoring in telecommunications, from Nottingham University in the United Kingdom and is currently working towards his CCIE certification. He lives in Vancouver, Canada, with his wife Sylvie and daughter Chloe. When not skiing on the local mountains, Mark can be reached at marc_carter@yahoo.com.

Bradley Dunsmore (A+, Network+, i-Net+, MCDBA, MCSE+I, and CCNA) is currently working for Cisco Systems in Raleigh, North Carolina. He is a Technical Trainer in the Service Provider Division where he develops and issues training to the solution deployment engineers. He has eight years of computer experience with the last four in enterprise networking. Bradley has had stints with Bell Atlantic, Adtran Telecommunications, and Electronic Systems Inc., a Virginia-based systems integrator. He specializes in TCP/IP and LAN/WAN communications in both small and large business environments.

Brian Feeny (CCNP and CCDP) is a Network Engineer for ShreveNet Inc., based in Shreveport, Louisiana. Brian has extensive experience in working with Unix/Linux–based operating systems and networking technologies commonly deployed at ISPs. In his off time, Brian enjoys spending time with his girlfriend Scarlett and her daughter Candace, playing with numerous routers, hammering out PERL code, and making small Linux boxes accomplish big things. Brian can be reached via email at signal@shreve.net.

Michael Flannagan (CCNA and CCDA) is a Senior Cisco Engineer for Clear Channel Communications in San Antonio, Texas. He is a Cisco Sales Expert (SMB) and has passed the Cisco Internetwork Design Exam. He is currently preparing to take the CCIE/Design exam, the newest track available for CCIE Certification.

Prior to joining Clear Channel Communications, he was a Senior Consultant working with one of the world's largest pharmaceutical companies on an extensive Quality of Service project. His background also includes lead roles in several major network design projects throughout the United States and Western Europe.

Andre' Paree-Huff (CCNP, CCDA, MCSE+I, ASE, A+, Network+, and i-Net+) has been working in the computer field for over eight years. He is currently working for Compaq Computer Corporation as a Network Support Engineer level III for the North America Customer Support Center in Colorado Springs, Colorado. Andre' troubleshoots network hardware, specializing in Layer 2 and 3 of the OSI model. Andre' has co-authored four network-related technical manuals and has been a technical editor on many others. He is currently working toward his CCIE.

Debra Littlejohn Shinder (MCSE, MCP+I, and MCT) is an instructor in the AATP program at Eastfield College, Dallas County Community College District, where she has taught since 1992. She is Webmaster for the cities of Seagoville and Sunnyvale, Texas, as well as the family Web site at www.shinder.net. She and her husband, Dr. Thomas W. Shinder, provide consulting and technical support services to Dallas area organizations. She is also the proud mom of a daughter, Kristen, who is currently serving in the U.S. Navy in Italy, and a son, Kris, who is a high school chess champion. Deb has been a writer for most her life and has published numerous articles in both technical and non-technical fields. She can be contacted at deb@shinder.net.

Bob Watkins (MCSE, CCNA, MCP+I, and A+) has been a consultant since 1997 in the networking and ISP disciplines. He has been a lead engineer on Y2K compliance projects, ISP backbone migrations, PLC QA, Database migration and backup/disaster recovery projects. Most recently, he worked on packaging over 2,000 software titles for delivery via SMS to 10,000 Windows 2000 Professional desktops with eight other members of his drop team. This current project is for a Fortune 50 oil company in the midwest, planning the assembly of a larger team for future Microsoft Windows 2000 Desktop and Server deployment projects.

Bob is currently pursuing his CCDA to plan and implement an infrastructure to support these projects. Bob is also the Webmaster for six Web sites including shop-r-mall.com and ContractMCSE.com, which his wife owns. They enjoy woodworking and reading on the porch in the mountains of Maryland. He can be reached at contractmcse@mindspring.com.

Bradley J. Wilson (CCNA, CCDA, MCSE, MCP+I, CNX-A, NNCSS, MCT, and CTT) is an independent contractor based out of Boston, Massachusetts, and a graduate of the University of Michigan-Flint. Following a two-year term at Bay Networks as a course developer and technical trainer, Bradley now straddles the fence between the technical training and the network engineering worlds. As a trainer, his clients have included Learning Tree, Glow Training Center, Interspeed, Niche Networks, and the Center for Advanced Networking. As a network engineer, Bradley has maintained networks for IBM/Lotus, Raytheon, Linguistic Systems Inc., and Millenium Digital Media and can be reached at analogkid01@mindspring.com.

Technical Editor

Bradley Dunsmore (A+, Network+, i-Net+, MCDBA, MCSE+I, and CCNA) is currently working for Cisco Systems in Raleigh, North Carolina. He is a Technical Trainer in the Service Provider Division where he develops and issues training to the solution deployment engineers. He has eight years of computer experience with the last four in enterprise networking. Bradley has had stints with Bell Atlantic, Adtran Telecommunications, and Electronic Systems Inc., a Virginia-based systems integrator. He specializes in TCP/IP and LAN/WAN communications in both small and large business environments.

Series Editor

Mark Buchmann (CCIE and CCSI) is a Cisco Certified Internetworking Expert (CCIE) and has been a Certified Cisco Systems Instructor (CCSI) since 1995. He is the owner of MAB Enterprises, Inc., a company providing consulting, network support, training, and various other services. Mark is also a co-owner of www.CertaNet.com, a company providing on-line certification assistance for a variety of network career paths including all the various Cisco certifications.

In his free time, he enjoys spending time with his family and boating. He currently lives in Raleigh, North Carolina. Mark is Series Editor for Syngress Media Cisco Certification titles.

ACKNOWLEDGMENTS

We would like to thank the following people:

- All the incredibly hard-working folks at Osborne/McGraw-Hill: Brandon Nordin, Scott Rogers, Gareth Hancock, Tim Green, and Jessica Wilson for their help in launching a great series and being solid team players.
- Laurie Stewart and Maureen Forys for their help in fine-tuning the project.

CONTENTS

13 Configuring Point-to-Point Protocol 267

14 Configuring Frame Relay Services 293

PREFACE

This book's primary objective is to help you prepare for and pass the CCNA Cisco Certified Network Associate exam (640-507), so you can reap the career benefits of certification. We believe that the only way to do this is to help you increase your knowledge and build your skills. After completing this book, you should feel confident that you have reviewed and practiced the necessary skills that Cisco has established for the exam.

In This Book

This book is organized in such a way as to serve as a review for the Cisco Certified Network Associate exam. Each chapter covers a major aspect of the exam, with an emphasis on the "why" as well as the "how to" of working with and supporting Cisco products.

In Every Chapter

We've created a set of chapter components that call your attention to important items, reinforce important points, and provide helpful exam-taking hints. Take a look at what you'll find in every chapter.

Test Yourself Objectives

Every chapter begins with a list of Test Yourself Objectives—what you need to know in order to pass the section on the exam dealing with the chapter topic. Each objective in this list will be discussed in the chapter and can be easily identified by the clear headings that give the name and corresponding number of the objective, so you'll always know an objective when you see it! Objectives are drilled down to the most important details— essentially what you need to know about the objectives and what to expect from the exam in relation to them. Should you find you need further review on any particular objective, you will find that the objective headings correspond to the chapters of Osborne/McGraw-Hill's *CCNA Cisco Certified Network Associate Study Guide*.

Exam Watch Notes

Exam Watch notes call attention to information about, and potential pitfalls in, the exam. These helpful hints are written by authors who have taken the exams and received their certification; who better to tell you what to worry about? They know what you're about to go through!

Practice Questions and Answers

In each chapter you will find detailed practice questions for the exam, followed by a Quick Answer Key where you can quickly check your answers. The In-Depth Answers section contains full explanations of both the correct and incorrect choices.

The Practice Exam

If you have had your fill of explanations, review questions, and answers, the time has come to test your knowledge. Turn toward the end of this book to the Test Yourself Practice Exam where you'll find a simulation exam. Lock yourself in your office or clear the kitchen table, set a timer, and jump in.

About the Web Site

Syngress Media and Osborne/McGraw-Hill invite you to download one free practice exam for the CCNA exam (640-507). Please visit www.syngress.com or www. certificationpress.com for details.

INTRODUCTION

This introduction covers the importance of your CCNA certification and prepares you for taking the actual examination. It gives you a few pointers on methods of preparing for the exam, including how to study and register, what to expect, and what to do on exam day.

CATCH THE WAVE!

Congratulations on your pursuit of Cisco certification! In this fast-paced world of networking, few certification programs are as valuable as the one offered by Cisco.

The networking industry has virtually exploded in recent years, accelerated by nonstop innovation and the Internet's popularity. Cisco has stayed at the forefront of this tidal wave, maintaining a dominant role in the industry.

The networking industry is highly competitive, and evolving technology only increases in its complexity, so the rapid growth of the networking industry has created a vacuum of qualified people. There simply aren't enough skilled networking people to meet the demand. Even the most experienced professionals must keep current with the latest technology in order to provide the skills that the industry demands. That's where Cisco certification programs can help networking professionals succeed as they pursue their careers.

Cisco started its certification program many years ago, offering only the designation Cisco Certified Internetwork Expert (CCIE). Through the CCIE program, Cisco provided a means to meet the growing demand for experts in the field of networking. However, the CCIE tests are brutal, with a failure rate of over 80 percent. (Fewer than 5 percent of candidates pass on their first attempt.) As you might imagine, very few people ever attain CCIE status.

In early 1998, Cisco recognized the need for intermediate certifications, and several new programs were created. Four intermediate certifications were added: CCNA (Cisco Certified Network Associate), CCNP (Cisco Certified Network Professional),

CCDA (Cisco Certified Design Associate), and CCDP (Cisco Certified Design Professional). In addition, several specialties were added to the CCIE certifications; currently CCIE candidates can receive their CCIE in five areas: Routing and Switching, WAN Switching, ISP-Dial, SNA/IP Integration, and Design.

CCNA Advice: *We would encourage you to take beta tests when they are available. Not only are the beta exams less expensive than the final exams (some are even free!), but also, if you pass the beta, you will receive credit for passing the exam. If you don't pass the beta, you will have seen every question in the pool of available questions and can use this information when you prepare to take the exam for the second time. Remember to jot down important information immediately after the exam if you didn't pass. You will have to do this after leaving the exam area, since materials written during the exam are retained by the testing center. This information can be helpful when you need to determine which areas of the exam were most challenging for you as you study for the subsequent test.*

WHY VENDOR CERTIFICATION?

Over the years, vendors have created their own certification programs because of industry demand. This demand arises when the marketplace needs skilled professionals and an easy way to identify them. Vendors benefit because it promotes people skilled in their product. Professionals benefit because it boosts their careers. Employers benefit because it helps them identify qualified people.

In the networking industry, technology changes too often and too quickly to rely on traditional means of certification, such as universities and trade associations. Because of the investment and effort required to keep network certification programs current, vendors are the only organizations suited to keep pace with the changes. In general, such vendor certification programs are excellent, with most of them requiring a solid foundation in the essentials, as well as their particular product line.

Corporate America has come to appreciate these vendor certification programs and the value they provide. Employers recognize that certifications, like university degrees, do not guarantee a level of knowledge, experience, or performance; rather, they establish a baseline for comparison. By seeking to hire vendor-certified employees, a company can assure itself that not only has it found a person skilled in networking, but also it has hired a person skilled in the specific products the company uses.

Technical professionals have also begun to recognize the value of certification and the impact it can have on their careers. By completing a certification program, professionals gain an endorsement of their skills from a major industry source. This endorsement can boost their current position, and it makes finding the next job even easier. Often a certification determines whether a first interview is even granted.

Today a certification may place you ahead of the pack. Tomorrow it will be a necessity to keep from being left in the dust.

CCNA
@dvice

CCNA Advice: Signing up for an exam has become easier with a Web-based test registration system. To sign up for the CCNA exams, access http://www.2test.com and register for the Cisco Career Certification path. You will need to get an Internet account and password if you do not already have one for 2test.com. Just select the option for first-time registration, and the Web site will walk you through that process. The registration wizard even provides maps to the testing centers, something that is not available when you call Sylvan Prometric on the telephone.

CISCO'S CERTIFICATION PROGRAM

Cisco now has a number of certifications for the Routing and Switching career track, as well as for the WAN Switching career track. While Cisco recommends a series of courses for each of these certifications, they are not required. Ultimately, certification is dependent upon a candidate's passing a series of exams. With the right experience and study materials, you can pass each of these exams without taking the associated class.

Cisco has recently changed the certification track for the CCNA and CCNP exams. They have updated the exam tracks to accommodate changes in Cisco technology. The new tracks are called "CCNA 2.0" and "CCNP 2.0" and it replaces the former tracks, called "CCNA 1.0" and "CCNP 1.0." Table 1 shows the Cisco CCNP 1.0 track. Table 2 shows the Cisco CCNP 2.0 exam track.

TABLE 1

CCNP 1.0 Track

Exam Name	Exam Number
CCNA 1.0 or CCNA 2.0	640-407 or 640-507
Advanced Cisco Router Configuration (ACRC)*	640-403
Cisco LAN Switch Configuration (CLSC)*	640-404
Configuring, Managing, and Troubleshooting Dialup Services (CMTD)*	640-405
Cisco Internetwork Troubleshooting (CIT)	640-440
* The Foundation Routing and Switching exam (640-409) can be taken in place of the ACRC, CLSC, and CMTD exams.	

TABLE 2

CCNP 2.0 Track

Exam Name	Exam Number
CCNA 1.0 or CCNA 2.0	640-407 or 640-507
Routing*	640-503
Switching*	640-504
Remote Access*	640-505
Support	640-506
* The new Foundation Routing and Switching exam (640-509) can be taken in place of the Routing, Switching, and Remote Access exams.	

As you can see, the CCNA is the foundation of the Routing and Switching track, after which candidates can pursue the Network Support path to CCNP and CCIE, or the Network Design path to CCDA, CCDP, and to CCIE Design.

Cisco recommends that any new candidate planning to achieve Cisco certification follow the 2.0 exam track. Cisco retired the 1.0 exam track on July 31, 2000.

CCNA
Online

CCNA Online: In addition to the technical objectives that are being tested for each exam, you will find much more useful information on Cisco's Web site at http://www.cisco.com/warp/public/10/wwtraining/certprog. You will find information on becoming certified, exam-specific information, sample test questions, and the latest news on Cisco certification. This is the most important site you will find on your journey to becoming Cisco certified.

CCNA
Advice

CCNA Advice: When I find myself stumped answering multiple-choice questions, I use my scratch paper to write down the two or three answers I consider the strongest, and then underline the answer I feel is most likely correct. Here is an example of what my scratch paper looks like when I've gone through the test once:

21. B or <u>C</u>
33. <u>A</u> or C

It is extremely helpful to mark the question and then continue. You can return to the question and immediately pick up your thought process where you left off. Use this technique to avoid having to re-read and re-think questions.

You will also need to use your scratch paper during complex, text-based scenario questions to create visual images to help you understand the question. For example, during the CCNA exam you will need to draw multiple networks and the connections between them or calculate a subnet mask for a given network. By drawing the layout or working the calculation while you are interpreting the question, you may find a hint that you would not have found without your own visual aid. This technique is especially helpful if you are a visual learner.

COMPUTER-BASED TESTING

In a perfect world, you would be assessed for your true knowledge of a subject, not simply how you respond to a series of test questions. But life isn't perfect, and it just isn't practical to evaluate everyone's knowledge on a one-to-one basis. (Cisco actually does have a one-to-one evaluation, but it's reserved for the CCIE Laboratory exam, and the waiting list is quite long.)

For the majority of its certifications, Cisco evaluates candidates using a computer-based testing service operated by Sylvan Prometric. This service is quite popular in the industry, and it is used for a number of vendor certification programs, including Novell's CNE and Microsoft's MCSE. Thanks to Sylvan Prometric's large number of facilities, exams can be administered worldwide, generally in the same town as a prospective candidate.

For the most part, Sylvan Prometric exams work similarly from vendor to vendor. However, there is an important fact to know about Cisco's exams: They use the traditional Sylvan Prometric test format, not the newer adaptive format. This gives the candidate an advantage, since the traditional format allows answers to be reviewed and revised during the test. (The adaptive format does not.)

CCNA
ⓐdvice

CCNA Advice: Many experienced test takers do not go back and change answers unless they have a good reason to do so. You should change an answer only when you feel you may have misread or misinterpreted the question the first time. Nervousness may make you second-guess every answer and talk yourself out of a correct one.

To discourage simple memorization, Cisco exams present a different set of questions every time the exam is administered. In the development of the exam, hundreds of questions are compiled and refined, using beta testers. From this large collection, a random sampling is drawn for each test.

Each Cisco exam has a specific number of questions and test duration. Testing time is typically generous, and the time remaining is always displayed in the corner of the testing screen, along with the number of remaining questions. If time expires during an exam, the test terminates, and incomplete answers are counted as incorrect.

CCNA Advice: I have found it extremely helpful to put a check next to each objective as I find it is satisfied by the proposed solution. If the proposed solution does not satisfy an objective, you do not need to continue with the rest of the objectives. Once you have determined which objectives are fulfilled you can count your check marks and answer the question appropriately. This is a very effective testing technique!

At the end of the exam, your test is immediately graded, and the results are displayed on the screen. Scores for each subject area are also provided, but the system will not indicate which specific questions were missed. A report is automatically printed at the proctor's desk for your files. The test score is electronically transmitted back to Cisco.

In the end, this computer-based system of evaluation is reasonably fair. You might feel that one or two questions were poorly worded; this can certainly happen, but you shouldn't worry too much. Ultimately, it's all factored into the required passing score.

Question Types

Cisco exams pose questions in a variety of formats, most of which are discussed here. As candidates progress toward the more advanced certifications, the difficulty of the exams is intensified, through both the subject matter and the question formats.

CCNA Online: In order to pass these challenging exams, you may want to talk with other test takers to determine what is being tested, and what to expect in terms of difficulty. The most helpful way to communicate with other CCNA hopefuls is the Cisco mailing list. With this mailing list, you will receive email every day from other members, discussing everything imaginable concerning Cisco networking equipment and certification. Access http://www.cisco.com/warp/public/841.html to learn how to subscribe to this source of a wealth of information.

True/False Questions

The classic true/false question format is not used in the Cisco exams, for the obvious reason that a simple guess has a 50 percent chance of being correct. Instead, true/false questions are posed in multiple-choice format, requiring the candidate to identify the true or false statement from a group of selections.

Multiple-Choice Questions

Multiple choice is the primary format for questions in Cisco exams. These questions may be posed in a variety of ways.

Select the Correct Answer

This is the classic multiple-choice question, in which the candidate selects a single answer from a minimum of four choices. In addition to the question's wording, the choices are presented in a Windows radio button format, in which only one answer can be selected at a time. The question will instruct you to "Select the best answer" when they are looking for just one answer.

Select the Three Correct Answers

The multiple-answer version is similar to the single-choice version, but multiple answers must be provided. This is an all-or-nothing format; all the correct answers must be selected, or the entire question is incorrect. In this format, the question specifies exactly how many answers must be selected. Choices are presented in a check box format, allowing more than one answer to be selected. In addition, the testing software prevents too many answers from being selected.

Select All That Apply

The open-ended version is the most difficult multiple-choice format, since the candidate does not know how many answers should be selected. As with the multiple-answer version, all the correct answers must be selected to gain credit for the question. If too many answers or not enough answers are selected, no credit is given. This format presents choices in check box format, but the testing software does not advise the candidates whether they've selected the correct number of answers.

CCNA Online: Make it easy on yourself and find some "braindumps." These are notes about the exam from test takers, which indicate the most difficult concepts tested, what to look out for, and sometimes even what not to bother studying. Several of these can be found at http://www.dejanews.com. Simply do a search for CCNA and browse the recent postings. Another good resource is at http://www.groupstudy.com. Beware however of the person that posts a question reported to have been on the test and its answer. First, the question and its answer may be incorrect. Second, this is a violation of Cisco's confidentiality agreement, which you as a candidate must agree to prior to taking the exam. Giving out specific information regarding a test violates this agreement and could result in the revocation of your certification status.

Freeform Response

Freeform responses are prevalent in Cisco's advanced exams, particularly where the subject focuses on router configuration and commands. In the freeform format, no choices are provided. Instead, the test prompts for user input, and the candidate must type the correct answer. This format is similar to an essay question, except the response must be specific, allowing the computer to evaluate the answer.

For example, the question

Type the command for viewing routes learned via the EIGRP protocol.

requires the answer:

```
show ip route eigrp
```

For safety's sake, you should completely spell out router commands, rather than using abbreviations. In this example, the abbreviated command SH IP ROU EI works on a real router, but is counted as wrong by the testing software. The freeform response questions almost always are answered by commands used in the Cisco IOS. As you progress in your track for your CCNA, you will find these freeform response questions increasingly prevalent.

Fill-in-the-Blank Questions

Fill-in-the-blank questions are less common in Cisco exams. They may be presented in multiple-choice or freeform response format.

Exhibits

Exhibits, usually showing a network diagram or a router configuration, accompany many exam questions. These exhibits are displayed in a separate window, which is opened by clicking the Exhibit button at the bottom of the screen. In some cases, the testing center may provide exhibits in printed format at the start of the exam.

Scenario-based Questions

While the normal line of questioning tests a candidate's "book knowledge," scenarios add a level of complexity. Rather than asking only technical questions, they apply the candidate's knowledge to real-world situations.

Scenarios generally consist of one or two paragraphs and an exhibit that describes a company's needs or network configuration. This description is followed by a series of questions and problems that challenge the candidate's ability to address the situation. Scenario-based questions are commonly found in exams relating to network design, but they appear to some degree in each of the Cisco exams.

CCNA
advice

CCNA Advice: You will know when you are coming to a series of scenario questions because they are preceded by a blue screen, indicating that the following questions will have the same scenario, but different solutions. You must remember that the scenario will be the same during the series of questions, which means that you do not have to spend time reading the scenario again.

STUDYING TECHNIQUES

First and foremost, give yourself plenty of time to study. Networking is a complex field, and you can't expect to cram what you need to know into a single study session. It is a field best learned over time, by studying a subject and then applying your knowledge. Build yourself a study schedule and stick to it, but be reasonable about the pressure you put on yourself, especially if you're studying in addition to your regular duties at work.

CCNA
advice

CCNA Advice: One easy technique to use in studying for certification exams is the 30-minutes-per-day effort. Simply study for a minimum of 30 minutes every day. It is a small but significant commitment. On a day when you just can't focus, then give up at 30 minutes. On a day when it flows completely for you, study longer. As long as you have more of the flow days, your chances of succeeding are extremely high.

Second, practice and experiment. In networking, you need more than knowledge; you need understanding, too. You can't just memorize facts to be effective; you need to understand why events happen, how things work, and (most important) how and why they break.

The best way to gain deep understanding is to take your book knowledge to the lab. Try it out. Make it work. Change it a little. Break it. Fix it. Snoop around "under the hood." If you have access to a network analyzer, like Network Associate Sniffer, put it to use. You can gain amazing insight to the inner workings of a network by watching devices communicate with each other.

Unless you have a very understanding boss, don't experiment with router commands on a production router. A seemingly innocuous command can have a nasty side effect. If you don't have a lab, your local Cisco office or Cisco users' group may be able to help. Many training centers also allow students access to their lab equipment during off-hours.

Another excellent way to study is through case studies. Case studies are articles or interactive discussions that offer real-world examples of how technology is applied to meet a need. These examples can serve to cement your understanding of a technique or technology by seeing it put to use. Interactive discussions offer added value because you can also pose questions of your own. User groups are an excellent source of examples, since the purpose of these groups is to share information and learn from each other's experiences.

The Cisco Networker's conference is not to be missed. Although renowned for its wild party and crazy antics, this conference offers a wealth of information. Held every year in cities around the world, it includes three days of technical seminars and presentations on a variety of subjects. As you might imagine, it's very popular. You have to register early to get the classes you want.

Then, of course, there is the Cisco Web site. This little gem is loaded with collections of technical documents and white papers. As you progress to more advanced subjects, you will find great value in the large number of examples and reference materials available. But be warned: You need to do a lot of digging to find the really good stuff. Often your only option is to browse every document returned by the search engine to find exactly the one you need. This effort pays off. Most CCIEs I know have compiled six to ten binders of reference material from Cisco's site alone.

SCHEDULING YOUR EXAM

The Cisco exams are scheduled by calling Sylvan Prometric directly at (800) 829-6387. For locations outside the United States, your local number can be found on Sylvan's Web site at http://www.prometric.com. Sylvan representatives can schedule your exam, but they don't have information about the certification programs. Questions about certifications should be directed to Cisco's training department.

This Sylvan telephone number is specific to Cisco exams, and it goes directly to the Cisco representatives inside Sylvan. These representatives are familiar enough with the exams to find them by name, but it's best if you have the specific exam number handy when you call. After all, you wouldn't want to be scheduled and charged for the wrong exam (for example, the instructor's version, which is significantly harder).

Exams can be scheduled up to a year in advance, although it's really not necessary. Generally, scheduling a week or two ahead is sufficient to reserve the day and time you prefer. When you call to schedule, operators will search for testing centers in your area. For convenience, they can also tell which testing centers you've used before.

Sylvan accepts a variety of payment methods, with credit cards being the most convenient. When you pay by credit card, you can even take tests the same day you call—provided, of course, that the testing center has room. (Quick scheduling can be handy, especially if you want to retake an exam immediately.) Sylvan will mail you a receipt and confirmation of your testing date, although this generally arrives after the test has been taken. If you need to cancel or reschedule an exam, remember to call at least one day before your exam, or you'll lose your test fee.

When you register for the exam, you will be asked for your ID number. This number is used to track your exam results back to Cisco. It's important that you use the same ID number each time you register, so that Cisco can follow your progress. Address information provided when you first register is also used by Cisco to ship certificates and other related material. In the United States, your Social Security number is commonly used as your ID number. However, Sylvan can assign you a unique ID number if you prefer not to use your Social Security number.

Table 3 shows the available CCNA and CCNP 2.0 exams and the number of questions and duration of each. This information is subject to change as Cisco revises the exams, so it's a good idea to verify the details when you register for an exam.

TABLE 3	Exam Title	Exam Number	Number of Questions	Duration (minutes)	Exam Fee (US$)
Cisco Exam Lengths and Question Counts	CCNA 2.0	640-507	70–80	90	$100
	Routing 2.0	640-503	80	90	$100
	Switching 2.0	640-504	80	90	$100
	Remote Access 2.0	640-505	80	90	$100
	Support 2.0	640-506	80	90	$100

In addition to the regular Sylvan Prometric testing sites, Cisco also offers facilities for taking exams free of charge at each Networkers Conference in the United States. As you might imagine, this option is quite popular, so reserve your exam time as soon as you arrive at the conference.

ARRIVING AT THE EXAM

As with any test, you'll be tempted to cram the night before. Resist that temptation. You should know the material by this point, and if you're too groggy in the morning, you won't remember what you studied anyway. Instead, get a good night's sleep.

Arrive early for your exam; it gives you time to relax and review key facts. Take the opportunity to review your notes. If you get burned out on studying, you can usually start your exam a few minutes early. On the other hand, I don't recommend arriving late. Your test could be canceled, or you might be left without enough time to complete the exam.

When you arrive at the testing center, you'll need to sign in with the exam administrator. In order to sign in, you need to provide two forms of identification. Acceptable forms include government-issued IDs (for example, passport or driver's license), credit cards, and company ID badge. One form of ID must include a photograph.

Aside from a brain full of facts, you don't need to bring anything else to the exam. In fact, your brain is about all you're allowed to take into the exam. All the tests are closed book, meaning that you don't get to bring any reference materials with you.

You're also not allowed to take any notes out of the exam room. The test administrator will provide you with paper and a pencil. Some testing centers may provide a small marker board instead.

Calculators are not allowed, so be prepared to do any necessary math (such as hex-binary-decimal conversions or subnet masks) in your head or on paper. Additional paper is available if you need it.

Leave your pager and telephone in the car, or turn them off. They only add stress to the situation, since they are not allowed in the exam room, and can sometimes still be heard if they ring outside the room. Purses, books, and other materials must be left with the administrator before you enter. While you're in the exam room, it's important that you don't disturb other candidates; talking is not allowed during the exam.

In the exam room, the exam administrator logs onto your exam, and you have to verify that your ID number and the exam number are correct. If this is the first time you've taken a Cisco test, you can select a brief tutorial for the exam software. Before the test begins, you will be provided with facts about the exam, including the duration, the number of questions, and the score required for passing. Then the clock starts ticking, and the fun begins.

The testing software is Windows-based, but you won't have access to the main desktop or to any of the accessories. The exam is presented in full screen, with a single question per screen. Navigation buttons allow you to move between questions. In the upper right corner of the screen, counters show the number of questions and time remaining.

The Grand Finale

When you're confident with all your answers, finish the exam by submitting it for grading. After what will seem like the longest ten seconds of your life, the testing software will respond with your score. This is usually displayed as a bar graph, showing the minimum passing score, your score, and a PASS/FAIL indicator.

If you're curious, you can review the statistics of your score at this time. Answers to specific questions are not presented; rather, questions are lumped into categories, and results are tallied for each category. This detail is also given on a report that has been automatically printed at the exam administrator's desk.

As you leave the exam, you'll need to leave your scratch paper behind or return it to the administrator. (Some testing centers track the number of sheets you've been given, so be sure to return them all.) In exchange, you'll receive a copy of the test report.

This report will be embossed with the testing center's seal, and you should keep it in a safe place. Normally, the results are automatically transmitted to Cisco, but occasionally you might need the paper report to prove that you passed the exam. Your personnel file is probably a good place to keep this report; the file tends to follow you everywhere, and it doesn't hurt to have favorable exam results turn up during a performance review.

RETESTING

If you don't pass the exam, don't be discouraged—networking is complex stuff. Try to have a good attitude about the experience, and get ready to try again. Consider yourself a little more educated. You know the format of the test a little better, and the report shows which areas you need to strengthen.

If you bounce back quickly, you'll probably remember several of the questions you might have missed. This will help you focus your study efforts in the right area. Serious go-getters will reschedule the exam for a couple of days after the previous attempt, while the study material is still fresh in their minds.

Ultimately, remember that Cisco certifications are valuable because they're hard to get. After all, if anyone could get one, what value would it have? In the end, it takes a good attitude and a lot of studying, but you can do it!

CISCO CERTIFIED NETWORK ASSOCIATE

1

Introduction to Internetworking

I n order to become a CCNA, you will need to have a solid working knowledge of the OSI model, which defines the hierarchical structure of data packets as well as each of the layers within that seven-layer model. It is not our intention to tell you that certain layers are more important than others, but as the CCNA is a certification that demonstrates foundational knowledge of internetworking and Cisco equipment, the lower (or more fundamental) layers will likely be the ones about which you should possess the most knowledge. Everything starts with Layer 1. Switching happens at Layer 2, and routing at Layer 3. These are the fundamental concepts that you will use for the rest of your internetworking life.

TEST YOURSELF OBJECTIVE 1.01

The Internetworking Model

Internetworking is the process and methodology of connecting multiple networks without regard to their individual physical topology. Although certain internetworking technologies have distance limitations, the overall concept of internetworking is not specifically concerned with physical distance as it relates to interconnectivity. Interconnectivity means, very simply, connecting two things regardless of what is between them. The Internet is the world's largest internetwork and provides interconnectivity to millions of people, whether they use Macintosh or IBM-compatible computers, Ethernet or token ring LAN technologies, or T1s or 14.4 modems. The ability to interconnect many disparate technologies depends upon the concept of interoperability. Interoperability is the methodology applied to make data understandable to computers that use proprietary, or simply different, operating systems and languages.

The OSI model is a seven-layer protocol suite model that provides a hierarchical tool for understanding networking technology, as well as a basis for current and future network developments. The OSI model layers are Application (7), Presentation (6), Session (5), Transport (4), Network (3), Data-Link (2), and Physical (1). A common mnemonic device for remembering these seven layers is **All People Seem To Need Data Processing.** As data is passed down through the layers, each layer wraps the data in a header. This is known as *wrapping the data* or, more officially, as *encapsulation.*

■ Internetworking is the process and methodology applied to connecting multiple networks, regardless of their physical topologies and distance.

- Interconnectivity is the means of transporting information between computers—inclusive of the physical media, the data packaging mechanism, and the routing between multiple network equipment pieces—from the starting node to the destination node.

- Interoperability is the methodology applied to make data understandable to computers that use proprietary, or simply different, computer operating systems and languages.

- The OSI model provides a hierarchical tool for understanding networking technology, as well as a basis for current and future network developments.

- The OSI model is a seven-layer protocol suite model.

- Encapsulation is the process of adding a header to the data or wrapping the data.

exam **Watch**

So, exactly what is Layer 3 switching? In a word: routing. The differences between Layer 3 switching and routing are largely irrelevant. For the majority of Cisco products out there, Layer 3 switching is really a clever way of saying "we stuck a router into a switch," so don't be confused if you've never worked with Layer 3 switching before and see a question about it.

QUESTIONS

1.01: The Internetworking Model

1. A customer needs you to help him understand the difference between a switch and a router. You explain to him that, unlike a switch, a router is a device that functions at which layer of the OSI model?

   A. Layer 1

   B. Layer 2

   C. Layer 3

   D. Layer 4

2. What is an internetwork?
   A. The connection of more than one network
   B. The connection of three or more networks
   C. The connection of five of more networks
   D. All of the above

3. What is the proper order of the OSI model layers, from highest to lowest?
   A. Physical, Data-Link, Network, Transport, Session, Presentation, Application
   B. Application, Presentation, Session, Transport, Network, Data-Link, Physical
   C. Data-Link, Physical, Session, Transport, Network, Presentation, Application
   D. Application, Physical, Session, Transport, Network, Presentation, Data-Link

TEST YOURSELF OBJECTIVE 1.02

Physical and Data-Link Layers

The Physical layer, Layer 1, defines the mechanical and electrical specifications for a bit stream (1s and 0s) and synchronizes network timing. Layer 1 defines the way data is transferred to the wire (Cat5 Cable, Fiber, etc.). V.35 is a standard Physical layer interface suitable for relatively low-speed connections to a packet network at speeds up to 48 Kbps, and beyond, even to 4Mbps. HSSI, on the other hand, is a DTE/DCE interface that handles high-speed communication over WAN links. Layer 2, the Data-Link layer (or the *link layer*), consists of two sublayers. The upper is the LLC and the lower is the MAC. Also note that encapsulated data at a layer is called a *frame*.

There are some differences in specifications that you should keep in mind when taking your CCNA exam. The IEEE's standard for Ethernet, 802.3, identifies the standard for the framing of Ethernet (the MAC layer of Layer 2, LLC) and the physical cabling. DIX Ethernet does not conform to this standard and instead defines the entire link and Physical layer attributes. IBM Token Ring networks are nearly identical to and compatible with the IEEE 802.5 specification that was developed later and based on IBM's Token Ring. The FDDI standard specifies the physical and MAC portions of the Data-Link layers for a token passing, dual-ring topology using fiber optic media at 100 Mbps.

When dealing with serial connections, especially ISDN connections, here are a few other things to keep in mind as you head into the CCNA exam: SLIP is a legacy link layer protocol for providing serial connections between two networks, or between a network and a remote node. PPP includes enhancements such as encryption, error control, authentication, dynamic IP addressing, multiprotocol support, and automatic connection negotiation. PPP will work over serial lines, regardless of speed.

- The Physical layer, or Layer 1, defines the mechanical specifications and electrical databit-stream.

- The Data-Link layer, or Layer 2, is also known as the link layer. It consists of two sublayers. The LLC is the upper level and the lower level is the MAC.

- The V.35 standard is a Physical layer protocol suitable for connections to a packet network at speeds up to 48 Kbps, and beyond, even to 4 Mbps.

- HSSI is a DTE/DCE interface that handles high-speed communication over WAN links.

- BRI is an ISDN term for an ISDN connection consisting of two B channels at 64 Kbps and one D channel at 16 Kbps.

- 802.3 specifies different Physical layer MAC address portions of the layer. The DIX Ethernet specifies one entire physical and Data-Link layer. 802.3 specifies different Physical layers, but DIX Ethernet specifies just one.

- Token Ring networks are compatible with the IEEE 802.5 specification developed later, which was based on IBM's Token Ring.

- The FDDI standard specifies the physical and MAC portion of the Data-Link layers for a token passing, dual-ring topology using fiber optic media at 100 Mbps.

- Synchronizing network timing is handled at the Physical layer of the OSI model.

- SLIP is a legacy Unix Data-Link layer protocol for providing serial connections between two networks, or between a network and a remote node.

- PPP includes enhancements such as encryption, error control, security, dynamic IP addressing, multiple protocol support, and automatic connection negotiation. PPP will work over serial lines, ISDN, and high-speed WAN links.

- Frame Relay is a widely used packet-switched WAN protocol standardized by the ITU-T. Frame Relay relies on the Physical and Data-Link layer interface between DTE and DCE devices.

exam
ⓦatch

Remember when you had to learn that multiplication table in third grade? Why not just get a calculator, right? Memorizing standards like 802.3 and 802.5 will probably make you feel the same way. Why not just write them down somewhere and look at the piece of paper if you ever need to know? The quick answer is that you can't take that piece of paper into your CCNA exam. You should spend some time learning these and know the differences.

QUESTIONS

1.02: Physical and Data-Link Layers

4. What standard defines Ethernet?

   A. 802.3

   B. 802.5

   C. 802.7

   D. 802.11

5. What type of technology is used for 802.3 Ethernet?

   A. Token passing

   B. CSMA/CD

C. Token passing with a dual-ring topology

D. CSMA/CD with token passing

6. What technology is being configured in the following example?

```
Router# conf t
Router(config)# interface E0/0
```

A. Token passing

B. CSMA/CD

C. Token passing with dual-ring topology

D. Wireless LAN

TEST YOURSELF OBJECTIVE 1.03

Network Layer and Path Determination

The Network layer, Layer 3, is where addressing is most important. The main function of this layer is to provide logical addressing of the node and network segments of a network. Routed protocols are used by end nodes to encapsulate data into packets along with Network layer addressing information, so it can be relayed through an internetwork.

The most common example of this is the Internet. Everything connecting to the Internet, whether it is a PC, router, switch, or mobile phone, must be assigned a Layer 3 address (an IP address) that is globally unique. We could use MAC addresses for this purpose, but they tend to get "messy." Instead, we use IP addresses. They are far more intuitive but allow the same functionality: packets get from Point A to Point B. The same is true on any network, except that on private networks the address must only be unique to that network, not globally unique.

So, how do those packets get from Point A to Point B? In most internetworks they are routed, which is a Layer 3 function. To determine the best way to send traffic from IP address A to IP address B, a router runs a routing algorithm that defines the best path. The algorithm that is run depends upon the routing protocol being used, but, regardless of the algorithm, the best path-routing selection is made. Note that, at Layer 3, encapsulated data is called a *packet*.

- ■ The main services provided at the Network layer are logical addressing of the node and network segments.
- ■ Layer 3, or the Network layer, is where addressing is most important.
- ■ Routed protocols are used by end nodes to encapsulate data into packets along with Network layer addressing information, so it can be relayed through the internetwork.
- ■ A routing algorithm is the calculation that the routing protocol uses to determine the best route to a destination network.

exam
ⓦatch

There is a big difference between a routing protocol and a routed protocol. A routing protocol (such as EIGRP, RIP, or OSPF) is what routers use to exchange information about a network; whereas, a routed protocol (such as TCP/IP) is the traffic that routers actually send, using the path determined by the routing protocol.

QUESTIONS

1.03: Network Layer and Path Determination

7. Your somewhat technically lacking customer needs you to help him select a routing protocol. He gives you a list of four that he is considering. Which of the following can you eliminate immediately because it is a routed protocol?

   A. EIGRP

   B. TCP/IP

   C. RIP

   D. OSPF

8. What is the main function of Layer 3?

    A. To provide link layer addressing

    B. To provide transport services

    C. To add application headers to data

    D. To provide logical addressing

9. When running a dynamic routing protocol, which of the following is run to determine the best path for data to travel from Point A to Point B?

    A. The administrative distance

    B. The routed protocol

    C. A routing algorithm

    D. A routing protocol

TEST YOURSELF OBJECTIVE 1.04

Transport Layer

The Transport layer, Layer 4, provides data transport services and effectively shields upper-layer protocols from data transfer issues. The main function of the Transport layer is to provide error recovery, if requested. TCP is considered a reliable, connection-oriented protocol and requests that Layer 4 provide error checking and correction for its data. UDP, on the other hand, is connectionless and unreliable and will not ask for any error checking or correction. It is important to note that, like most protocols, TCP/UDP do not conform exactly to the OSI model. Remember, the OSI model is a suggested model, but it is not a requirement that protocols function exactly as specified in the model.

■ The Transport layer provides data transport services, effectively shielding the upper layers from data transfer issues.

■ TCP is considered a reliable, connection-oriented protocol. UDP is unreliable and connectionless.

exam
⚠atch

It is important to understand why TCP and UDP are different, and what their benefits and limitations are. At first glance, you might say that all of your data must be reliable. You want to error check it all, so why not use TCP for everything? Error checking adds overhead, and that means delay—the enemy of all network administrators. Streaming video is a case where it is acceptable to sacrifice a few dropped video frames in order to guarantee speed. For streaming video, UDP is a great choice. On the other hand, financial data being uploaded to a mainframe can handle some delay but must be absolutely accurate, so TCP would be the proper choice for that data transmission.

QUESTIONS

1.04: Transport Layer

10. Your customer requests that you help determine him the best way to send weekly accounting updates to the finance directors at each of his regional offices. What should you tell him to do?

   A. Select a TCP solution because it doesn't have error correction and will get your data there much faster.

   B. Select a UDP solution because it doesn't have error correction and will get your data there much faster.

   C. Select a TCP solution because it has error correction and will be more reliable.

   D. Select a UDP solution because it has error correction and will be more reliable.

11. What is encapsulated data called at Layer 4?

   A. Frame

   B. Packet

   C. Segment

   D. Transport

12. What does the following diagram illustrate?

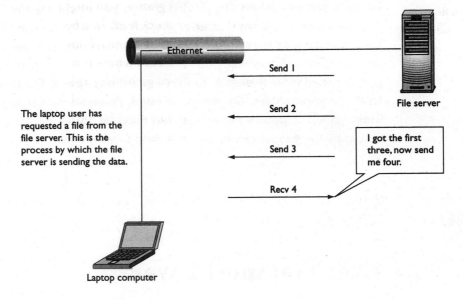

A. A TCP connection

B. A UDP connection

C. A connection-oriented protocol

D. A connectionless protocol

Upper-Layer Protocols

The term "upper-layer protocols" refers to the Session, Presentation, and Application layer protocols. The Session layer (Layer 5) is responsible for establishing, controlling, and tearing down sessions (conversations). The Presentation layer (Layer 6) defines data formats, such as ASCII, JPEG, and HTML. Layer 6 also defines encryption. The Application layer (Layer 7) defines applications that are capable of communications (e.g., if an application is capable of transferring a file, it is a Layer 7 application).

FTP, Telnet, and email programs are all examples of applications that function at Layer 7.

- The term "upper-layer protocols" refers to the Session, Presentation, and Application layer protocols.

- The Application layer provides basic services such as file transfer and network management to applications.

- The Presentation layer handles the formatting or presentation of the data.

- The Session layer establishes, maintains, and terminates the session between two network nodes.

exam
ⓦatch

Because the CCNA exam is an entry-level certification exam, it is going to focus heavily on fundamental concepts. You should not only know the order of the OSI model layers, but you should also be prepared to discuss what happens at each layer. You should also know what encapsulated data is called at each layer.

QUESTIONS

1.05: Upper-Layer Protocols

13. Which of the following is *not* an upper-layer in the OSI model?

   A. Session

   B. Network

   C. Presentation

   D. Application

14. Your client is a graphic designer. She wants to know which layer defines the format for a JPEG file. A JPEG is an example of a file format that is defined at which OSI layer?

   A. Session

   B. Transport

C. Presentation

D. Application

15. Which layer is responsible for establishing, controlling, and tearing down connections?

A. Application

B. Presentation

C. Session

D. Transport

TEST YOURSELF OBJECTIVE 1.06

Cisco Routers, Switches, and Hubs

Depending on the model, Cisco routers may support a combination of Ethernet, Fast Ethernet, Gigabit Ethernet, token ring, FDDI, T1/E1/PRI, T3, OC-3, ATM, and various other types of interfaces. Regardless of the types of interfaces that are supported on any given router, almost all Cisco routers run IOS software. It is this IOS software that truly provides the functionality for Cisco products. Most people would agree that Cisco only sells routers and switches to run their "real" product, IOS software. .

It's no surprise, then, that Cisco will want you to know a great deal about configuring their software, and the commands required to do so, for the CCNA exam. IOS has the following major modes: User EXEC, Privileged EXEC, Global Configuration, and Interface/Line Configuration. There are other modes, such as Access List Configuration, but those four are the most commonly referred to by name. It is extremely important for you to know the differences between each of these modes.

■ Cisco routers support any combination of the following interface types: ATM, channelized T3/E3, FDDI/CDDI, multichannel T1/E1/PRI, BRI, HSSI, Packet OC-3, synchronous/asynchronous serial interfaces, token ring, and Ethernet/Fast Ethernet/Gigabit Ethernet.

■ Cisco IOS software is the software that runs on Cisco products. This platform is integral to the interoperations of network devices in a Cisco internetwork.

exam
Watch

Don't get caught by the difference between the Global Configuration mode and more specific configuration modes, such as the Interface Configuration mode. Just keep in mind that the Global Configuration mode makes changes that affect the entire router, not specific aspects of the router; while, for example, the Interface Configuration mode makes changes that affect a specific interface.

QUESTIONS

1.06: Cisco Routers, Switches, and Hubs

16. A client wants to buy a Cisco router. He says, "If I know how to use one model, I know how to use them all. IOS is the same on every piece of Cisco equipment, right?" You tell him that this is

   A. True. All Cisco routers run IOS.

   B. False. Some Cisco router models do not run IOS.

   C. True. All Cisco routers and switches run IOS.

   D. False. No Cisco switches run IOS.

17. Which Cisco router mode is shown in the following example?

   ```
   Router(config-if)#
   ```

   A. User EXEC mode

   B. Privileged EXEC mode

   C. Global Configuration mode

   D. Interface Configuration mode

18. Once in Line Configuration mode, what is the easiest way to get back to the Privileged EXEC mode?

   A. Type **exit**.

   B. Type **quit**.

   C. Press CTRL-Z.

   D. Press the UP ARROW.

Configuring a Cisco Switch and Hub

Keep in mind that there are specifications to be met (both site and device) when installing hardware at a location. It is important to understand these before deploying the equipment on site. For example, when patching a router's Ethernet port to a hub or switch, be certain that you are using a straight-through cable, not a crossover cable. Additionally, the type of electrical interface that you order from the telephone company (e.g., V.35, RJ-45, etc.) must match the interface on your CSU. If, for example, an internal CSU is being used, you would order an RJ-45 handoff.

- There are specifications that need to be met when installing hardware at the site. It is important to follow these before deploying the equipment on site.

- When using patch cables, be aware of the different types: straight-through and crossover.

exam
Watch

There are not likely to be many questions on Cisco exams about cabling, but don't be surprised if you are asked to differentiate between a crossover cable and a straight-through cable. It's really only important to know, for the CCNA exam, that a crossover cable cannot be used to connect a router to a switch, but could be used to connect two routers back to back (between Ethernet ports, of course).

QUESTIONS

1.07: Configuring a Cisco Switch and Hub

19. Ron is trying to connect a crossover cable to a 3640 router's Ethernet0/0 port. What is Ron doing wrong?

   A. He is connecting a non-Ethernet cable to an Ethernet port.

   B. He is connecting a crossover cable to a port that is already crossed over.

C. He is connecting a crossover cable to a port that requires a straight-through connection.

D. He might not be doing anything wrong. In order to know if his action is correct, you need more information about what is going to be on the other end of the Ethernet cable.

20. Next, Ron is trying to connect Ethernet ports of two routers back to back with a V.35 cable. What is Ron doing wrong?

A. Ron is attempting to make an Ethernet connection with a serial cable.

B. Ron is attempting to make a serial connection with an Ethernet cable.

C. Ron is attempting to make a connection that requires a crossover cable with a straight-through cable.

D. Ron is attempting to make a connection that requires a straight-through cable with a crossover cable.

21. If Ron has a Cisco 3640 with an Internet CSU/DSU, what type of handoff should you request from your T1 provider?

A. G.703

B. RJ-45

C. V.35

D. X.25

LAB QUESTION

Objectives 1.01–1.07

Lab Scenario: This chapter has reviewed the OSI model, its layers, and where hardware and protocols are located within them. It is very important that you know these things for the exam, as there will be numerous questions asking on which layer a specific hardware component or protocol will be located. There will also be questions asking you to define specific OSI layers.

Please complete the table below, filling in each section with as much information as you can remember. As you will notice, there is a section for layer name, layer definition, hardware, and protocols. The layers should be listed in descending order. You must also be able to list the five-step process of data encapsulation and de-encapsulation. Feel free to reference this chapter or the *CCNA, Second Edition Study Guide* if necessary.

Layer	Layer Name	Layer Definition	Hardware	Protocols
7				
6				
5				
4				
3				
2				
1				

QUICK ANSWER KEY

Objective 1.01

1. C
2. D
3. B

Objective 1.02

4. A
5. B
6. B

Objective 1.03

7. B
8. D
9. C

Objective 1.04

10. C
11. C
12. C

Objective 1.05

13. B
14. C
15. C

Objective 1.06

16. B
17. D
18. C

Objective 1.07

19. D
20. A
21. B

IN-DEPTH ANSWERS
1.01: The Internetworking Model

1. ☑ **C.** A router functions at Layer 3 (a switch functions at Layer 2).

    ☒ **A** is incorrect because Layer 1 defines physical characteristics. **B** is incorrect because Layer 2 defines Data-Link layer functions, such as switching. **D** is incorrect because Layer 4 defines transport services.

2. ☑ **D.** Technically, **A** is the most correct definition of an internetwork, but all of these answers are correct because they all qualify as "more than one network."

3. ☑ **B.** This is the only answer that is in the correct order.

    ☒ **A**, **C**, and **D** are not correct because they do not follow the correct order. They also cannot fit into the mnemonic device "All People Seem To Need Data Processing."

1.02: Physical and Data-Link Layers

4. ☑ **A.** 802.3 defines the standard for Ethernet.

    ☒ **B** is incorrect because it is the standard for token ring. **C** and **D** make an interesting point relating to the CCNA exam. Until now you have probably never even seen 802.7 or 802.11. When taking the exam (provided you've studied an adequate amount), if you also see some bizarre number or term you've never seen before, chances are it isn't the right answer. **C** is incorrect because 802.7 defines Broadband LAN, and D is incorrect because 802.11 defines wireless LAN.

5. ☑ **B.** Carrier Sense Multiple Access/Collision Detection is the correct answer.

    ☒ **A** is incorrect because token passing would be a feature of token ring or FDDI. **C** is incorrect because a token passing technology with a dual-ring topology would be FDDI. **D** is incorrect because these two technologies are mutually exclusive and do not ever coexist on a network.

6.   ☑   **B.** Ethernet is a CSMA/CD technology.

☒   **A** is incorrect because that would be a Token Ring Interface. **C** is incorrect because that would be a FDDI Interface. **D** is incorrect because that would be an interface in a wireless device.

1.03: Network Layer and Path Determination

7.   ☑   **B.** Only TCP/IP is a routed protocol.

☒   **A**, **C**, and **D** are incorrect because they are routing protocols.

8.   ☑   **D.** The main function of the Network layer is to provide logical addressing.

☒   **A** is incorrect because link layer addressing is a Data-Link layer (Layer 2) function. **B** is incorrect; transport services are provided by the Transport layer (Layer 4). **C** is incorrect because application headers are added only by the Application layer.

9.   ☑   **C.** A routing algorithm is run to convert the information learned from other routers in the internetwork into usable information about the best path to a given destination.

☒   **A** is incorrect because the administrative distance is something that is set by the network administrator, not something that is run. **B** is incorrect because the routed protocol determines the way data is encapsulated for transmission. **D** is incorrect because a routing protocol determines how routers exchange information about paths to various networks, but that exchange is not enough to determine the best path. In order to determine the best path, the routing algorithm must be run.

1.04: Transport layer

10.   ☑   **C.** TCP has error correction and will be more reliable.

☒   **A** is incorrect because TCP does have error correction. **B** is not the best choice because accounting data must be accurate and should use a protocol with error correction. **D** is incorrect because UDP does not have error correction.

11. ☑ **C.** Encapsulated data at Layer 4 is called a *segment*.

    ☒ **A** is incorrect because a frame is encapsulated data at Layer 2. **B** is incorrect because a packet is encapsulated data at Layer 3. **D** is incorrect because transport is the name of the layer, not the name of encapsulated data at that layer.

12. ☑ **C.** This illustrates a connection-oriented protocol.

    ☒ **A** might be correct, but there is no way of knowing if this is TCP or some other connection-oriented protocol, so A is not the best choice. **B** and **D** are incorrect because connectionless protocols (like UDP) would give no acknowledgments. The illustration clearly shows a forward acknowledgment.

1.05: Upper-Layer Protocols

13. ☑ **B.** The Transport layer is not part of the upper layers.

    ☒ **A**, **B**, and **C** are incorrect choices because they are the three layers that are defined as the upper-layer protocols.

14. ☑ **C.** The Presentation layer defines JPEG as well as many other formats.

    ☒ **A** is incorrect because the Session layer establishes, controls, and tears down connections. **B** is incorrect because the Transport layer is responsible for any error correction that is requested by connection-oriented protocols. **D** is incorrect because the Application layer defines applications that communicate with other computers.

15. ☑ **C.** The Session layer is the correct answer.

    ☒ **A** is incorrect because the Application layer defines applications that are capable of communicating with other computers. **B** is incorrect because the Presentation layer defines file formatting. **D** is incorrect because the Transport layer provides error-checking and correction.

16. ☑ **B.** Most Cisco routers run Cisco IOS, but there are some (such as the 700 series routers) that do not. Don't get caught on the CCNA exam by questions like this. With Cisco, there is an exception to almost every rule.

    ☒ **A** is incorrect because certain models do not run IOS. **C** is incorrect because some router models, and many Cisco switch models, do not run IOS. **D** is incorrect because certain Cisco switch models, like the 29xx-XL series, run IOS-based code.

17. ☑ **D.** The "config-if" portion tells you that this is an Interface Configuration mode.

    ☒ **A** is incorrect; that prompt would be "Router>." **B** is incorrect; that prompt would be "Router#." **C** is incorrect; that prompt would be "Router(config)#."

18. ☑ **C.** Pressing CTRL-Z will immediately return you to the Privileged EXEC mode.

    ☒ **A** is incorrect because that command will return you to the Global Configuration mode. **B** is incorrect for the same reason. **D** is incorrect because that command shows you the last command entered from the buffer.

1.07: Configuring a Cisco Switch and Hub

19. ☑ **D.** It depends upon what is on the other end of the Ethernet cable. If he is connecting to another router's Ethernet port, a crossover cable is required. If he is connecting to a switch or hub, a straight-through cable is required.

    ☒ **A** is incorrect because a crossover cable is an Ethernet cable. **B** is incorrect because Ethernet ports are not crossed over. **C** is incorrect because the Ethernet port doesn't determine the type of cable required. The end-to-end connection determines the type of cable that is required.

20. ☑ **A.** A V.35 cable is for serial connections and may not be used for Ethernet connections.

    ☒ **B** is incorrect because a V.35 cable is not an Ethernet cable. **C** is incorrect because a V.35 cable is not a straight-through cable in the sense that this section discusses.

21. ☑ **B.** An RJ-45 connection from the DMARC to the CSU would be the best solution because a standard straight-through cable could be used.

    ☒ **A** is in correct because G.703 is a European Standard Interface. **C** is incorrect because a V.35 handoff would require a V.35 cable and some type of converter for the physical interface. **D** is incorrect because X.25 is a type of WAN technology, not a type of physical interface.

LAB ANSWER
Objectives 1.01–1.07

Layer	Layer Name	Layer Definition	Hardware	Protocols
7	Application	Responsible for all application-to-application communications. User information maintained at this layer is *user data*.	Gateways	FTP, SMB, TELNET, TFTP, SMTP, HTTP, NNTP, CDP, GOPHER, SNMP, NDS, AFP, SAP, NCP
6	Presentation	Responsible for the formatting of the data so that it is suitable for presentation. Responsible for character conversion (ASCII/ EBCDIC), Encryption/ Decryption, Compression, and Virtual Terminal Emulation. User information maintained at this layer is called *messages*.		ASCII, EBCDIC, POSTSCRIPT, JPEG, MPEG, GIF
5	Session	Responsible for the setup of the links, maintaining of the link, and the link tear-down between applications.		RADIUS, RPC, DNS, ASP
4	Transport	Responsible for the guaranteed delivery of user information It is also responsible for error detection, correction, and flow control. User information at this layer is called *datagrams*.		TCP, UDP, SPX, Netbios, ATP

Layer	Layer Name	Layer Definition	Hardware	Protocols
3	Network	Responsible for the routing of user data from one node to another through the network including the path selection. Logical addresses are used at this layer. User information maintained at this layer is called *packets*.	Routers	IP, IPX, ICMP, OSPF, IGRP, EIGRP, RIP, BOOTP, DHCP, IS-IS, ZIP, DDP, X.25
2	Data-Link	Responsible for the physical addressing of the network via MAC addresses. There are two sublevels to the Data-Link layer, MAC and LLC. The Data-Link layer has error detection, frame ordering, and flow control. User information maintained at this layer is called *frames*.	Bridges, switches	L2F, PPTP, L2TP, PPP, SLIP, ARP, RARP, SLARP, IARP, SNAP, BAP, PAP, CHAP, LCP, LZS, MLP, Frame Relay, Annex A, Annex D, HDLC, BPDU, LAPD, ISL
1	Physical	Responsible for the physical transmission of the binary digits through the physical medium. This layer includes things such as the physical cables, interfaces, and data rate specifications. User information maintained at this layer is called *bits* (the 1s and 0s).	Hubs, repeaters, cables	10BaseT, 100BaseT, 1000BaseT, 10Base2, 10Base5, OC-3, OC-12, DS1, DS3, E1, E3, ATM, BRI, PRI

Encapsulation:

1. Layer 7: User data
2. Layer 4: Datagrams
3. Layer 3: Packets
4. Layer 2: Frames
5. Layer 1: Bits

De-Encapsulation:

1. Layer 1: Bits
2. Layer 2: Frames
3. Layer 3: Packets
4. Layer 4: Datagrams
5. Layer 7: User data

2

Bridging and Switching Concepts

T his chapter will cover questions on bridging and switching. Some of the important things to remember for the exam are the differences between the collision and broadcast domains and how to manipulate them using different devices. You must also know how to segment the LAN to provide more bandwidth per user. Understanding traffic flow with full- and half-duplex Ethernet is essential to passing the exam. You will need to know VLANs, BPDUs, loops, bridge and switch operations, and the Spanning-Tree Protocol. Lastly, you will need to know cut-through and store-and-forward switching methods.

TEST YOURSELF OBJECTIVE 2.01

Collision and Broadcast Domains

Collision domains refer to a single half-duplex Ethernet system. In a single collision domain, if two or more devices transmit at the same time, a collision will occur. Once a collision occurs, each of the colliding devices must back off and then attempt to gain access to the wire according to the Carrier Sense Multiple Access with Collision Detection (CSMS/CD) mechanism. Degradation in performance may occur under increasing load. However, this situation can be elevated with careful network design using bridges or switches to partition a network into multiple collision domains that distribute load and minimize collisions.

- It is important to realize that collisions are a normal part of Ethernet operation. However, as collision rates increase, useful bandwidth decreases. This means that applications must re-try more often, causing longer response times for users.

- When two stations simultaneously transmit in Ethernet the frames from each station collide and are damaged. Hubs and repeaters will propagate these damaged frames, but not LAN switches, routers or bridges, which discard them. The area within the Ethernet topology over which these frames spread is known as the *collision domain*.

- Reducing the number of users per collision domain effectively increases the bandwidth on that segment. By keeping traffic local to a network segment, users have more bandwidth and better response times than if all users were on one large segment.

- Collisions consume bandwidth.

■ Broadcasts are useful. They may be used to distribute route information, resolve addresses, or find network services. Most networking protocols use broadcasts as a mechanism to tell all interested listeners (network devices) where a specific service is and what route to take to get there.

■ Just as in a radio broadcast, listeners tune into the same frequency and receive the program; so in our network, all end stations on the same segment receive the broadcast. However, when an end station receives the broadcast frame, its processor must stop what it is doing (for example, word processing), examine the frame, and discard it. Therefore, we wish to segment our LAN in order to decrease the size of our broadcast domain. Remember, broadcasts consume bandwidth.

exam
ⓦatch

In the exam, you may be asked about the differences between a bridge and a switch. Cisco likes to try and trick you with this one. A switch is essentially a multiport bridge that interconnects individual devices rather than networks. A bridge and a switch create collision domains on each port. Depending on the configuration of the device, both are capable of creating multiple broadcast domains. Routers, by comparison, block broadcasts, and since each interface on a router is a separate collision domain, a network of routers will have several broadcast and collision domains.

QUESTIONS

2.01: Collision and Broadcast Domains

1. End users in the Graphics Department are complaining about a network slowdown and degradation on the local area network. After investigation, it has been determined that a particular workstation is very chatty. What should you do?

   A. Move the workstation to another LAN segment where you know there are fewer users.

   B. Disable the computer and ask the user to do some other work instead.

   C. Replace the NIC (network interface card) because it is causing "jabber" (chatter) on the network.

   D. Move the workstation to another broadcast domain.

2. How many collision domains and how many broadcast domains are there in this bridge and router illustration?

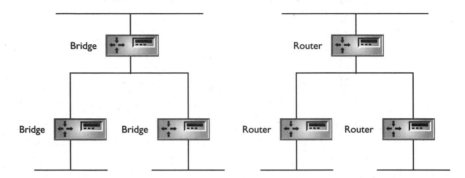

A. The bridge graphic has four collision domains and one broadcast domain. The router graphic has four collision domains and four broadcast domains.

B. The bridge graphic has three collision domains and three broadcast domains. The router graphic has three collision domains and one broadcast domain.

C. The bridge graphic has two collision domains and two broadcast domains. The router graphic has one collision domain and four broadcast domains.

D. The bridge graphic has one collision domain and four broadcast domains. The router graphic has four collision domains and one broadcast domain.

TEST YOURSELF OBJECTIVE 2.02

Local Area Network (LAN) Segmentation

It's always ideal to segment the LAN to achieve more bandwidth per user and support traffic between same-segment nodes. The three main methods of segmenting an Ethernet LAN to increase bandwidth are bridges, routers, and switches. These devices will only achieve proper segmentation if they are correctly placed in the network. Each segment on the network becomes a separate collision domain, which supports traffic between same-segment nodes without interference from nodes attached to other segments. Reducing the number of users per collision domain increases the bandwidth on the network segment. By keeping the traffic local to the network segment, users experience a better response time and more available bandwidth than with one large backbone.

- Segmenting LANs is the way to provide users additional bandwidth without replacing all user equipment. In this case, the network is broken into a number of smaller portions, which are connected with internetworking equipment.

- Repeaters, bridges, routers, and switches are the devices that help extend networks. These devices are also used when it comes to manipulating the domains and facilitating LAN segmentation.

- Repeaters are the devices that can overcome the borders of a single segment. These devices operate on a Physical layer of the OSI model. They know nothing about MAC addresses or IP. They amplify the signal and remove the undesirable aspects of a signal, such as noise.

- Bridges operate on Layer 2 of the OSI model, or the Data-Link layer. They have information about MAC addresses. Bridges analyze the MAC header of every frame and decide whether to forward the frame or to discard it, building a special table of devices attached to different ports. Thus, the bridge separates one big collision domain into two smaller ones but maintains one and the same broadcast domain. The correct use of only one bridging device almost doubles the network performance and increases the maximum network diameter.

- Basically, a switch is a multiport bridge. Switches also make their switching tables (just like bridges and their bridging tables), where MAC addresses correspond with ports. A typical switch allows you to create a few collision domains but only one broadcast domain per VLAN.

- Routers are the devices that work on the Network layer of the OSI model. Just like bridges, routers use special tables—called routing tables—to decide to which interface it should forward the frame. As distinct from bridges and switches, in the routing tables, routers usually keep the information about whole networks, not about particular devices.

- It is appropriate to use routers in large networks. They almost always benefit from scalability, flexibility, and intelligence of routing. Here are some advantages of routers: broadcast filtering, support of wide range of interfaces, and optimal and flexible path selection.

Bridges have a latency (the time it takes for the frame to be processed by the device) of 20 to 30 percent for acknowledged based protocols and 10 to 20 percent for sliding window protocols. Bridges forward multicast and broadcast frames and operate at the Data-Link layer. Routers have a latency of 30 to 40 percent for acknowledged based protocols and 20 to 30 percent for sliding window protocols. They operate at the Network layer and block broadcasts. However, the main advantages of segmenting with routers are manageability, flow control, explicit packet lifetime control, and multiple active paths.

QUESTIONS

2.02: Local Area Network (LAN) Segmentation

3.   What are we trying to achieve when we segment the LAN?

   A.   Decrease the number of routers in a segment.

   B.   Decrease the size of the collision domain.

   C.   Increase the number of nodes in a segment.

   D.   Use repeaters where possible.

4.   What are the advantages of segmenting a LAN with a repeater?

   A.   Repeaters isolate broadcast traffic by logically separating the LAN.

   B.   Repeaters extend the physical distance of the LAN by amplifying the electrical signal.

   C.   Repeaters physically separate LANs and filter non-local and broadcast traffic from local traffic.

   D.   A repeater performs a rich set of functionality, allowing security and multi-protocol environments.

5. With reference to the following illustration, a repeater has been correctly placed
    in the network to increase the distance of the LAN. However, the cable length
    on the left side has reached 90 meters. Where would you place the next repeater
    in order to extend the LAN further?

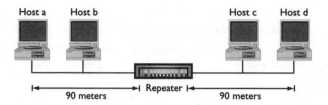

A. Between Host c and d

B. Between Host a and b

C. After Host d

D. Before Host a

Full- and Half-Duplex Ethernet

Full-duplex Ethernet allows simultaneous transmission and reception but requires a
switched connection, not a hub, between two end nodes. This implementation will
significantly improve network performance without requiring expensive new media.
Full-duplex Ethernet uses point-to-point connections on separate transmit and receive
circuits and is therefore collision free. A 10-Mbps, full-duplex Ethernet operating bi-
directionally on the same port has a theoretical aggregate throughput of 20 Mbps.
Full-duplex can now be used on 10BaseT, 100BaseT, and 100BaseFL media to
provide point-to-point connections. However, it is important to remember that the
network interface card (NIC) on both ends of the connection must be capable of full-
duplex operation.

■   Full-duplex Ethernet provides a collision-free environment. It can transmit and
    receive frames simultaneously, but this mode can only be reached if two
    stations are connected using a point-to-point, dedicated cable.

■ Half-duplex Ethernet describes the shared medium of the Ethernet. When one station is sending frames to another station, the transmitting process is performed on a transmitting station and the receiving station is the only one actively receiving.

exam
⦿atch
The circuits for full and half duplex are different. The full-duplex circuit has the collision detection and loopback portion disabled. Full-duplex Ethernet offers a significant performance improvement over shared half-duplex Ethernet, uses point-to-point connections, and is collision free. Frames sent by two connected end nodes couldn't collide because they transmit and receive on separate copper pairs. Watch out for half duplex being described as a "narrow, one-way bridge"—in this case, Cisco's analogy is with a road bridge!

QUESTIONS

2.03: Full- and Half-Duplex Ethernet

6. In order to implement full-duplex Ethernet, which of the following do you require? (Choose all that apply.)

   A. Loop-back and collision detection disabled

   B. Automatic detection of full-duplex operation

   C. Full-duplex NICs

   D. Multiple paths between multiple stations on a link

7. Which of the following media can full duplex be implemented on? (Choose all that apply.)

   A. 10BaseT

   B. 100BaseT

   C. 100BaseFL

   D. FDDI

8. With reference to the following illustration, what kind of circuit does it represent?

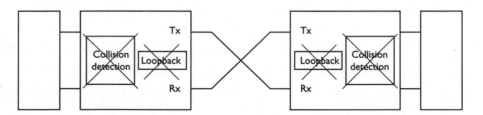

A. Half-duplex

B. Full-duplex

C. SONET

D. FDDI

Bridge and Switch Operations

Bridges, like repeaters, regenerate signals, but they also learn MAC addresses and determine if the destination computer is on the local segment or another network segment. If that computer is on the local segment, the bridge won't forward the frame. If it's not on the local segment, the bridge will forward the frame to all other network segments. Bridges have a latency of 20 to 30 percent due to processing and filtering frames. Bridges forward broadcasts and can therefore cause broadcast storms, as these broadcasts can propagate throughout the network. Switches can operate in full-duplex mode and are essentially an extremely fast multiport bridge. An end station transmitting to a switch will send a frame only to a specific port on the switch.

■ Bridges and switches are the devices that connect and pass packets between two network segments that use the same communications protocol. These devices operate at the Data-Link layer (Layer 2) of the OSI model. Generally speaking, they filter, forward, or flood an incoming frame based on the destination MAC address of that frame.

■ Bridges and switches use special algorithms to build bridging and switching tables that they use to make forwarding or filtering decisions.

■ Frame filtering occurs when the source and destination reside on the same interface, or if the address is in the filtering table compiled by a network administrator. Such a table usually contains so-called filtering information that operates on many fields inside the data frame.

e x a m **!**
   ⓦ a t c h

Switches are capable of running in 10/100 Mbps half- or full-duplex mode and can have a separate VLAN on each port. If you create five VLANs, you create five virtual bridge functions within the switch. Each bridge function is logically isolated from the others. A switch uses bridge technology; it creates collision domains on each port. Both a bridge and a switch can create collision domains on each port and multiple broadcast domains, depending on the configuration.

QUESTIONS

2.04: Bridge and Switch Operations

9. Which of the following devices works at the Physical layer?

   A. Repeaters

   B. Bridges

   C. Routers

   D. Switches

10. What is the name of the protocol that bridges use to communicate with each other?

    A. STP

    B. STA

    C. BPDU

    D. MAC

11. What method can switches use to create smaller broadcast domains?

   A. VLANs

   B. Virtual Trunking Protocol

   C. STP

   D. Routing

TEST YOURSELF OBJECTIVE 2.05

Spanning-Tree Protocol (STP)

In a Layer 3 routing environment, the routing protocol is responsible for telling the rest of the network that a link has failed and finding an alternative route. The Spanning-Tree Protocol (STP) provides a similar service in a Layer 2 switched environment. Bridge Protocol Data Units (BPDUs) accomplish this, and are sent out every two seconds on every port to ensure a stable, loop-free topology. Initially, STP takes the port through four states: blocking, listening, learning, and forwarding. Time taken to move through these four states is 50 seconds. A single instance of STP runs on each VLAN.

■ STP is a complex protocol developed by DEC and later modified and incorporated into IEEE's standard as 802.1d.

■ The main function of STP is loop prevention. It allows bridges to transfer data from one bridge to another to discover physical loops in the network. Then it specifies an algorithm that bridges use to create a loop-free logical topology.

■ The bridge identifier, the port priorities, and the path costs are three important parameters that influence the way STP goes to block some ports and to forward others. It is necessary to remember that STP does not provide the optimal configuration; it creates a loop-free environment. Thus, sometimes a network administrator has to take time to configure certain parameters on some bridges and switches included in a network to optimize the network.

!

exam
ⓌatchＷａｔｃｈ

STP runs on all ports of a switch. However, you do not always want this to happen. Cisco has therefore created several techniques to accelerate the STP performance, which you must understand for the exam. PortFast is used for workstations or servers that are not part of the switching fabric, to allow the port to enter the forwarding state immediately, allowing instant access to the Layer 2 network. UplinkFast is used for fast, STP uplink convergence in less than five seconds for inter-switch connects. Complimentary to UplinkFast is BackboneFast, in case of indirect failures in the core of the backbone.

QUESTIONS

2.05: Spanning-Tree Protocol (STP)

12. You have set up a group of users in your company and placed their workstations and servers in a separate VLAN. Which of the following is true regarding STP?

   A. Now you have multiple instances of STP.

   B. Only one instance of STP per VLAN is allowed.

   C. Only one instance of STP is allowed per switch.

   D. You have up to 64 instances of STP per VLAN.

13. What protocol is used to describe the STP specification to prevent loops in a network?

   A. 802.2

   B. 802.1

   C. 802.1d

   D. 802.11d

14. You have designed and set up your network, with built-in redundancy, as in the following illustration. Everything looks good except that Spanning-Tree has blocked three of the four redundant links between the backbone switches to prevent loops. What can you do to utilize these links and provide more aggregate throughput between the backbone switches?

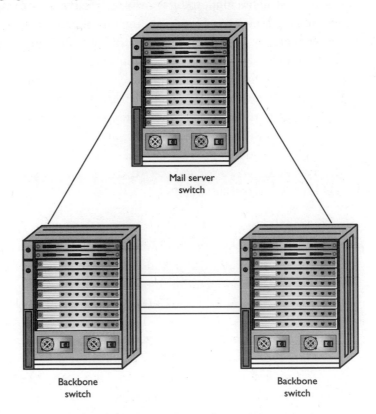

Mail server
switch

Backbone
switch

Backbone
switch

A. Configure PortFast on these ports connecting the backbone switches together.

B. Configure BackboneFast on these ports.

C. Configure UplinkFast on these ports.

D. Configure fast etherchannel.

TEST YOURSELF OBJECTIVE 2.06

Switching Types

Different switches support different switching types, and some switches support several switching types. Understanding the differences between switching types is fundamental to passing the CCNA exam. Cut-through (real-time) switching streams data through a switch so that the leading edge of a packet exits the switch at the output port before the packet finishes entering the input port. In the store-and-forward technique, frames are completely processed before being forwarded out the appropriate port. Fragment-free switching combines some of the best qualities of the two. Like cut-through, it does not wait until the entire frame is received; instead, it forwards a frame after the first 64 octets of the frame have been received. Analyzing the first 64 octets of a packet received, it is almost always possible to tell whether the whole packet is corrupt.

- The advantages of fragment-free switching mode are low latency and the good possibility of detecting errored packets quickly.

- Store-and-forward switching mode is the only choice if your source and destination segments use different media speeds, since you have to cache the data and then send it to the segment at another speed.

exam
Watch

Of the switching modes discussed, it may seem that the store-and-forward switching type is the best because it reads the entire frame and checks the CRC before forwarding. However, it has an increased latency that varies according to frame length. Cut-through, although it has no error-control mechanism, maybe the correct type, depending on network requirements. On the Cisco 5505s, the default switching method is store-and-forward.

QUESTIONS

2.06: Switching Types

15. What method of switching has less latency through the switch?

    A. VLAN

    B. Cut-forward

    C. Cut-through

    D. Store-and-forward

16. Which method of switching has the best error-checking?

    A. Fragment free

    B. Cut-through

    C. Store-and-forward

    D. Cut-forward

LAB QUESTION

Objectives 2.01–2.06

Your company is in the process of upgrading the network infrastructure, which involves moving from a 10BaseT to a 100BaseT network. STP will be used in the network for loop avoidance. As a member of the data network team, you are asked to take care of a portion of this upgrade. How would you provide the best desktop connectivity for end users, and the fastest possible throughput and security for the Payroll Department? In addition, decide what devices to use in the closet.

A QUICK ANSWER KEY

Objective 2.01
1. C
2. A

Objective 2.02
3. B
4. B
5. D

Objective 2.03
6. A and C
7. A, B, and D
8. B

Objective 2.04
9. A
10. C
11. A

Objective 2.05
12. B
13. C
14. D

Objective 2.06
15. C
16. C

IN-DEPTH ANSWERS

2.01: Collision and Broadcast Domains

1. ☑ **C.** The only solution to the problem of a bad NIC on the LAN segment is to replace it. From time to time a NIC may malfunction and cause a lot of collisions in the collision domain; the segment will experience slowdown and a degradation of service.

   ☒ **B** is incorrect because the user may be a VP in the company and this action may result in late promotion. **D** is incorrect because the other segment maybe in the wrong broadcast domain and your user will not be able to access the resources that were available to him before. **A** is incorrect because moving the user to another LAN segment would cause the same problem on that segment.

2. ☑ **A.** The bridge illustration has four collision domains. Although bridges interconnect collision domains, allowing independent collision domains to appear as if they were connected, they do not propagate collisions between them. Bridges forward broadcast frames; therefore, there is one broadcast domain. Routers do not forward broadcast domains; therefore, there are four broadcast domains and four collision domains in the router graphic.

   ☒ **B, C,** and **D** incorrectly describe the number of collision and broadcast domains.

2.02: Local Area Network (LAN) Segmentation

3. ☑ **B.** Each collision domain supports traffic between same-segment nodes without interference from nodes attached to other segments.

   ☒ **A** is incorrect because limiting the number of routers would increase the collision and broadcast domains. **C** is incorrect because increasing the number of nodes in a segment would increase the size of the collision domain. **D** is incorrect because repeaters extend the physical distance of the LAN.

4. ☑ **B.** Repeaters amplify the electrical signal of the LAN allowing greater physical distance, extending the LAN.

   ☒ **A** is incorrect because a repeater does not logically separate the LAN. **C** is incorrect because a repeater does not perform any filtering of LAN traffic. **D** is incorrect because a repeater does not offer security or other such functionality.

5. ☑ **D.** By placing the repeater before host a, you are extending the segment another 100 meters (ideal conditions).

   ☒ **A** is incorrect because placing the repeater between host c and d would not extend the LAN on the left side of the segment. **B** is incorrect. Although placing the repeater between a and b would extend the LAN, it is a bad design. The timing of the 10BaseT is such that the maximum number of segments you could extend is five (using four repeaters), and of those five segments, only three of them can actually be populated with nodes. This is referred to as the 5-4-3 rule. **D** is incorrect because placing the repeater after host d would not extend the LAN on the left of the illustration.

2.03: Full- and Half-Duplex Ethernet

6. ☑ **A** and **C** are the correct answers. Full duplex requires the loopback and collision detection circuits of the NIC to be disabled (there are no collisions in full-duplex Ethernet), so this is a full-duplex NIC.

   ☒ **B** is incorrect because auto detection is not required; it is just a feature of some full-duplex NICs. **D** is incorrect because multiple paths between multiple stations are not required.

7. ☑ **A, B,** and **D** are correct. Full-duplex operation is available on 10BaseT, 100BaseT, and 100BaseFL.

   ☒ **D** is incorrect because full-duplex operation is not available for FDDI.

8. ☑ **B.** The transmit is directly wired to the receive, and the collision domain and loopback circuits have been disabled.

   ☒ **A** is incorrect because half-duplex would require the collision domain and the loopback enabled. **C** and **D** are incorrect because the graphic does not represent SONET or FDDI circuits.

2.04: Bridge and Switch Operations

9. ☑ **A.** Repeaters work at Layer 1, the Physical layer.

   ☒ **B** and **D** are incorrect because bridges and switches are Layer 2 (Data-Link layer) devices. **C** is incorrect because routers work at Layer 3 (Network layer) of the OSI model.

10. ☑ **C.** Bridges communicate with each other with Bridge Protocol Data Units (BPDUs).

    ☒ **A** is incorrect. STP is the Spanning-Tree Protocol used for avoiding loops. **B** is incorrect. STA is the Spanning-Tree algorithm used to calculate the network topology. **D** is incorrect. MAC is the media access control address.

11. ☑ **A.** VLANs are used to create smaller broadcast domains in a switched network.

    ☒ **B** is incorrect. Trunking is a method of carrying traffic of multiple VLANs over a single link. **C** is incorrect. STP is the Spanning-Tree Protocol used to calculate loop avoidance. **D** is incorrect. Routing is used by routers at Layer 3 of the OSI model.

2.05: Spanning-Tree Protocol (STP)

12. ☑ **B.** There is only one instance of STP per VLAN allowed.

    ☒ **A.** Is incorrect because there are never multiple instances of STP allowed. **D** and **C** are wrong because a switch can have several VLANs and therefore several instances of STP.

13. ☑ **C.** 802.1d is the IEEE standard for the STP.

    ☒ **A** is incorrect because 802.2 is the IEEE specification that specifies the Data-Link layer for various media access methods. **B** is incorrect because the 802.11d is for wireless LANs. **D** is incorrect because 802.1 is the IEEE specification for network management.

14. ☑ **D.** Cisco provides this mechanism for redundant links to allow parallel links to be treated by STP as one physical link.

☒ **A** is incorrect because PortFast is used for ports connected to end stations. **B** is incorrect because BackboneFast is used when a switch receives an inferior BPDU from another switch. **C** is incorrect because UplinkFast is used from the closet switch to the backbone switch.

2.06: Switching Types

15. ☑ **C.** The cut-through switching method forwards the frame after only the destination physical address is read, and therefore has the less latency through the switch.

☒ **A** is incorrect because VLAN is not a switching method. **B** is incorrect because cut-forward is not a switching method. **D** is incorrect because this switching method has the longest latency through the switch.

16. ☑ **C.** The store and forward switching method has the best error checking, since it reads the entire frame before forwarding.

☒ **A**, **B**, and **D** are incorrect because none of these methods have error-checking.

LAB ANSWER
Objectives 2.01–2.06

Your best choice of device to use in the closet would be a switch. The desktops for end users should have their NICs configured for 100-Mbps full duplex to provide the best desktop connectivity. Use VLANs (in addition to some router configuration) to provide the Payroll Department with added security. However, to provide the fastest possible throughput, you will have to select a switch that will provide the cut-through switching method. Using a switch will also ensure that the payroll department will be in a separate broadcast domain and that each end station will be in a separate collision domain.

Configure the switches with the following configuration:

```
Closet Switch # speed 100

Closet Switch # duplex full

Closet Switch # set spanning-tree portfast

Closet Switch # set spanning-tree uplinkfast

Backbone Switch # set spanning-tree backbonefast
```

PortFast is configured on the closet switch to enable the end user stations to obtain an IP address from the DHCP server.

CCNA
CISCO CERTIFIED NETWORK ASSOCIATE

3

Cisco Catalyst 1900 IOS Software Basics

One of the major revisions to the CCNA certification exam is the inclusion of bridging, switching, and the Catalyst 1900 product line. The CCNA candidate must be familiar with the basics of Catalyst 1900 switch operation, including the menu-driven user interface, the basics of switch operation (including switching modes, Spanning-Tree, and VLANs), other configuration methods such as TFTP and HTTP, and methods of upgrading switch software.

A couple of Cisco proprietary protocols will also be introduced in this chapter: CGMP (Cisco Group Management Protocol), which helps streamline multicasting through the Catalyst switch, and CDP (Cisco Discovery Protocol), which allows Cisco devices (both routers and switches) to identify themselves to one another and create a very basic network map.

TEST YOURSELF OBJECTIVE 3.01

User Interface

The default interface for the Catalyst 1900 switch family is a menu-driven interface. This menu interface comes with the Standard Edition software. This interface is extremely primitive but usable, and you'll pretty much be able to teach yourself how to use it. Just like the Cisco routers, Catalyst switches also come with a login password, which may optionally be set to a null password. However, it is very bad practice not to assign login passwords to your network devices. There is no User mode or Privileged mode on a Catalyst 1900 switch running Standard Edition software; so if a malicious user (or an uneducated user) gains access to a Catalyst switch with no login password, he has full rights to make any changes to your switch's running configuration. The Catalyst switch also provides you with the ability to assign a single IP address to the switch (and encourages you to do so) for management purposes.

- The 1900 series uses a menu interface by default.

- In order to secure the switch from unauthorized access, you must set a Console Password.

- The Console Password must be between four and eight characters. It is not case sensitive.

- Once you set the Console Password and configure an IP address on the switch, the Management Console menu will only contain the Menus option.

One of the most annoying feats of memorization Cisco will make you perform is to remember which Catalyst switch family runs on which type of default interface. Menu-driven? Set commands? IOS? Well, fortunately, the CCNA only requires you to know the 1900 family, which runs on either one of two default interfaces. With the Standard Edition software, the default interface is the menu-driven interface. If the switch is upgraded to the Enterprise Edition, it will be using a more familiar Cisco IOS–like CLI for the Catalyst product.

QUESTIONS

3.01: User Interface

Questions 1–2   This scenario should be used to answer questions 1 and 2.

You connect a HyperTerm session to the console port of a Catalyst 1900 switch. You power up the switch and see the following menu come up:

```
[M] Menus

[I] IP Configuration
```

1. What has not been configured on this switch? (Choose two of the following.)

    A. A default port speed

    B. A password

    C. An IP address

    D. A base MAC address

2. From reading the situation, choose which edition of software is running on the Catalyst switch.

    A. Enterprise Edition

    B. Desktop Edition

    C. Spanning-Tree Edition

    D. Standard Edition

3. The maximum number of 100-Mbps ports on a Catalyst 1924 is

   A. 1

   B. 2

   C. 12

   D. 24

TEST YOURSELF OBJECTIVE 3.02

Switch Basics

The Catalyst 1900 switch is a fairly simple device, and the number of configuration options are minimal compared those featured on a Cisco router. The Catalyst 1900 is meant to be a Plug-and-Play device, meaning you can drop it in the place of a hub and it will, by its very nature, improve network performance. The majority of the ports will provide 10-Mbps half-duplex service to any attached device, and also provide two 100-Mbps full-duplex ports, meant to be used for dedicated servers or router uplinks. Very little real configuration can be done beyond this point, except for VLAN configuration, Spanning-Tree Protocol configuration, switching method changes, and IP address assignment. There are a couple new protocols we also need to become familiar with: CGMP and CDP. We'll also take a look at the LEDs on the Catalyst switch that can be used for troubleshooting and diagnostic purposes.

- The Catalyst 1900 series switch was designed for Plug-and-Play operation.
- The 1900 series can utilize Cisco Group Management Protocol (CGMP), which is used to prevent the flooding of multicast packets to all ports in a VLAN.
- This switch supports full-duplex operation on its 100-Mbps ports.
- STP is implemented on the 1900 series. STP is used to prevent and remove redundant links in your switched network topology.
- The 1900 series can be purchased with either 12 or 24 10BaseT ports.
- The Catalyst 1900 uses LEDs to display the status of the switch and its ports.
- This switch employs three methods of frame forwarding: cut-through, store-and-forward, and modified cut-through (also known as fragment-free).
- CDP (Cisco Discovery Protocol) was developed to allow Cisco devices to communicate with each other.

exam

Watch

A couple of quick and easy-to-remember facts about the Catalyst 1900 family: A Catalyst with 12 10baseT ports is called the 1912, and the model with 24 10baseT ports is called a 1924. Both have two 100-Mbps full-duplex uplink ports. Remember that with Catalyst LEDs, green is good, amber is bad (except in the case of STP).

The three methods of frame forwarding are store-and-forward (oldest method, and slowest), cut-through (an improvement over store-and-forward, but prone to problems), and fragment-free (the newest method, which is a combination of the first two. Make sure you realize that the method is called fragment free, not error free).

QUESTIONS

3.02: Switch Basics

4. A Catalyst switch receives a frame on a port, takes the entire frame in, performs a checksum on the frame, and forwards it out a destination port. Which switching method is being described here?

   A. Cut-through

   B. Store-and-forward

   C. Fragment-free

   D. Spanning-Tree

5. The CDP protocol is used to:

   A. Allow Cisco devices to identify themselves to one another

   B. Allow Cisco devices to identify themselves to one another, and exchange CAM table information

   C. Allow Catalyst switches to detect bridging loops and disable ports accordingly

   D. Provide a method of tagging frames that need to be transported over trunk links between various vendors' switches

6. **Current Situation:** Steven is the administrator of a small network that is centered around a Catalyst 1912 switch. He would like to connect his seven users to dedicated 10baseT half-duplex ports on the Catalyst switch. He would also like to connect their proxy server to a 100baseTX port on the switch.

   Required Result: Connect each user to a dedicated 10baseT half-duplex port on the Catalyst 1912 switch.

   Optional Desired Result: Connect the company's proxy server to a 100baseTX port on the Catalyst 1912 switch.

   Proposed Solution: Connect the seven users into ports 1 through 7 on the switch and connect the proxy server to port 12 on the switch.

   A. The proposed solution produces the required result and the optional result.

   B. The proposed solution produces the required result but not the optional result.

   C. The proposed solution produces neither the required result nor the optional result.

   D. The proposed solution produces the optional result but not the required result.

TEST YOURSELF OBJECTIVE 3.03

Initial Configuration

This section deals with some of the information that the Catalyst switch provides to you while it is powering up and while it is functioning normally. The LEDs above each port on the switch give you different information, depending on the setting of the Mode switch on the front of the Catalyst 1900 chassis. While in Stat mode (the default), the port LEDs will show green for a link, will flicker with activity on the link, or will show amber if there is a fault or if the port has been blocked by STP. In UTL mode, the series of lights (1 through 12 or 1 through 24, depending on which model you're using) will show the overall utilization of the switch. The more LEDs turned on, the busier the switch is. In FDUP mode, a green LED indicates that the port is operating in full-duplex mode, while a dark LED indicates half-duplex mode.

■ The 1900 series performs a POST when it is first powered on.

■ The POST results are communicated via the Port LEDs as well as the Management console.

■ The System Status LED communicates the basic status of the device. If the LED is off, the switch is off. If it is green, the switch is operating normally. If it is amber, then a fault has been detected.

■ The RPS LED indicates the status of a connected redundant power system.

■ The Port LEDs are multipurpose. By default, they display the status of the individual ports. They can also display the bandwidth utilization of the switch and the full-duplex operation of the ports.

■ By default, the switch does not have an IP address configured. The 1900 series can utilize DHCP to get an IP address.

exam
ⓦatch

There are two ways to approach this section of the exam: memorization or understanding functionality. Don't spend a lot of time memorizing which power on self test corresponds to which LED turning amber. Rather, spend your time understanding how the LEDs provide you with valuable information in the various modes of the switch. Also, understand how the Catalyst switch employs IP for management purposes (using SNMP, HTTP, and Telnet).

QUESTIONS

3.03: Initial Configuration

7. During the initial power-up of the Catalyst switch, you may notice that all of the port LEDs turn green, flicker on and off, then eventually all turn off. What is the flickering an indication of?

A. Dynamic VLANs being configured on the switch

B. The Spanning-Tree Protocol running and blocking ports

C. The power on self test checking various system components

D. Ports auto-configuring themselves for full- or half-duplex operation

8. What would be the quickest way to determine the current load on the switch?

    A. Connect a terminal to the console port, log in to the user interface, and view the port statistics in the menu system.

    B. Connect a sniffer to one of the ports on the switch and capture packets over a five-minute time frame.

    C. Use a tool such as Microsoft Performance Monitor to gauge network traffic.

    D. Set the Mode button on the front of the Catalyst chassis to UTL and look at the port LEDs on the front of the switch.

9. What is the recommended method of assigning an IP address to the Catalyst switch?

    A. Assign an IP address manually using the user interface on the console port.

    B. Assign an IP address manually using the HTTP interface.

    C. Use DHCP to assign an IP address to the switch dynamically.

    D. It is not possible to assign an IP address to a Catalyst switch, since it is a Layer 2 device.

TEST YOURSELF OBJECTIVE 3.04

Configuration Methods

There isn't much to the various configuration methods available for the Catalyst 1900 switch, but what makes this section complex is remembering which methods are available with which firmware package, as listed below:

	Menu-based	IOS CLI	HTTP	SNMP	TFTP	Telnet
Standard Edition	X		X	X		X
Enterprise Edition		X	X	X	X	X

Note that the HTTP, SNMP, TFTP, and Telnet options assume that an IP address has been assigned to the switch.

■ There are three primary configuration methods: menu-based interface (or Management console), Web-based (HTTP), and SNMP.

■ The CLI is available with the Enterprise Edition software.

■ You can access the menu-based configuration via the console port or from Telnet.

■ You can access the Web-based configuration from a Web browser, such as Internet Explorer or Netscape Communicator.

■ Some changes on the Web console are not immediate. You need to apply them for the setting to become active.

■ You can configure the switch using an SNMP-based product, such as CiscoWorks.

exam
ⓦatch
As simple as this section is, keep in mind the two different aspects of making the connection to the Catalyst switch: the method of making the connection to the switch and the choice of user interface. There are four main methods of making the actual connection to the switch: connecting to the console port, Telnetting, using SNMP commands, and using the HTTP service. Once you've connected to the switch, the possible interfaces are the menu-based CLI, the IOS-based CLI, or the Web interface.

QUESTIONS

3.04: Configuration Methods

10. You've connected via a Telnet session to your Catalyst switch. When the session is established, you see the following on your screen:

    ```
    [M] Menus
    [I] IP Configuration
    ```

    Which user interface are you connected to?

    A. Web browser

    B. The default user interface with Standard Edition software

    C. The default user interface with Enterprise Edition software

    D. The SNMP Browser

11. What is the minimum version of Internet Explorer that is required to use the HTTP service on the Catalyst 1900?

    A. 3.0

    B. 4.0

    C. 4.7

    D. 5.0

12. How do you save any configuration changes made via the menu-driven interface?

    A. Type **copy run start** at the CLI.

    B. Choose System | Save from the menu hierarchy.

    C. Type **save config** at the CLI.

    D. You don't. Configuration changes are saved automatically.

TEST YOURSELF OBJECTIVE 3.05

Catalyst 1900 IOS Software Upgrades

This section covers two basic topics: the features made available by the Enterprise Edition software and the methods of delivering a new version of code to the Catalyst switch (TFTP download). Keep in mind that TFTP download requires a valid IP address to be assigned to the switch. It's not important to know what each Enterprise Edition feature does (for example, Fast EtherChannel or Uplink Fast STP), but it is important to know that these features are specific to the Enterprise Edition.

■ The Enterprise Edition software adds additional functionality to the switch. Additional features are as follows: VLANs, Fast EtherChannel, Uplink Fast STP, TACACS+, configuration file upload, and the CLI.

■ The CLI allows you to configure all the options for the switch. Some Enterprise features are not available from the menu-based or Web-based interfaces.

■ You can update the firmware of your switch by downloading the code from a TFTP server.

Don't expect to see many questions on this topic on the exam. TFTP downloads to the Catalyst switch usually transpire without a hitch. If the power gets interrupted during the transfer, the documentation included with the Enterprise Edition will help you get the switch back to a working state. If you do not have the documentation, the Cisco TAC will be able to assist you to get the switch back to a working state.

QUESTIONS

3.05: Catalyst 1900 IOS Software Upgrades

13.   What is required to transfer a new firmware revision to the Catalyst switch?

   A.   A password on the switch

   B.   At least one VLAN

   C.   A port configured for full-duplex operation

   D.   An IP address

14.   Which features are included with the Enterprise Edition of Catalyst software? (Choose all that apply.)

   A.   VLAN support

   B.   HTTP server

   C.   TACACS+

   D.   IOS CLI

15.   What is the default speed of the console port?

   A.   1200 baud

   B.   2400 baud

   C.   4800 baud

   D.   9600 baud

LAB QUESTION

Objectives 3.01–3.05

You have been given the task of installing a new Catalyst switch into your production network. The eventual goal for this switch is to be configured for multiple VLANs and HTTP server support, but for now your goal is simply to get it up and running and ready to configure. With that in mind, your tasks are to access the user interface and install the Enterprise Edition (which you have, except that the switch is only running Standard Edition) on the switch.

What steps will you take to reach your goal of installing Enterprise Edition onto your Catalyst switch?

A QUICK ANSWER KEY

Objective 3.01
1. **B** and **C**
2. **D**
3. **B**

Objective 3.02
4. **B**
5. **A**
6. **B**

Objective 3.03
7. **C**
8. **D**
9. **A**

Objective 3.04
10. **B**
11. **B**
12. **D**

Objective 3.05
13. **D**
14. **A, C,** and **D**
15. **D**

IN-DEPTH ANSWERS

3.01: User Interface

1. ☑ **B** and **C** are correct. With no password configured, the user will not be prompted to enter one. When no IP address has been configured, the menu shown will be displayed initially.

   ☒ **A** is incorrect. The default port speed for the ports on the switch is either 10 Mbps or 100 Mbps, depending on the port. **D** is incorrect. A base MAC address has already been assigned to the switch from the factory and cannot be changed.

2. ☑ **D.** The Standard Edition of Catalyst software offers a menu-driven interface by default.

   ☒ **A** is incorrect because the Enterprise Edition offers a more IOS-like environment. **B** is incorrect because Desktop is a flavor of Cisco IOS for routers only. **C** is incorrect because there is no such thing as Spanning-Tree Edition.

3. ☑ **B.** The Catalyst 1924 comes with 24 10-Mbps half-duplex ports for regular station connections. It also comes with two 100-Mbps ports, either 100baseTX, 100baseFX, or one of each.

   ☒ **A, C,** and **D** are incorrect. These two 100-Mbps ports are the most you can have on a Catalyst 1924.

3.02: Switch Basics

4. ☑ **B.** Store-and-forward switching involves taking the entire packet in and verifying its integrity before making a decision about how to forward the packet.

   ☒ **A** is incorrect because cut-through switching involves reading the destination MAC address, and forwarding the frame before the entire frame has been received. **C** is incorrect because fragment-free switching involves reading the first 64 bytes of the frame and, after making sure that it is not a runt frame produced by a collision, forwarding the frame out a destination port before the rest of the frame has been received. **D** is incorrect because Spanning-Tree is not a switching method.

5. ☑ **A.** The CDP protocol is a Layer 2 protocol that simply identifies one Cisco device to another.

   ☒ **B** is incorrect because CAM tables are not exchanged via this protocol. **C** is incorrect. It describes the function of the Spanning-Tree Protocol. **D** is incorrect. It describes the 802.1q protocol.

6. ☑ **B.** Ports 1 through 12 on a Catalyst 1912 switch are all 10baseT half-duplex ports. A Catalyst 1912 switch also has two 100-Mbps ports, labeled A and B. To fulfill the optional requirement, Steven should connect the proxy server to either the A port or the B port.

   ☒ **A, C,** and **D** are incorrect. The proposed solution produces the required result but not the optional result.

3.03: Initial Configuration

7. ☑ **C.** The flicker means the power on self test is checking the system components. During the POST, some of the LEDs represent various system components. If one of the components fails the POST, its corresponding port LED will turn amber. The exact error may be viewable via the command-line interface.

   ☒ **A** is incorrect because port LEDs do not give any information regarding VLAN configuration. **B** is incorrect because Spanning-Tree does not run during the initial power-up, and will turn the LED amber when a port is blocked. **D** is incorrect. The ports are already configured with default duplex operation.

8. ☑ **D.** Setting the mode to UTL on the front of the switch will give you a rough idea of how busy the switch is.

   ☒ **A, B,** and **C** are incorrect. These methods may be viable options, but they are not the *fastest* way to determine the load on the switch.

9. ☑ **A.** Assigning an IP address manually is recommended.

   ☒ **B** is incorrect because it is not possible to use the Web management feature without an IP address assigned to the switch. **C** is incorrect because using DHCP might be counter-productive; if you can't find out what your switch's IP address is, you won't be able to Telnet into it or use the Web management feature. **D** is incorrect because the Catalyst switch does have IP functionality for management purposes; it simply does not use Layer 3 information to perform packet forwarding.

3.04: Configuration Methods

10. ☑ **B.** The default user interface with Standard Edition software.

    ☒ **A** is incorrect because the Web Browser interface is not accessed via Telnet. **C** is incorrect. The Enterprise Edition offers an IOS-like CLI, not a menu-driven interface. **D** is incorrect because using SNMP does not involve an interface on the Catalyst switch.

11. ☑ **B.** Internet Explorer 4.0 is the minimum version required to use the HTTP service on the Catalyst switch.

    ☒ **A, C,** and **D** are incorrect. Versions higher than 4.0 may also be used, but 4.0 is the minimum version.

12. ☑ **D.** Any configuration changes made via the menu-driven interface are saved automatically.

    ☒ **A** is incorrect. COPY RUN START is typically used on a Cisco router. **B** is incorrect because System and Save are nonexistent choices in the menu-driven interface. **C** is incorrect. SAVE CONFIG is not a command used in any Cisco product.

3.05: Catalyst 1900 IOS Software Upgrades

13. ☑ **D.** An IP address.

    ☒ **A** is incorrect. A password is strongly recommended, but not required to transfer a file to the Catalyst. **B** is incorrect because it's not possible to configure a VLAN unless the Enterprise Edition has been installed on the router. **C** is incorrect. The transfer can take place over a port running at either half- or full-duplex.

14. ☑ **A, C,** and **D** are correct. VLAN support, TACACS+, and IOS CLI are all features included with the Enterprise Edition of Catalyst software.

☒ **B** is incorrect. The HTTP server feature is included in the Standard Edition.

15. ☑ **D.** The default console port speed is 9600 baud.

☒ **A, B,** and **C** are incorrect default speeds.

LAB ANSWER
Objectives 3.01–3.05

You will need to work from the ground up to get this switch ready for use on your network.

1. You first must make the initial connection to the switch. Do this by connecting the RJ-45 end of a console cable (which will come with your switch) to the console port on the Catalyst switch, and connecting the DB-9 end to the Com port on a PC running HyperTerm or some other terminal emulation program. With the HyperTerm program set to 9600-8-N-1, power on the switch. Observe the status of the LEDs during the POST, and watch for any anomalies. Assuming there is no password yet assigned to the switch, you will see the menu interface come up on your HyperTerm window, and step 1 will be complete.

2. This involves assigning an IP address to the switch, attaching a PC to the switch, and testing connectivity. Since TFTP is an IP protocol, IP must be running on your switch in order to make the transfer. Navigate through the menu hierarchy to the IP Management menu, and assign a valid IP address and subnet mask to the switch. Using a straight-through RJ-45 cable, attach a PC to a port on the front panel of the switch. Depending on what type of station this is in your network, you may need to plug into either one of the 10baseT ports, or one of the 100baseT ports. If this is simply a user station, a 10baseT port will suffice. If it is an enterprise server, a 100baseT port might be more appropriate. Be sure to check your duplex settings as well. Assuming this PC has a valid IP address on the same subnet as the Catalyst switch, you should now be able to ping between the switch and the PC.

3. At this point, you want to make the actual TFTP transfer of the Enterprise Edition software. Start the TFTP server on the PC, and make sure the Catalyst software is copied into the appropriate directory. On the switch, you will need to tell the switch the IP address of the TFTP server from which to get the new software. Assuming IP connectivity has been tested and established, you can now initiate the transfer procedure, which the switch will automate. The switch will notify you when the transfer is complete. It's a good idea not to perform this task during a period of power instabilities, such as a lightning storm, or in a place where the power is not reliable.

CISCO CERTIFIED NETWORK ASSOCIATE

4

Cisco Router IOS Software Basics

TEST YOURSELF OBJECTIVES

This chapter will focus on the way in which you will interface with the router, such as via Telnet and the console port. You will be asked questions that test your knowledge of the basic methods by which you can configure a router and perform certain tasks, such as the initial configuration of a router. This chapter will provide very tightly focused material that will give you a good review for the CCNA exam, and provide you with an idea of what areas you need to brush up on before the exam.

The material provided in this chapter is fairly fundamental, but do not underestimate the importance of it. A working knowledge of the fundamental methods of interfacing with and configuring a Cisco router will be imperative when you sit down to take the CCNA exam.

TEST YOURSELF OBJECTIVE 4.01

User Interface

The most common ways to interface with a Cisco router (or switch) is through the command-line interface (CLI). We won't discuss it here, but most Cisco products can also be configured, in a limited manner, through a Web interface.

You can Telnet to the router to access the CLI, or you can access the CLI via the console port. Basic information about the router, including show commands, can be accessed in User EXEC mode, but no configuration changes can be made. The Privileged EXEC mode is the router mode where changes to the configuration can be made. Privileged EXEC mode is accessed by typing **enable**, so it is sometimes called Enable mode.

- The most common way to interact with the router is through the command-line interface provided by the Cisco IOS software.

- In order to begin working with the router from the console, you may need to log in to access User EXEC mode.

- The highest level of access to the router is Privileged EXEC mode, sometimes called Enable mode, because the command you use to get into this mode is ENABLE.

You will find that exam terminology is often not the same as everyday terminology that you hear around your office. If you have hands-on experience with Cisco routers, you are probably accustomed to calling Privileged EXEC mode "Enable mode." In casual conversation, this will be the way that most people will refer to the Privileged EXEC mode, but when studying to take your Cisco Career Certification Exams, you will want to make sure that you remember that the modes are officially called User EXEC mode and Privileged EXEC mode.

QUESTIONS

4.01: User Interface

1. You have just unpacked a Cisco router at a customer's office. The vendor performed some very basic configuration, including setting the VTY password to *Cisco*, but you are ready to configure the majority of the router's operations via your laptop computer. List two possible ways to connect to that Cisco router, without any special configuration.

   A. Telnet to Line Console 0 and Telnet to Line VTY 0 4

   B. Connect directly to Line Console 0 and connect directly to Line VTY 0 4

   C. Telnet to Line Console 0 and connect directly to Line VTY 0 4

   D. Connect directly to Line Console 0 and Telnet to Line VTY 0 4

2. What is the most common way to interface with a Cisco router?

   A. Command-line interface (CLI)

   B. Cisco line interface (CLI)

   C. User EXEC mode

   D. Privileged EXEC mode

3. Which router mode is shown in the following example?

```
Router#
```

   A. User EXEC mode

   B. Privileged EXEC mode

   C. Global Configuration mode

   D. Interface Configuration mode

4. By default, how many VTY lines are available on a Cisco router?

   A. Two

   B. Three

   C. Four

   D. Five

TEST YOURSELF OBJECTIVE 4.02

Router Basics

Cisco router hardware is comprised of lines (such as Console and VTY), interfaces (Ethernet, FDDI, Serial, etc.), the processor, and memory. All Cisco routers test their hardware each time they are booted. This test is typically referred to as a power on self test (POST), but may also be referred to as bootstrap.

Once the router is powered on and you have logged on to the User EXEC mode, there are a variety of non-disruptive commands (meaning commands that will not change the way that the router functions) that can be entered. If you would like to see the list of available commands, you can type a question mark (**?**) at the prompt and press ENTER. You can also find the options (also known as arguments) for any command by typing that command, followed by a question mark (for example, **show ?**). Disruptive commands, meaning commands that affect the configuration of the router, are available in Privileged EXEC mode.

Cisco routers do not require the configuration of an enable password or an enable secret password, but configuring them is a good security policy, so most administrators do so. If there is an enable password, but no enable secret password, you will be required to enter the enable password to access the Privileged EXEC mode. If an enable secret password is configured, or an enable secret and an enable password are configured, you will be asked for the enable secret password when attempting to enter Privileged EXEC mode. To enter the Privileged EXEC mode, type the command **enable**. Once in Privileged EXEC mode, you can go back to User EXEC mode by typing **disable**. To completely exit your session, type **exit**, **logout**, or **quit**.

- ■ To access the router's Privileged EXEC mode, the user will be prompted for the router's enable secret password.

- ■ To leave Privileged EXEC mode and revert to User EXEC mode, use the command DISABLE.

- ■ To log out of the router entirely and end your console session, use the command EXIT, LOGOUT, or QUIT.

- ■ If you want to know all the commands available to you at any time, just type a question mark (**?**) at the router prompt.

- ■ Many commands you will be using have required parameters or *arguments*.

- ■ The hardware components of the router include memory, processor, lines, and interfaces.

- ■ Some of the most common router interfaces are serial interfaces, which generally connect the router to WAN and LAN interfaces including Ethernet, token ring, and FDDI.

- ■ The router's command executive has a hierarchy of modes that limit and organize the commands to configure the router.

- ■ When you power up your router, it first needs to test its hardware including memory and interfaces.

exam
watch

The Cisco command structure is such that certain nondisruptive commands are available in User EXEC mode, Disruptive Router-level commands are available in Privileged EXEC mode, and Disruptive Interface-level or Line-level commands are available in Interface Configuration mode and Line Configuration mode, respectively. Both Interface and Line Configuration modes are accessible only after you have entered Privileged EXEC mode. This structure should be carefully noted, since commands entered in the wrong mode will not have the desired affect and may not work at all.

QUESTIONS

4.02: Router Basics

5. If you are in Privileged EXEC mode, what is the command that you type to go to User EXEC mode?

   A. ENABLE

   B. DISABLE

   C. QUIT

   D. EXIT

6. You are at a client's corporate office and need to log on to the core router. The client has given you a password list that shows that this router has both an enable password and an enable secret password. Once you have logged on to User EXEC mode, what will you need to do to enter Privileged EXEC mode?

   A. Type **enable**, followed by the enable password.

   B. Type **enable**, followed by the enable secret password.

   C. Type **enable**, followed by the enable password and the enable secret password.

   D. Type **enable**, followed by either the enable password or the enable secret password.

TEST YOURSELF OBJECTIVE 4.03

Initial Configuration

Once in Privileged EXEC mode, you can enter Global Configuration mode by typing **configure terminal** (usually called config-t). In Global Configuration mode, the commands that you type affect the router's running configuration. These are changes that affect the router as a whole, not an individual interface (such as an Ethernet or Serial connection). Once configuration changes are made, typing **exit** or pressing CTRL-Z will take you back to Privileged EXEC mode.

A variety of commands will work in Privileged EXEC mode, but are not allowed in Global Configuration mode. The PING command is especially useful for testing network layer connectivity; the TRACEROUTE command will show you the path, hop by hop, that you traffic is taking through the internetwork; and the DEBUG command (which has a variety of options) is great for troubleshooting. Unfortunately, none of these tools can be used in Global Configuration mode. If you're in the middle of configuring something, you'll have to exit Global Configuration mode to use any of the three tools just mentioned.

- Once you are in Privileged EXEC mode, you then enter Global Configuration mode to make changes to the router's running configuration.

- The commands used to view the status of router memory elements, interfaces, and processes are known collectively as SHOW commands.

    - PING is a tool that tests connectivity at the network layer only.

    - TRACEROUTE provides information about which path your traffic is taking through the internetwork, hop by hop, as well as how long each hop is taking.

- DEBUG is a tool you can use to get detailed diagnostic information from your router about routing processes and messages the router is receiving, sending, or acting upon.

exam ⓦatch

It is especially important to note the fact that commands are specific to certain modes. For example, an interface may only be configured from Interface Configuration mode, and a globally significant command like IP CLASSLESS may only be entered from Global Configuration mode. As with all exams, be sure to read the questions on the CCNA exam very carefully to make sure that whatever command you're being asked about is being entered in the correct router mode. If it is not, the command will not work.

QUESTIONS

4.03: Initial Configuration

7. Your client asks you to configure an FDDI interface. Great! Except you can barely spell FDDI and certainly don't have a clue on how to configure an FDDI interface. Given your understanding of how to configure other interfaces, you should be able to make an educated guess at how to find the commands to configure a FDDI interface. What would you do?

   A. Type **interface ?** in Global Configuration mode.

   B. Type **fddi ?**.

   C. Type **show fddi ?** in Global Configuration mode.

   D. Type **show fddi ?** in Privileged EXEC mode.

8. Use the following example to answer the question below.

   ```
   Router(config-if)#
   ```

   What is the fastest way to enter the command SHOW INTERFACE SERIAL0?

   A. Type **exit**.

   B. Press CTRL-P, then press ENTER.

   C. Press CTRL-Z.

   D. Type **shutdown**, followed by **no shutdown**.

TEST YOURSELF OBJECTIVE 4.04

Configuration Methods and Modes

Each type of physical interface, such as Ethernet or Serial, will show slightly different information when you enter the SHOW INTERFACES command. The reason for the subtle differences is that each type of physical interface connects to a slightly different physical medium, and will, therefore, have slightly different data-link information.

Regardless of the medium connecting two Cisco devices, if Cisco Discovery Protocol (CDP) is enabled on each device, valuable information can be learned by typing **show cdp neighbors** or **show cdp neighbors detail** for more complete information. CDP is a Layer 2 media and protocol-independent protocol; it is enabled by default on all Cisco routers, switches, and access servers. If CDP is turned off, you would type **cdp enable** in Global Configuration mode to enable it. CDP can also be turned off on a specific interface with the NO CDP RUN command.

Of course, in large internetworks, administrators do not have console access to all of the routers, so Cisco routers have a Telnet application in the IOS. Typically, you will find the configuration for the Telnet (VTY) ports under Line VTY 0 4. The 0 4 indicates the first and last available Telnet lines and, while the default is five (0 to 4), this is configurable. In order for any of these lines to accept a Telnet connection, a password must be configured on that line.

■ Each type of physical interface, such as Ethernet or Serial, has slightly different information in its SHOW INTERFACE display that is specific to that data-link technology.

■ Cisco Discovery Protocol (CDP) is one of the best methods of understanding your network topology. CDP is a Layer 2 media- and protocol-independent protocol that runs by default on all Cisco routers, switches, and access servers.

■ In a large network with remote locations, an administrator cannot gain direct console access to a router to check the router's status or to change its configuration; therefore, Cisco routers have a Telnet application included in the IOS.

■ In order for a router to accept an incoming Telnet session, at least one of its VTY lines must be configured with a password.

■ The Cisco IOS software includes several commands that can be used to test basic connectivity in an IP network.

exam
ⓦatch

It is important to take note of the fact that access to VTY lines can be restricted using Standard Access Control Lists (ACLs). These ACLs are configured exactly like an ACL that you would apply to an interface, but they are not applied in the same way. ACLs for interfaces are applied with the ACCESS-GROUP command, whereas ACLs are applied to VTY lines using the ACCESS-CLASS command. The syntax is the same, but don't forget that the command is different. These ACLs may be applied inbound or outbound, but the effect is not the same as on a regular (LAN/Serial) interface. On the inbound, the router will filter based upon source address; on the outbound, the router will filter based upon the destination address.

QUESTIONS

4.04: Configuration Methods and Modes

9. Is it possible to configure more than five VTY lines on a Cisco router?

    A. Yes

    B. No

    C. Only on low-end routers

    D. Only on high-end routers

10. A customer with two office locations (San Antonio, TX, and Houston, TX) needs to have a highly secure network, and all possible measures need to be taken to make sure that unauthorized access to the routers is impossible. The routers at each location are in a physically secure area. All of the networking staff is in the San Antonio office. What is the best way to do this?

    A. VTY access lists on all routers and enable secret passwords

    B. VTY access lists on all routers in the Houston office, console-only access in the San Antonio office

    C. VTY access lists on all routers in the San Antonio office, no remote access to routers in the other office

    D. Console-only access in both offices

TEST YOURSELF OBJECTIVE 4.05

Sources for Cisco IOS Software

The Cisco IOS image can be loaded for three sources. For typical router operations, you will want to load the image either from a TFTP server or from Flash memory. Alternatively, you can load the small version of IOS stored in ROM. There are two ways to tell the router where to find its IOS image. The first way is through the router's 16-bit software configuration register (much older routers had a hardware configuration register, set using jumpers). The second and more common way is using the BOOT SYSTEM command. The two most common commands are as follows:

BOOT SYSTEM FLASH *<filename>*   This command tells the router to load a specific filename from Flash memory. The BOOT SYSTEM FLASH command, with no filename specified, will load the first IOS image in Flash.

BOOT SYSTEM TFTP *<tftp server IP address> <filename>*   This command tells the router to look on a specific TFTP server for a specific filename.

- Cisco routers have a 16-bit configuration register that is used to help the router find the Cisco IOS. This configuration register is stored in NVRAM.

- You can place BOOT SYSTEM commands in the router's configuration file that will instruct it where to look for its IOS image.

exam
Watch

You will want to pay particular attention to the various options for loading an IOS image during boot. You can configure the router to load the full IOS from Flash memory or a TFTP server, and you can also configure the router to select from multiple IOS images. Additionally, you can configure the router to load the bootstrap Image In the event that no full IOS image is available. You should know how to configure a router to go through a list and first attempt to load the IOS from a TFTP server, then from a backup TFTP server, and finally from Flash. This is a process that you should be comfortable with.

QUESTIONS

4.05: Sources for Cisco IOS Software

11. What effect will the following command, entered in global configuration mode, have on the operation of the router?

```
boot system 10.1.1.1 1600-ios-image
```

A. It will load the image named "1600-ios-image" from Flash.

B. It will load the image named "1600-ios-image" from TFTP server 10.1.1.1.

C. It will load the image named "1600-ios-image" from ROM.

D. This command will have no effect.

TEST YOURSELF OBJECTIVE 4.06

Maintaining the Cisco IOS Software

Cisco routers and most Cisco switches have the ability to copy IOS images and configuration files to and from TFTP servers. The command to copy an IOS image to a TFTP server in most Cisco routers and all IOS-based Cisco switches is COPY FLASH TFTP. To copy the IOS image from the TFTP server, the command is COPY TFTP FLASH. To copy a startup configuration to a TFTP server, the command is COPY STARTUP-CONFIGURATION TFTP, and to copy the configuration from the TFTP server, just enter **copy tftp startup-configuration**. Each of these commands will lead to the router prompting you for further information, such as the IP address of the TFTP server and various filenames. These commands can be useful when initially configuring a router, backing up a configuration, restoring a lost configuration, or updating the IOS image.

- A router has the capability to copy its configuration to and from a TFTP server.

- A router has the capability to backup, restore, or upgrade Cisco IOS images to and from a TFTP server.

- The router may also copy its configuration contents in RAM to the NVRAM by running the COPY RUNNING-CONFIG STARTUP-CONFIG command. Any time you do any significant changes, you should copy the configuration contents over or you will lose the settings upon the next reboot.

exam
ⓦatch

When evaluating the skills of prospective employees, one of the "gotcha" questions that I always include is about copying an IOS image to or from an FTP server. It is important to note the difference between an FTP server and a TFTP server. If you are asked a question about copying IOS images and router configurations, on the CCNA exam or elsewhere, it's a safe bet that any answer involving an FTP server is not the correct answer.

QUESTIONS

4.06: Maintaining the Cisco IOS Software

Questions 12–14   Use the following illustration and information to answer questions 12, 13, and 14.

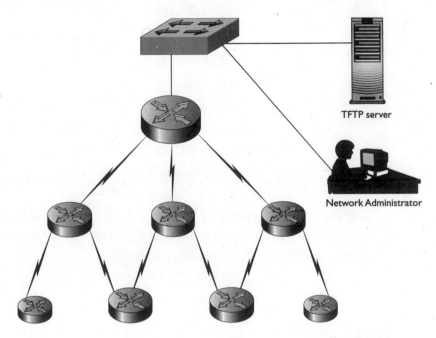

TFTP server

Network Administrator

12. Assume that all routers have been issued the COPY RUNNING-CONFIGURATION STARTUP-CONFIGURATION command since the last configuration changes were made to them. The network administrator would like to perform the task of backing up each router's configuration to the TFTP server. Which command should be entered on each router?

   A. COPY FLASH TFTP

   B. COPY TFTP FLASH

   C. COPY STARTUP-CONFIGURATION TFTP

   D. COPY TFTP STARTUP-CONFIGURATION

13. Assume that one of the routers in the preceding question has lost its configuration. What steps would need to be taken to restore the image from the TFTP server?

    A. Perform a basic configuration to establish connectivity, and then type **copy tftp flash**.

    B. Perform a basic configuration to establish connectivity, and then type **copy tftp startup-configuration**.

    C. Perform a basic configuration to establish connectivity, and then type **copy startup-configuration tftp**.

    D. Perform a basic configuration to establish connectivity, and then type **copy tftp flash**.

14. Your customer asks you to evaluate the placement of the TFTP server in the previous illustration. What should you tell him? (Choose all that apply.)

    A. The placement appears optimal, since the TFTP server appears to be at your core location.

    B. The placement appears optimal, since the TFTP server appears to be at the same location as your network administrator.

    C. While it appears to be correct, there is not enough information here regarding typical traffic flow to and from the server to make an absolute statement regarding the placement.

    D. The placement of the TFTP server should be in the most centralized location possible to avoid transferring large IOS images across multiple WAN links and consuming WAN bandwidth.

LAB QUESTION

Objectives 4.01–4.06

Your customer, who we met in questions 12–14, has some more complex issues and has asked for your assistance. Please review the more detailed network diagram that he has provided and use it to answer the following question.

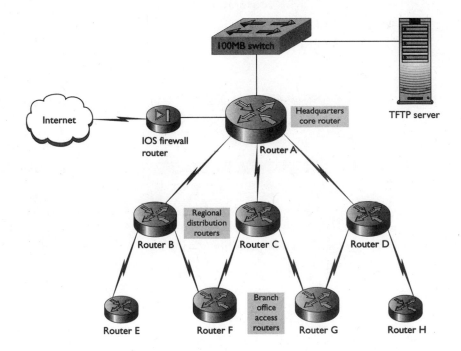

Your customer would like to apply as much security as possible to his network to prevent internal users from being able to access networking equipment. While security is important to him, firewalls are expensive, and he feels that they are overkill. In addition to security, he would like to minimize the effort required to update IOS images and needs to implement regular backups of router configuration files to enable him to recover in the event of a router failure. Please suggest a solution that will address each of his issues.

A QUICK ANSWER KEY

Objective 4.01

1. **D**
2. **A**
3. **B**
4. **D**

Objective 4.02

5. **B**
6. **B**

Objective 4.03

7. **A**
8. **C**

Objective 4.04

9. **A**
10. **B**

Objective 4.05

11. **D**

Objective 4.06

12. **C**
13. **B**
14. **A, B, C,** and **D**

IN-DEPTH ANSWERS
4.01: User Interface

1. ☑ **D.** You can use a console cable to connect directly to the console port of the router, which is represented in IOS by the Line Console 0. D would not have been a correct choice if the vendor had not preset the VTY password before delivering the router.

   ☒ **A** is incorrect because you cannot Telnet to the console port. **B** is incorrect because VTY lines are virtual lines and cannot be connected to directly. **C** is incorrect for the same reasons that A and B are incorrect.

2. ☑ **A.** Command-line interface (CLI) is correct.

   ☒ **B** is incorrect; there is no Cisco line interface. **C** and **D** are also incorrect. User EXEC mode and Privileged EXEC mode are both modes that you use to enter commands while you're interacting with the router, but they are not the mechanism by which you interact with the router.

3. ☑ **B.** Privileged EXEC mode is shown in this example, as indicated by the # in the router prompt.

   ☒ **A** is incorrect. The hostname would have looked like Router> for User EXEC mode. **C** and **D** are also incorrect. You can't enter any configuration commands at the # prompt.

4. ☑ **D.** There are five VTY lines (0 to 4) configured by default on Cisco routers.

   ☒ Based on the above correct answer, **A**, **B**, and **C** are incorrect.

4.02: Router Basics

5. ☑ **B.** The DISABLE command will return you to User EXEC mode.

   ☒ **A** is incorrect because typing **enable** from Privileged EXEC mode will have no effect; you'll remain in Privileged EXEC mode. **C** and **D** will both end your session with the router, not return you to User EXEC mode.

6. ☑ **B.** You would enter the ENABLE command. You will then be prompted for a password, which must be the enable secret password if one is configured.

    ☒ **A** is correct if there is an enable password, but no enable secret password. **C** and **D** are incorrect; the router requires the enable secret password only.

4.03: Initial Configuration

7. ☑ **A.** You already know that to configure an Ethernet interface, you'd type **interface Ethernet x**, so logic would tell you that an FDDI interface would be similar. Typing **interface ?** at the prompt in Global Configuration mode will show you the command to enter the Interface Configuration mode for an FDDI interface. Once in Interface Configuration mode, you can type **?** to see a list of available FDDI interface commands.

    ☒ **B** is incorrect because that will only show you commands that begin with FDDI, and what you are looking for here is how to enter Interface Configuration mode for an FDDI interface. **C** is an illegal command; you can't type **show commands** from Global Configuration mode. **D** might help you look at some information about the FDDI interfaces on the router, but will not allow you to configure the interface.

8. ☑ **C.** Pressing CTRL-Z will get you back to Privileged EXEC mode.

    ☒ **A** is incorrect because, as mentioned earlier, typing **exit** from Line Configuration mode will return you to Global Configuration mode, and SHOW commands cannot be entered in Global Configuration mode. **B** is incorrect because that keystroke is used to recall previously entered commands. **D** is incorrect because shutting down the interface will be of no help in trying to type a SHOW command.

4.04: Configuration Methods and Modes

9. ☑ **A.** Most Cisco routers can be configured with more than five VTY lines by typing the command **line vty x**, where x is the number or range of numbers for the additional VTY lines.

10. ☑ **B.** This is a subjective question, but the general "best practice" guideline would be to follow method B. The reason for this choice is that, if your routers are in a physically secure location, forbidding all but console access is the most secure method of accessing the router. In the example, however, the networking staff is all in San Antonio, and it is not feasible to think that they would travel to Houston just to perform basic router functions. It would, in this case, be a good idea to allow Telnet access to the Houston routers, but restrict it as much as possible by using VTY access lists. All four answers will technically work, but this question was looking for a "best practice" solution.

4.05: Sources for Cisco IOS Software

11. ☑ **D.** This command will have no effect, because the syntax is incorrect. The proper syntax for this command would be BOOT SYSTEM TFTP 10.1.1.1 1600-IOS-IMAGE. Without the TFTP keyword, this command is not a legal configuration command.

4.06: Maintaining the Cisco IOS Software

12. ☑ **C.** This command will copy the startup configuration (which was considered the same as the running-configuration for this example) to the TFTP server.

    ☒ **A** and **B** are incorrect because they have to do with the IOS image, not the configuration. **D** is incorrect because it would be used to copy the configuration from the TFTP server to the router.

13. ☑ **B.** You would want to configure the router just enough to establish connectivity to the TFTP server, and then download the configuration from the TFTP server to the startup configuration. Once the startup configuration is correct, you can reload the router, and the router will load with the proper configuration.

    ☒ **A** and **D** are incorrect because they deal with the IOS image, not the configuration. **C** is incorrect because it would copy the very basic configuration that you performed to establish connectivity to the TFTP server.

14. ☑ **A, B, C,** and **D** are correct. All of these statements are true statements.

LAB ANSWER
Objectives 4.01–4.06

The first step is to clearly identify all of the issues that need a resolution.

- Prevent internal users from accessing the routers. Firewalls are not an option.
- Minimize effort required to update IOS images.
- Implement regular backups of router configuration files.

The first issue can be addressed by the use of an access list, applied with the ACCESS-CLASS command, preventing Telnet access to the routers except from certain network management workstations.

The second issue can be addressed by using the TFTP server to load IOS images on boot. Don't forget to use Flash and ROM as backup options for image loading. This will mean that the local IOS images will only need to be updated when new functionality is implemented or a major bug is fixed. Minor IOS updates that do not affect critical router performance or functionality would not require an upgrade of the IOS images stored in each router's Flash. Use caution with this solution, however, and be certain the WAN links shown are fast enough to accommodate the loading of an IOS image via the WAN. If they are not, a local TFTP server at each location could be considered, but that would require almost as much effort as updating the Flash image directly. When you need to configure the boot sequence, don't forget that you can use the Global Configuration command BOOT SYSTEM ? to see all of the available options.

The third issue can be easily resolved using the TFTP server. Configuration files are extremely small, and the backup of configuration files can be done manually through the use of a script running on a server, or through a Network Management tool. Typically, you would back up the startup-configuration, and all networking staff should be careful to always write the running configuration to the startup configuration, using the command COPY RUNNING-CONFIGURATION STARTUP-CONFIGURATION after any changes.

CCNA
CISCO CERTIFIED NETWORK ASSOCIATE

5

TCP/IP
Protocol Suite

TEST YOURSELF OBJECTIVES

This chapter is a summary of the requirements for the CCNA certification exam. It will test your knowledge and abilities with regard to the TCP/IP suite and its components. You must know several of the reserved TCP and UDP ports and their purposes, and also the correlation between the TCP/IP suite and the OSI reference model. You will be expected to know several of the basic commands to configure a Cisco router. This will include enabling and configuring an interface, as well as saving and restoring a configuration. Make sure you are able to correlate the TCP/IP model to the OSI model and know how each layer operates on both models.

TEST YOURSELF OBJECTIVE 5.01

Application Layer Services

The Application layer services are those that interact with the user at the highest layer of the TCP/IP stack. You must be able to describe this layer in detail and be familiar with the well-known ports, such as port 80 for HTTP and ports 20 and 21 for FTP. You will need to know which layer of the TCP/IP stack corresponds with the OSI model layer.

- For internetworks consisting of heterogeneous computer systems that communicate with each other, TCP/IP stands out as the common denominator across all types of platforms.

- The TCP/IP suite has four major layers, which roughly correspond to the seven layers of the OSI reference model.

- Applications function at the OSI reference model Layer 7 or Layer 4 of the TCP/IP suite.

- The TCP/IP model does not have a formal Presentation or Session layer in general.

- RPCs are a method for executing programs (here called *procedures*) on the other network nodes so that they appear to be executing locally.

- Berkeley Sockets is a Session layer API.

- Windows Sockets (Winsock) runs on computer systems that use the Microsoft TCP/IP-32 stack.

- TLI ensures that the Transport layer will retain its independence from the Session, Presentation, and Application layer services.

- The Network Basic Input/Output System (NetBIOS) encountered in Microsoft environments is a Session layer API, not a protocol.

- In the Microsoft model NetBIOS can bind to TCP/IP, IPX, or NetBEUI.

The TCP and UDP ports are very important topics on the Cisco test. You will need to know the most important ones, such as POP3, SNMP, SMTP, and FTP. Know which ones are UDP and which are TCP, as well as their respective port numbers.

QUESTIONS

5.01: Application Layer Services

1. You are trying to configure your firewall to allow administrators who work from home to monitor the network in the same fashion as they do when they are in the office. Which port must you open to allow administrators to manage the network, and which protocol or protocols are used for this? (Choose all that apply.)

   A. SMTP

   B. SNMP

   C. Port 443

   D. Port 161

2. **Current Situation:** You have 350 users who work in the office. Over the next sixty days your office is going to move approximately 100 of them to home offices in order to cut back on office space. At the current time you have a very closed network, meaning that your firewall is blocking everything possible without stopping company production.

   Required Result: Users must be able to access the company's email system.

   Optional Desired Results:

   1. Users must be able to connect to the internal Web page of the company.

   2. Users have requested that IRC be used to communicate with other staff, both in the office and at home.

Proposed Solution: Open the firewall to ports 110 and port 25. Install an IRC server so that the users in the office can connect to it. The home-based employees will utilize a public external IRC server.

Which result does the proposed solution produce?

A. The proposed solution produces the required result and both optional results.

B. The proposed solution produces the required result and only one of the optional results.

C. The proposed solution produces the required result and none of the optional results.

D. The proposed solution does not produce the required result.

3. In the following illustration, which port settings will be used for server connections?

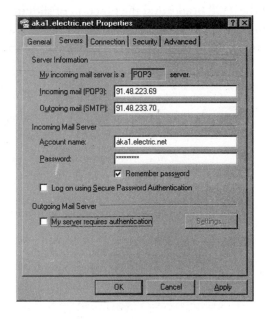

A. POP3 port 110 and SMTP port 25

B. POP3 port 10 and SMTP port 125

C. POP3 port 25 and SMTP port 110

D. POP3 port 23 and SMTP port 123

4. What is the predecessor of DHCP and which port does it use? (Choose all that apply.)

   A. TFTP

   B. BOOTP

   C. 67 and 68

   D. 20 and 21

TEST YOURSELF OBJECTIVE 5.02

Detailed Protocol Structure

It's important for the CCNA exam to understand reliable/unreliable, connection-oriented as well as connectionless packet transmission. You must be able to describe in detail the TCP header and the function of sliding windows. You will be expected to be able to trace packets from one station to another across the network, to know how packets are acknowledged, and to know what causes retransmissions.

- The function of the Transport layer is to provide the reliable transport of data between two systems, regardless of the underlying networks in between.

- The TCP is defined in RFC 793 and defines a reliable, connection-oriented, full-duplex byte stream for user processes.

- In TCP, efficient transmission over the network and flow control between senders and receivers are achieved by using a variable sliding window mechanism.

- A well-tuned sliding window protocol can keep the network completely saturated with packets and obtain substantially higher throughput.

- UDP provides a connectionless, unreliable datagram service.

- UDP flooding uses the IEEE 802.1d spanning tree algorithm to forward packets in a controlled manner.

Be careful when reading the questions and answers not to trip up on the port numbers such as list UDP port 21 for FTP instead of TCP port 21. Be aware that the UDP port x and TCP port x are not the same port.

QUESTIONS

5.02: Detailed Protocol Structure

5. In the following illustration of a TCP header, which part of the header (marked with the Xs) is missing?

Source port	Destination port
XXXXXXXXXXXXXXX	
Acknowledgment number	

Data offset	RSVD	Flags	Window
			Urgent pointer

Options + Padding
Data (variable length)

    A. Port number of destination host

    B. Clocking information

    C. IEEE802.2 packet type

    D. Sequence number

6. A UDP packet is said to be _____ and _____. (Choose two of the following.)

    A. Reliable

    B. Connectionless

    C. Connection-oriented

    D. Unreliable

7. Arrange the following four layers of the TCP/IP model, from top to bottom.

   1. Network

   2. Host-to-Host

   3. Application

   4. Internet

   A. 3, 2, 1, 4

   B. 3, 2, 4, 1

   C. 3, 4, 2, 1

   D. 3, 1, 2, 4

8. You have been asked to increase security at your company due to evidence that one or more employees have been accessing the systems to broadcast spam mail via your SMTP server. Your manager tells you that there is no budget for a firewall until next quarter—but you must do it now.

   Required Result: Keep unauthorized persons from using your SMTP server but allow authorized users to send mail.

   Optional Desired Results:

   1. Keep unauthorized persons from accessing your Web server.

   2. Keep unauthorized persons from posting to your NNTP server.

   Proposed Solution: Shut down your SMTP server and utilize only POP3 mail, change the port number for your Web server to port 8081, and change the port number for your NNTP server to port 119.

   Which of the following is correct?

   A. The proposed solution produces the required result and both of the optional results.

   B. The proposed solution produces the required result and only one of the optional results.

   C. The proposed solution produces the required result and none of the optional results.

   D. The proposed solution does not product the required result.

Network Layer

The Network layer is responsible for addressing. You must know how systems acquire their address via DHCP or RARP, or how they find another system's MAC address. You will need to understand the ICMP messages, what the different ICMP types are, and how they are used.

- ■ The second approach that can be used to forward UDP broadcasts is the IP helper address.

- ■ The Network layer deals primarily with addressing.

- ■ IP may be thought of as a delivery mechanism that moves packets from one host to another.

- ■ The protocol used to map IP addresses to MAC addresses on broadcast networks is called the ARP.

- ■ The RARP is used by systems that know their hardware address but do not yet know their IP address.

- ■ The InARP is generally used in non-broadcast networks such as Frame Relay. The goal is to dynamically associate a remote DLCI with an IP address.

- ■ ICMP messages are contained within IP packets. This ensures that the ICMP message will be able to find its way to the appropriate host within a group of subnets.

exam

ⓦatch

Go into the test knowing the definitions of ARP, RARP, SLARP, and AARP, and how and when they are used. Also be aware of the different ICMP packet field types.

QUESTIONS

5.03: Network Layer

9. Which protocol is implemented by Cisco to dynamically assign an IP address to a serial port based on the IP address of the neighboring router?

    A. ARP

    B. RARP

    C. SLARP

    D. AARP

10. What is ICMP primarily used for?

    A. Establish a Telnet connection

    B. PING (echo)

    C. Managing a network

    D. ARP

11. What is the flow control mechanism used to tell the originating host to reduce the rate at which packets are being sent?

    A. Source quench

    B. Back off

    C. Window size

    D. Router flow control

Operating System Commands

Knowledge of the basic commands of the Cisco router is required to successfully pass the CCNA exam. You must be able to log in as well as configure an interface for simple packet transmission, such as adding an IP address to an interface. You will need to know how to look at the configuration on the router as well as how to save the configuration to the router and also a TFTP server.

■ Some of the most common protocol commands are FTP and PING.

■ One of the first operating systems to include TCP/IP was BSD UNIX.

■ TCP/IP commands were incorporated as part of the 32-bit Microsoft operating systems, such as Windows NT, Windows 95, and Windows 98.

exam
ⓦatch

When reading the questions, be aware of the operating system that is being referred to. Remember that IPCONFIG does not work on Windows 95 systems but does work on Windows 98 and NT, whereas WINIPCONFIG works on Windows 95 and Windows 98 but not on Windows NT. Also know the commands used once you create an FTP session, such as "GET," "PUT," "MGET," "MPUT," "BIN," and "LS." When typing in commands for the test, remember that Unix questions require case-sensitive entries.

QUESTIONS

5.04: Operating System Commands

12. What command is used to display the collection of MAC addresses that are cached in the local system running a Microsoft Windows operating system?

    A. ARP a

    B. APR–a

    C. APR/a

    D. ARP|more

13. What command would be used to display the system name on a Unix system?

    A. HOSTNAME

    B. Show Host

    C. Host /d

    D. NETSTAT –R

14. A user calls in after moving his work PC from the office to his home, for full-time work. He tells you that he is not able to connect to any systems or browse the network when he dials up using his 33.6K modem connection. He informs you that when he uses his personal system at home, as he sometimes did when working from home only part-time, he is able to connect, but email can take 30 to 60 minutes to download. The new system is unable to do anything after connecting. Even when using his personal system he is unable to browse the Internet when dialing in to work, but can when he dials into his ISP. He tells you that he took the modem out of their "personal" PC to use in the work PC, because it did not have one. What is the reason for his problem? Office systems are configured with a static IP address, and people who work at home must use DHCP so that it does not hinder them from dialing into their ISP.

    Required Result: User is able to access required systems in office.

    Optional Desired Results:

    1. Decrease the time to download email.

    2. Enable user to browse Internet.

    Proposed Solution: Reconfigure the TCP/IP settings on the user's work PC for DHCP. Install a higher speed modem to decrease the time required to download email. Configure his browser to use the company proxy server.

    A. The proposed solution produces the required result and both optional result.

    B. The proposed solution produces the required result and only one of the optional result.

    C. The proposed solution produces the required result and none of the optional result.

    D. The proposed solution does not produce the required result.

Questions 15–17 This scenario should be used to answer questions 15, 16, and 17.

Your company has ten remote sites as well as the corporate office. The corporate office has approximately 100 users in the office and another 150 who work from home, both full- and part-time. Each remote site has 15 systems, and all of those users work in-office. The main office maintains a Web server set behind a firewall so that you can control access. You have several Cisco routers as well as four NT servers and two Novell NetWare servers. The users in the corporate office all run on Windows NT 4.0 systems. The home-based users have a mixture of Windows 95 and Windows 98 systems. The remote offices also have collections of Windows 95 and NT 4.0 systems; these Windows 95 systems in the remote offices are all Pentium 75MHz, whereas the NT systems are all running on Pentium IIIs. The home-based users connect via 56-Kbps dial-up connection or 128-Kbps ISDN, depending on their location. The remote offices all have Cisco routers connecting them to the corporate office via T1 lines. All except for the DNS, DHCP, and the serial connections on the corporate routers are provided with IP address by some dynamic fashion such as DHCP or BOOTP. The corporate office has installed a Unix system that acts as a mail server as well as a holding site for documents that the users need to share. All employees use Outlook Express as their mail client.

15. A Cisco router in a field office needs to be replaced. When the new unit arrives, you instruct an employee as to how to replace the old one with the new. The unit powers up, but you are still unable to send data across the link. What could be the problem?

   A. The receive window size is not the same as the previous router.

   B. SLARP is not turned on.

   C. The problem was with the TI, not the router, so replacing it didn't solve the problem

   D. It requires a system running NT at the remote office in order to initiate the data transfer.

16. Work-from-home users report that they are unable to transfer files using FTP since the firewall was brought online. Which of the following is the most likely cause?

   A. The firewall is blocking ports 110 and 25. These ports need to be opened; they are required for users of FTP.

   B. The firewall is blocking ports 67 and 68. These ports need to be opened; they are required for users of FTP.

   C. The firewall is blocking ports 20 and 21. These ports need to be opened; they are required for users of FTP.

   D. The firewall is blocking port 80. This port needs to be opened; it is required for users of FTP.

17. What process is used by a system in the corporate office to send data to a system in the remote office when it has only the system's TCP/IP address?

   A. The PC in the corporate office will ARP for the MAC address of the PC in the remote office. Being on a remote network, it will receive the MAC address of the gateway and use that as the destination station in the data packet being sent. It will rely on the gateway to locate the MAC address of the destination PC.

   B. The PC in the corporate office will ARP for the MAC address of the PC in the remote office and then use that MAC address of the destination station in the data packets being sent.

   C. The PC in the corporate office will RARP for the MAC address of the PC in the remote office and then use that MAC address of the destination station in the data packets being sent.

   D. The PC in the corporate office will query the DNS server for the MAC address of the PC in the remote office and use that MAC address of the destination station in the data packet being sent.

LAB QUESTION

Objectives 5.01–5.04

You are a computer technician working for a large company. A user calls to report that she is unable to access company files. She has recently moved from the third to the ninth floor. You also find out that she has made the move herself. You will need to FTP the TCP/IP settings file off the FTP server (tech.ourcomopany.com) and compare those settings to the ones on the user's PC. Some of the floors have DHCP servers, and others have not been upgraded from static to dynamic IP configuration. You will need to make sure that the user has Outlook Express set up correctly in order to point to the POP3 and SMTP servers used for that floor. The server name is "pop3.9thfloor.ourcompany.com:110" and the SMTP is ".9thfloor.outcompany. com:25." The proxy server for that floor is "proxy-9.ourcompany.com:8080." What steps should you take to devise a solution to the problem?

A QUICK ANSWER KEY

Objective 5.01

1. **B** and **D**
2. **C**
3. **A**
4. **B** and **C**

Objective 5.02

5. **D**
6. **B** and **D**
7. **B**
8. **D**

Objective 5.03

9. **C**
10. **B**
11. **A**

Objective 5.04

12. **B**
13. **A**
14. **A**
15. **B**
16. **C**
17. **A**

IN-DEPTH ANSWERS

5.01: Application Layer Services

1. ☑ **B** and **D** are correct. SNMP is the Simple Network Management Protocol, and it uses TCP port 161.

   ☒ **A** is incorrect because SMTP is used for mail. **C** is incorrect because 443 is reserved for secured HTTP communications.

2. ☑ **C.** The proposed solution will allow home-based users to access the email systems by opening up ports 25 and 110. The optional results are not met because all users must use the same IRC server, or cluster of IRC servers, in order to access the same channels. A public IRC server will not be able to connect the home-based users to the internal IRC server. There is no solution to allow home-based users to reach the internal Web server.

   ☒ **A** and **B** are incorrect because neither of the optional results are met (see above). **D** is incorrect because the required result is met.

3. ☑ **A.** POP3 uses port 110 and SMTP uses port 25 for communications.

   ☒ **B, C,** and **D** are incorrect. They list incorrect ports: port 23 is used for Telnet and port 123 is used for NTP (Network Time Protocol).

4. ☑ **B** and **C** are correct. BOOTP was the predecessor of DHCP and used ports 67 and 68. BOOTP is still in use today, primarily for loading IP addresses on switches and routers. It does not have the ability to configure items such as DNS or WINS server addresses.

   ☒ **A** is incorrect. TFTP mainly used to load switches and routers. **D** is incorrect because ports 20 and 21 are used for FTP, not BOOTP.

5.02: Detailed Protocol Structure

5. ☑ **D.** The sequence number is missing from the illustration.

☒   **A** is incorrect because the destinations port number is listed. **B** is incorrect because clocking is not a part of a TCP header. **C** is incorrect because there is no IEEE801.2 packet field in the TCP header.

6.   ☑   **B** and **D** are correct. UDP is unreliable and connectionless, meaning that no acknowledgment of the reception of the packet is relayed back from the sending station.

☒   **A** and **C** are incorrect because they describe TCP, not UDP.

7.   ☑   **B.** The correct order appears in answer B.

☒   **A**, **C**, and **D** are all in the incorrect order.

8.   ☑   **D.** By shutting down your SMTP server you cannot send mail. Users cannot use POP3 to send mail; it is only used to receive mail from the mail server.

☒   **A**, **B**, and **C** are all incorrect because the required results are not met.

5.03: Network Layer

9.   ☑   **C.** SLARP or Serial Line Address Resolution Protocol is used by Cisco to dynamically assign an IP address to the serial port. When the router is powered up, the serial port will send out a SLARP request on its serial line. The neighboring router responds with its IP address and subnet mask. The router will then assign itself an IP address and mask based on the information provided.

☒   **A** is incorrect because ARP is used to determine the MAC addresses of a system when the IP address is known. **B** is incorrect because RARP is used by systems that know their MAC address to learn their IP address, such as with X-Windows stations. **D** is incorrect because AARP is Apple Talk's Address Resolution Protocol.

10.   ☑   **B.** PING (ICMP term is "echo") uses ICMP or Internet Control Message Protocol to see if a remote station is reachable.

☒   **A** is incorrect because ICMP has nothing to do with a Telnet connection. Telnet is purely TCP. **C** is incorrect; SNMP is used to manage a network. **D** is incorrect because ARP is its own protocol.

11. ☑ **A.** Source quench is the process that tells the originating or sending host to back off on packets because either the receiving host or the gateway is being overflowed. The sending host will reduce the number of packets sent until it stops receiving the source quench packets. After a while it may try to increase the packet rate again.

    ☒ **B** and **D** are incorrect. Back off and router flow control are not real terms. **C** is incorrect because the window size is determined when the connection is created between the two hosts.

5.04: Operating System Commands

12. ☑ **B.** The "–a" instructs the system to display the current MAC address cache on the system.

    ☒ **A, C,** and **D** are all incorrect because they are not valid switches for the ARP utility.

13. ☑ **A.** HOSTNAME is used to display the name currently configured on the Unix system.

    ☒ **B** and **C** are incorrect because they are not valid commands. **D** is incorrect because it is used to display the statistics and the state of the TCP/IP connections.

14. ☑ **A.** By changing the TCP/IP settings, from the IP address in the office to DHCP, the user will be able to acquire the correct IP address and mask. A 56K modem will increase the bandwidth and allow for quicker downloading of email. Reconfiguring the browser to use the company's proxy server will allow him to browse the Internet while connected to the company.

    ☒ **B** and **C** are incorrect because the proposed solutions met both of the optional results. **D** is incorrect because the proposed solution produced the required result.

15. ☑ **B.** More than likely SLARP is not configured. The scenario states that everything except for the DNS, DHCP, and corporate routers get their IP address dynamically, so, presumably, SLARP is being used to assign the IP address to the serial links on the routers.

☒   **A** is incorrect because the data window size is a setting that is determined during the call-setup phase and is down by the systems without operator intervention. **C** is incorrect, based on the answer above. **D** is incorrect because Cisco does not require a server or PC to bring a line up—only data, which could come from anywhere, including another router.

16.   ☑   **C.** Ports 20 and 21 are required for FTP processes to work correctly. If the firewall is blocking one or both of them, the FTP utility will not function correctly. Configuring the firewall to allow data on TCP ports 20 and 21 to pass through will allow users to utilize FTP.

☒   **A** is incorrect because TCP ports 25 and 110 are used for mail, not for FTP. **B** is incorrect because ports 67 and 68 are used for DHCP. **D** is incorrect because port 80 is used for HTTP traffic.

17.   ☑   **A.** The PC in the corporate office will ARP using the TCP/IP address of the remote system it wishes to reach. Since the PC is on a remote network it will receive the MAC address of the gateway and use that as the destination address. It will transmit data using the gateway's MAC address and rely on it to route the packet to the correct network.

☒   **B** is incorrect because the MAC address for the PC in the remote office is not known on the local network and therefore cannot be received by the corporate PC. **C** is incorrect because RARP is used when a station knows its MAC but needs its TCP/IP address. **D** is incorrect because the station has the TCP/IP address and therefore does not need to access the DNS in order to find it.

LAB ANSWER

1. You will need to access the TCP/IP. From the command prompt, type **ftptech.ourcompany.com**. Log in using your name and password.

2. Download the file using GET *<filename>* or MGET *<filename>*.

3. Close the connection.

4. Determine whether the user is to be using DHCP or static. In this case, we'll assume static with IP of 192.168.1.2 255.255.255.0 mask 192.168.1.1 gateway 243.22.59.1.

5. Go to the user's system. If it's Windows 95, type command prompt **winipconfig /all |more** to check the IP address. If it's Windows NT or Windows 98, type **ipconfig /all** at the command prompt to determine the IP address and configuration.

6. If the IP address is incorrect, right-click Network Neighborhood, choose Properties, and make the necessary changes.

7. Confirm settings for Outlook Express to be sure that the user is pointing to the correct SMTP and POP3 server for their area.

8. Confirm that the settings in the user's browser for proxy are configured for the correct proxy server.

9. Reboot the system after all changes have been made.

10. Clear the ARP cache to ensure that the system isn't trying to use a MAC address for a network not connected by type ARP–d.

11. Ping a station that you know is on the local network such as the mail server or gateway.

12. Ping a station you know is on another network in the office that the user should be able to reach.

13. Have the user access her email to confirm it works.

14. Have the user browse the Internet to ensure that she is able to do so.

CISCO CERTIFIED NETWORK ASSOCIATE

6

IP Addressing

T he cornerstone of the Internetworking environment today is IP addressing. A thorough understanding of IP addressing is not only essential for network connectivity, but also for passing the CCNA exam.

Several questions on the CCNA exam will demand immediate recognition of IP address classes, identifying correct and incorrect subnet masks, and computing correct subnet masks for various scenarios. You must be familiar with the rules of effective subnet planning, and the mechanics of complex subnetting solutions. The exam will also require knowledge of the Cisco IOS commands for assigning IP addresses and subnet masks. You will be required to recognize correct and incorrect syntax and input syntax lines as you would on a Cisco device. Finally, you should be familiar with some of the advanced techniques of configuring IP networks, including supernetting and variable-length subnet masking. After completing this section, you will have a well-rounded understanding of IP addressing both in theory and practice.

TEST YOURSELF OBJECTIVE 6.01

Classes of IP Addresses

IP addresses for individual end stations are divided into three main address classes: Class A, B, and C addresses. Keep in mind that there is a multicast range for the one-to-many type of traffic flow. There is also a reserved address range that is used for research and development. On the exam you will be given an address and asked to identify in which class the address belongs. It is recommended that you memorize the first-byte address ranges of each class, as listed here:

Class	First-Byte Address Range
A	0–126
B	128–191
C	192–223
D	224–239
E	240–255

Note: 127.*x.x.x* address range is reserved for loop-back functions and is not included in any specific address class.

You should also be able to identify how many networks and hosts are available within each standard class, as shown here:

Class	Number of Networks	Number of Hosts
A	126	16,777,214
B	16,384	65,534
C	2,097,152	254

See the *Study Guide* for the complete explanation on IP address class structure.

- The IP is used for end-to-end routing of data across a network, which may mean that an IP packet must travel across multiple networks and may cross several router interfaces to get to its destination.

- The implementation of address classes divided the address space into a limited number of very large networks (Class A), a much larger number of intermediate-sized networks (Class B), and a very large number of small networks (Class C).

- The 32-bit structure of an IP address is comprised of both a network address and a host address.

- Subnetting extends the network portion of the address to allow a single network to be divided into a number of logical sections (subnets).

- Certain addresses in the IP address space have been reserved for special purposes and are not normally allowed as host addresses.

- When all the bits in the host portion of an IP address are set to zero, it indicates the network, rather than a specific host on that network.

- The network address 127.x.x.x has been designated as a local loop-back address.

- When all the bits in an IP address are set to ones, the resulting address, 255.255.255.255, is used to send a broadcast message to all hosts on the local network.

- If you set all the host bits in an IP address to ones, this will be interpreted as a broadcast to all hosts on that network. This is also called a *directed broadcast*.

- You can determine the class of an IP address by looking at the first (most significant) octet in the address.

- If the highest bit in the first octet is a zero (0), the address is a Class A address.

- A Class B address is characterized by a bit pattern of 10 at the beginning of the first octet.

- A Class C address will have a bit pattern of 110 leading the first octet.

- Class D addresses have a bit pattern that begins with 1110. A Class D address refers to a group of hosts, who are registered as members of a *multicast group*.

- If the first four bits of the first octet are 1111, the address is a Class E Address.

exam
Ⓦatch

Be able to recognize addresses classes at a glance on the exam. Some questions will simply have you indicate the class of the address, more advanced questions will require you to make a subnet calculation. If you have associated the address with the incorrect class, this will translate into an incorrect subnet calculation. Know your classes!

QUESTIONS

6.01: Classes of IP Addresses

1. Given the IP address 156.11.99.0 and a subnet mask of 255.255.240.0, what IP address class does this address fall under?

   A. Class A

   B. Class B

   C. Class C—subnetted

   D. Class D

2. Which of the following is an example of a Class B address?

   A. 200.10.1.5

   B. 233.256.5.2

   C. 1.11.56.2

   D. 130.156.10.55

3. In the following illustration, which network is using a Class A address?

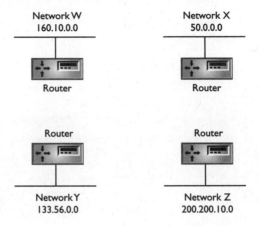

A. Network W

B. Network X

C. Network Y

D. Network Z

TEST YOURSELF OBJECTIVE 6.02

Subnetting and Subnet Masks

The subnet mask is a constant companion of the IP address. Each device uses the mask in order to determine the meaning of the address; specifically, is the address subnetted, and, if so, what bits in the address are reserved for subnetting? The CCNA exam will require you to interpret and calculate valid subnet masks for various scenarios. Be sure you understand the mechanics of subnetting; don't rely on simply memorizing the various masks.

■ An IP address cannot exist without an associated subnet mask. The subnet mask defines how many of the 32 bits that make up an IP address are used to define the network or the network and associated subnets.

- You can further segment a network into subnets by borrowing host address bits and using them to represent a portion of your network.

- To gain the economy and simplicity of a single network address, yet provide the capability to internally segment and route your network, use subnetting.

- In a subnetted network, each address contains a network address, a subnet portion, and a host address.

exam

⬙atch *The number one cause of network failure is the incorrect configuration of a subnet mask. As you go through the various questions on the exam, this should be the first configuration that you verify. Sometimes the solution to the problem is the most obvious!*

QUESTIONS

6.02: Subnetting and Subnet Masks

4. Which of the following is the default mask for a Class C address?

   A. 255.255.255.0

   B. 255.0.0.0

   C. 255.255.240.0

   D. 255.255.255.128

5. **Current Situation:** Your San Francisco-based company, Moth Balls, Inc., is expanding into two new cities, Chicago and Detroit. You need to install two new Cisco routers (one at each location) and configure their interfaces to be able to route back to your head office in San Francisco. You will be using Frame Relay, so each site has one Serial interface configured for the WAN cloud. Each site has a single Ethernet interface.

   Required Result: Your configuration will need connectivity on your WAN interfaces.

Optional Desired Result: You should be able to communicate between the Ethernet segments in San Francisco and Chicago, and San Francisco and Detroit.

Proposed Solution: Examine the following table for your implemented configuration.

City	WAN IP Address	WAN Subnet Mask	Ethernet Segment IP Address	Ethernet Segment Subnet Mask
San Francisco	199.10.10.1	255.255.255.0	156.11.11.193	255.255.255.192
Chicago	199.10.10.2	255.255.255.0	156.11.12.1	255.255.255.192
Detroit	199.10.10.3	255.255.255.0	156.11.13.1	255.255.255.192

Routing protocols have been activated and all routers are advertising their connected networks to each other. After a ping test from San Francisco to all ports, WAN and Ethernet, how many of the results were satisfied?

A. The proposed solution meets the required result and all of the optional results.

B. The proposed solution meets the required result and some of the optional results.

C. The proposed solution meets the required result and none of the optional results.

D. The proposed solution does not meet the requirements.

6. What is the decimal equivalent of the following binary mask?

11111111,11100000,00000000,00000000

A. 255.255.255.0

B. 255.0.0.0

C. 255.111.0.0

D. 255.224.0.0

TEST YOURSELF OBJECTIVE 6.03

Subnet Planning

Have you ever heard of the phrase, "Measure twice, cut once?" There is no substitute for properly planning out your IP strategy. The goals of effective planning are to maximize address space and meet the designated design requirements of a given network infrastructure. Poor planning can result in wasted IP addresses that can hamper the growth of a network. If an IP strategy is shown to be inadequate after it has been fully implemented into a network, the cost of redesign and re-implementation can be extremely high. Therefore it is crucial that you take extra time in the planning stage. The CCNA exam will zero in on your prowess at calculating correct subnet masks for particular host and network requirements.

- In choosing a subnet, the chief consideration is how many subnets you will need to support.

- Once you have determined the appropriate subnet mask, the next challenge is to determine the address of each subnet, and the allowable range of host addresses on each subnet.

exam
ⓦatch

Pay special attention to the particular multiple-choice answers to questions pertaining to correct subnet planning. Sometimes more than two answers may seem correct, but only one is the right answer. For example, the subnet masks 255.255.240.0 (14 subnets, 4094 hosts) and 255.255.248.0 (30 subnets, 2046 hosts) will both meet the requirement for allowing up to 12 possible networks for a Class B address. However, the 248 subnet does not maximize the number of hosts possible for the requirement of 12 networks, and so the first subnet mask would be the correct answer.

QUESTIONS

6.03: Subnet Planning

7. Once you have chosen an IP address space. In what sequence should the following steps be performed when planning out your IP architecture?

    1. Implement your solution.

    2. Calculate the needed subnet mask.

    3. Test the configuration in a pilot environment.

    4. Determine the maximum number of networks and hosts required.

    A. 1, 3, 2, 4

    B. 4, 2, 3, 1

    C. 4, 3, 2, 1

    D. 2, 3, 4, 1

8. What is the maximum number of hosts useable for each network with the IP address space 210.50.50.0 with the subnet mask of 255.255.255.248?

    A. 8

    B. 6

    C. 2046

    D. 2

9. **Current Situation:** You have been appointed the task of planning the IP address structure for a new company, Nuts 'n Bolts, Inc. They have obtained a Class B address space, 133.10.0.0, and have purchased all routers required for their LAN and WAN installation. They require connectivity for all networks and hosts across their LAN and WAN and have entrusted you with the task.

    Required Result: The company requires the IP configuration to accommodate 28 networks with the maximum of 750 hosts per network. They will not let the number of hosts exceed 750.

Optional Desired Results:

1. The company expects to require an additional 20 networks for a total of 48 networks, with the same host requirements.

2. The company does not want any of the addresses reconfigured when the expansion is required.

Proposed Solution: You sit down with the company's IT to verify their IP address design. The senior architect speaks up and declares that the network will be subnetted using the mask 255.255.248.0, showing that the solution is adequate for immediate implementation. You politely interject and suggest that the mask be changed to 255.255.252.0. Trusting your word, they implement the solution without testing. What requirements were met?

A. Your amended solution meets the required result and all of the optional results.

B. Your amended solution meets the required result and some of the optional results.

C. Your amended solution meets the required result and none of the optional results.

D. Your amended solution does not meet the requirements.

Questions 10–11   This scenario should be used to answer questions 10 and 11.

Company Y has grown extremely fast over the last five years, and they expect tremendous growth over the next five years. They are convinced that their current network infrastructure will not be able to support the future growth and have looked to you to explain the benefits of switching to an IP-based infrastructure. Furthermore, they seek your leadership and expertise to assist in the design, configuration, and implementation of the new IP architecture. It is paramount that as their needs change in the future, costs can be kept low on new configurations and overall performance not decrease over time.

10. What is the first task of the network architect when attacking this kind of project?

A. Communicate with the client to ascertain their exact needs, present and future.

B. Start a pilot network to test some configurations.

C. Design the IP address structure and hope it meets the needs of the client.

D. Inform the customer that planning is not really necessary.

11. The customer wishes to maintain high network performance and reduce the chance of broadcast storms bringing down the network. Which is the correct recommendation?

   A. Choose a Class A address to accommodate a huge amount of hosts, and have one large network.

   B. Carefully divide the network into smaller, manageable portions with subnetting.

   C. Purchase more powerful computers and servers.

TEST YOURSELF OBJECTIVE 6.04

Complex Subnetting

IP address space is precious. It was also expected that the Internetworking community would run out of IP addresses long ago. Well thanks to a few complex subnetting techniques like variable-length subnet masking and supernetting, the Internetworking community has managed to stretch their IP dollar a little farther. You should be able to understand and recognize configurations using VLSM and supernetting and understand why they are implemented. Refer to the *Study Guide* if you need to review how VLSM and supernetting work.

   ■ Whenever you use more than eight bits for subnets, you run into the issue of crossing octet boundaries.

   ■ If you could take one of your subnets, and further divide it into a second level of subnetting, you could effectively "subnet the subnet" and retain your other subnets for more productive uses. This idea of "subnetting the subnet" forms the basis for VLSM.

   ■ Supernetting removes bits from the default mask, starting at the right-most bits and working to the left.

exam
ⓦatch

Be cautious on the exam when examining particular configurations. VLSM and supernetting will allow for configurations that, on the surface, look incorrect. Make sure you double-check what the question is actually asking and don't mistake a VLSM or supernetting solution for a bad configuration. Questions on complex subnetting should be easy to spot if you know the terms.

QUESTIONS

6.04: Complex Subnetting

12. Which of the following is a complex subnetting technique that enables you to subnet a subnet and save you from wasting valuable host addresses?

    A. Variable-length supernetting

    B. Submarine netting

    C. Variable-length subnet masking

    D. Supernetting

13. Given the following contiguous Class C subnets, using supernetting, what mask could you use to advertise them all to the Internet as a single network?

200.10.224.0	224=11100000
200.10.225.0	225=11100001
200.10.226.0	226=11100010

    A. 255.255.255.0

    B. 255.255.255.252

    C. 255.255.252.0

    D. 255.0.0.0

14. What complex subnetting technique allows you to advertise contiguous subnets as one network?

    A. Variable-length subnet masking

    B. Supermasking

    C. Unmasking

    D. Supernetting

TEST YOURSELF OBJECTIVE 6.05

Configuring IP Addresses with Cisco IOS

You will prove your weight in gold on the exam and in real-life situations when you can transpose your theoretical knowledge of IP addressing, simple and complex subnetting, and subnet planning to Cisco hardware. Navigating effectively through Cisco's IOS for the purpose of configuration and troubleshooting will be relevant in any routing environment you encounter. For the exam, you will be required to recognize and provide the Cisco IOS commands for entering into Privileged mode on the router and entering in the addressing commands.

- Domain Name System (DNS) mapping is a process that allows user names for network hosts, rather than having to specify them by their IP addresses.

- Pocket Internet groper (PING) is a common utility used with IP to test connectivity between two IP hosts.

- You can use TraceRoute for route information, and Telnet, a terminal emulation program that will validate connectivity at higher protocol levels.

The CCNA exam will constantly try to trip you up on syntax, so be on the lookout! Commands will be reversed or missing, even though the configuration information might be correct. Also watch out for forgotten masks in the configuration.

QUESTIONS

6.05: Configuring IP Addresses with Cisco IOS

15. Which IOS command will correctly configure the e0 interface for the IP address 192.168.50.1 and mask 255.255.255.0? Assume you are already in config-t mode.

   A. `int s0`
      `ip address 192.168.50.1 255.255.255.0`

B. `int e0`

`address ip 192.168.50.1 255.255.255.0`

C. `int e0`

`ip address 192.168.50.1 255.255.255.0`

D. `int e0`

`ipaddress 192.168.50.1 255.255.255.0`

16. What IOS command will ensure that the interface is brought up when the configuration is loaded?

A. INTERFACE UP

B. NO SHUTDOWN

C. INTERFACE ON

D. E0 ON

17. **Current Situation:** A client is seeking to contract you to configure routers for five new offices. They would like to submit a sample configuration before granting you access to their network. They want you to configure two interfaces on a router, e0 and s0, and attempt to meet all of their criteria. If you achieve all their desired results, you will be hired as the technical lead. If you meet only the required results, you will assist in a minor roll. If you fail to meet the required result, you will not be hired.

Required Result: You must choose a Class B address for the s0 interface and a Class C address for the e0 interface.

Optional Desired Results:

1. The customer wishes you to subnet the Class B address in interface s0 to accommodate at least 25 networks and 2000 hosts.

2. All interfaces must come up when the router is turned on.

Proposed Solution: You accept the task with enthusiasm and set to work. Here is the configuration (interface portion) that you have submitted for review:

```
interface s0

    ip address 188.100.8.1 255.255.248.0

    no shutdown
```

```
interface e0

ip address 200.100.100.1 255.255.255.0

no shutdown
```

A. The proposed solution meets the required result and all of the optional results.

B. The proposed solution meets the required result and some of the optional results.

C. The proposed solution meets the required result and none of the optional results.

D. The proposed solution does not meet the required result.

LAB QUESTION
Objectives 6.01–6.05

Your customer wishes to migrate his IPX network to an IP network over the next year. The network is large, with a head office of over 5,000 users, as well as about 100 wide-area locations across the country. Many of the remote offices changed locations or are closed, and new offices have opened, so a tremendous amount of flexibility is required in the maintenance of their network.

As a network architect, it is your job to understand (and eventually design a configuration that will meet) all the customer expectations and needs. Your report should provide explanations of the relevant details of design and implementation that will apply to the customer's needs. Your answer should be structured in three stages: design, implementation, and maintenance. Using what you have learned from this section, come up with two or three important points or issues that arise in each step. This process forces you to look at the whole picture, not just the specifics of choosing or configuring a single address.

A   QUICK ANSWER KEY

Objective 6.01

1. B
2. D
3. B

Objective 6.02

4. A
5. C
6. D

Objective 6.03

7. B
8. B
9. A
10. A
11. B

Objective 6.04

12. C
13. C
14. D

Objective 6.05

15. C
16. B
17. A

IN-DEPTH ANSWERS

6.01: Classes of IP Addresses

1. ☑ **B.** It is a Class B address. Regardless whether or not it is subnetted, the first octet still indicates the class. 156 lies in the Class B range (128–191).

   ☒ **A** is incorrect because the Class A address range is from 1–126. **C** is incorrect because the address range for a Class C address is 192–223. **D** is incorrect because the address range for a Class D network is 224–239.

2. ☑ **D.** 130.156.10.55.

   ☒ **A** is incorrect because it is a Class C address. **B** is incorrect because it is an illegal address. **C** is incorrect because it is a Class A address.

3. ☑ **B.** Network X. The first octet is in the Class A range 0–127.

   ☒ **A** and **C** are incorrect because they are Class B addresses. **D** is incorrect because it is a Class C address.

6.02: Subnetting and Subnet Masks

4. ☑ **A.** The first three octets define the network portion of a Class C address.

   ☒ **B** is incorrect because it is a mask for a Class A network. **C** is incorrect because it is for a Class B network, plus it is subnetted. **D** is incorrect because it is for a Class C network, but it is subnetted.

5. ☑ **C.** The San Francisco configuration is correct on the LAN and WAN side. The WAN interfaces are all correctly configured on a Class C network with no subnetting. The Ethernet segments of Chicago and Detroit, however, are subnetting two bits into the fourth octet (indicated by the "192" subnet mask). It works in San Francisco because the Ethernet interface there has a valid host address for that subnet. The other two are addressed to "1," which makes it an illegal address.

☒   Therefore answers **A** and **B** are incorrect. **D** is incorrect because the minimum requirement of WAN connectivity was met.

6.   ☑   **D.** The second octet subnet using the first three bits is equal to 224 (128+64+32+0+0+0+0+0).

☒   **A** would contain all ones in the first three octets, so is incorrect. **B** would have ones only in the first octet and is also incorrect. **C** is not a valid mask.

6.03: Subnet Planning

7.   ☑   **B.** The correct order is as follows: determine the maximum number of networks and hosts required for your network, calculate the subnet mask for the network that will accommodate for number of networks and hosts, test configuration in a pilot environment, and implement the solution.

☒   **A**, **C**, and **D** are out of sequence.

8.   ☑   **B.** The mask indicates that the first five bits of the last octet are being used for the network portion of the address. That allows for eight possible binary values between 00000000 and 00000111, excluding 000 and the broadcast space 111.

☒   **A** is theoretically correct but not in practice. **C** would be the number of hosts for a Class B address subnetted with 255.255.248.0. **D** is a possible number of hosts, but not the maximum.

9.   ☑   **A.** The architect's solution would have met the main requirement of 28 networks (248 mask will accommodate 30 networks), but would have not accounted for the expansion. By using one more bit for the mask (252) the network possibility was increased to 62, giving ample room for expansion, plus it still meets the requirements of 750 hosts (1022 possible hosts with this configuration). Finally, your configuration will not have to be altered with the expansion. Had the senior architect's recommendation been taken, alterations would have to be made.

10. ☑   **A.** It is extremely important in any situation, either in new installations or when troubleshooting, to communicate with the customer and find out exactly what they want.

☒ **B** is a good practice to ensure that a configuration will work, but it is not the first step. **C** is incorrect because you do not design a solution with initial consultation. **D** is incorrect because it is irresponsible and will definitely not accomplish what the customer is looking for.

11. ☑ **B.** Carefully divide the network into smaller, manageable portions with subnetting.

☒ **A** is incorrect because a huge single address space with no divisions would create a huge broadcast domain, which would bring performance down and increase the change of network failure. **C** is great for individual users, but it will not reduce broadcast traffic or improve overall network performance.

6.04: Complex Subnetting

12. ☑ **C.** VLSM allows you effectively to "subnet the subnet" and retain your other subnets for more productive uses.

☒ **A** and **B** are nonsense answers. **D** is incorrect because supernetting is the technique of allowing you to advertise multiple contiguous addresses under one mask.

13. ☑ **C.** Supernetting allows you to borrow bits from, in this case, the third octet, to accommodate the differing bits. The first two bits will suffice; the rest of the numbers are the same across all networks, resulting in a mask of 255.255.252.0.

☒ **A** is incorrect because it is the standard subnet mask for a Class C address. **B** is incorrect because it would be an example of subnetting, not supernetting. **D** is incorrect because this is a Class A subnet mask.

14. ☑ **D.** Supernetting allows you to advertise contiguous subnets as one network.

☒ **A** is incorrect because VLSM is used for further subnetting a subnet. **B** and **C** are not complex subnetting techniques.

6.05: Configuring IP Addresses with Cisco IOS

15. ☑ **C.** This command is correct.

    ☒ The command in **A** is correct, but it is followed by the wrong interface number. **B** is incorrect because the syntax is backwards. **D** is incorrect because a space is missing between "ip" and "address" in the syntax.

16. ☑ **B.** The command NO SHUTDOWN will ensure that the interface is brought up when the configuration is loaded.

    ☒ **A, C,** and **D** are incorrect syntax.

17. ☑ **A.** The correct network classes were selected for each interface. The interface s0 has been subnetted to allow for 30 hosts and 2046 networks, and the NO SHUTDOWN command will ensure that the interfaces come up from when the router is turned on.

    ☒ **B, C,** and **D** are incorrect; you're hired!

LAB ANSWER
Objectives 6.01–6.05

You must take into consideration the immediate needs of the customers, plus the changing environment they will encounter in the life cycle of their network. Here are the various points that should be taken into account at each important step.

Step 1: Design

■ Assess the customer's present and future needs. To be able to anticipate future growth is crucial to an efficient IP design.

■ Take into account the number of hosts and networks that will likely be required in five years.

■ Determine the number of register addresses required.

Step 2: Implementation

■ The installer needs a strong command of Cisco's IOS in order to configure routers correctly.

■ A thorough understanding of IP addressing is crucial to overcoming routing, address, and sub-netting problems.

Step 3: Maintenance

■ Assess whether the design is continuing to support the infrastructure, or whether you need to start planning for future changes.

■ As the network grows and the customer's needs change, some advanced techniques may be required in order conserve addresses or consolidate address space.

■ If the network has been planned properly, large changes will not be necessary at this point.

CISCO CERTIFIED NETWORK ASSOCIATE

7

IP Routing Protocols

Routing packets from one network to another over an internetwork can be accomplished in one of two ways: static routing uses a routing table into which the routes to networks are manually entered. Dynamic routing uses routing protocols to automatically collect and update route information to create and maintain the routing table. This routing table is used to select the best route to get a packet to its destination. All routing tables contain the same basic information. This includes the destination network, the associated metric, the network address of next router or endstation, and the interface to exit the router (to reach that destination network).

Routing protocols are not to be confused with routed protocols. The latter term refers to the network/transport protocols used for end-to-end communication across the network. Examples of routed protocols include IP and IPX. Routing protocols are not used to send data; they are used by routers to share information for building and updating routing tables. Examples of routing protocols include the Routing Information Protocol (RIP), Open Shortest Path First (OSPF), and the Interior Gateway Routing Protocol (IGRP).

TEST YOURSELF OBJECTIVE 7.01

Why Routing Protocols?

Manual creation and updating of routing tables is time-consuming and inefficient. Routing protocols use routing algorithms to select the optimal path to the destination based on the metrics used. Routing algorithms provide low overhead in terms of network bandwidth and CPU usage, and quick convergence, or synchronization of the routing tables of all routers on the network. Each routing protocol uses a different metric or set of metrics to determine the best path to a destination. Some use hops, some use bandwidth, and others use cost.

- Internetworks use routing to get data from one network to another.
- Bridging is the capability to connect two or more physical network segments such that the connection is transparent to the network.

- Switching is a way to increase available bandwidth (as well as limit the amount of traffic a node encounters) by providing a dedicated channel for each switched port. Switching occurs at the Data-Link layer.

- Routing occurs at the Network layer and includes the capability to separate the management of the segments on the internetwork.

- There are two basic mechanisms that make up routing: learning and forwarding.

- One of the terms to be aware of for route determination is metric. A metric is the value of a variable, such as the network delay, after the routing protocol algorithm has computed it.

- Routing protocols both create and maintain a routing table.

- The routing update can consist of the router's entire routing table or only the portion that has changed.

- There are three major objectives of a routing algorithm: accuracy, low overhead, and quick convergence.

- Convergence is the process of all routers synchronizing their routing information tables, or the time it takes for a single routing change to be reflected in all routers.

- Some of the types of routing algorithms are static versus dynamic, interior versus exterior, and distance vector versus link state.

- Dynamic routing protocols include a method for dynamically configuring the routing information table.

exam
Watch

A router can support more than one routed protocol at the same time. The routing tables for all supported routed protocols can be maintained and updated independently. For example, separate routing tables are maintained for IP, IPX, and AppleTalk packets. The router can forward packets that use different routed protocols, over the same link. This is called separate and integrated multiprotocol routing.

QUESTIONS

7.01: Why Routing Protocols?

1. You are the network administrator of a small network that is expected to grow considerably in size over the next year due to a merger of your company with another firm. You are currently using static routing on the network, but are considering implementing dynamic routing when the network expands. Which of the following changes can you expect to occur as a result of implementing dynamic routing protocols on the network? (Choose all that apply.)

   A. Reduction in network bandwidth usage

   B. Easier administration

   C. Faster updates to routing tables or changes in network topology

   D. Better control over routing table entries

2. You have a TCP/IP network that uses a single network ID. There are 45 users on this network, and about eight of the users spend most of the day sending files with an average size of 145MB to each other over the network. This is significantly slowing down overall network performance for all users on the network. What would be the most cost-effective solution for solving network performance problems?

   A. Install an active hub.

   B. Install a bridge.

   C. Implement link state routing protocols.

   D. Implement distance vector routing protocols.

3. The process of all routers synchronizing their routing information tables, or the time it takes for a single routing change to be reflected in all routers, is the definition of:

   A. Hopping

   B. Triggered updates

   C. Convergence

   D. Route filtering

TEST YOURSELF OBJECTIVE 7.02

Static Routes and Dynamic Routes

Advantages of static routing include easy configuration when the internetwork is small, reduced overhead on routers (since no routing protocols are needed), and complete control over the route selection. However, static routes don't work well in large or frequently changing internetwork environments. Dynamic routing protocols send periodic updates throughout the internetwork, which are compared to the current routing table. If the topology has changed, the routers update the routing tables with the new best routes. A static route is a route that has been manually entered into the routing table.

- Hierarchical routing allows the limitation of routing information propagation throughout an entire internetwork.

- Static routing conserves bandwidth because there are no updates being sent by routers.

- Static routing provides security because the routers are only aware of those networks that you choose to manually enter into the routing table.

- Static routing is appropriate for configuring a route to a stub network (a network accessible by only one path).

exam
Watch

To configure a static route on a Cisco router, use the IP ROUTE command. The syntax is as follows:

IP ROUTE <network mask address | interface [distance]>

The network entry is the destination network (or subnet). The mask entry refers to the subnet mask. The address entry is the IP address of the next-hop router. The interface entry is the name of the interface that will be used to reach the network defined in the first (network) entry. The distance entry refers to the administrative distance. The administrative distance is a way of evaluating the reliability of a source, using a scale of 0 to 255 (with lower numbers representing higher reliability). The default administrative distance is 1 for static routes.

QUESTIONS

7.02: Static Routes and Dynamic Routes

4. You wish to configure a static route on a Cisco router for a remote network with network ID 173.35.2.0. The IP address of the next-hop router is 173.35.5.3 and the subnet mask is 255.255.255.0. Administrative distance is 120. What command should you type to enter this static route into the routing table?

   A. ROUTE 173.35.2.0 255.255.255.0 173.35.5.3 120

   B. ROUTE IP 173.35.5.3 255.255.255.0 173.35.2.0 120

   C. IP ROUTE 173.35.2.0 173.35.5.3 255.255.255.0 120

   D. IP ROUTE 173.35.2.0 255.255.255.0 173.35.5.3 120

5. Which of the following is true of static routing? (Choose all that apply.)

   A. Static routing is preferred for small networks.

   B. Static routing provides automatic reconfiguration of the routing tables in the event of a router failure.

   C. Static routing uses more network bandwidth than dynamic routing.

   D. Static routing does not use routing protocols.

6. You are configuring static routes from your terminal on a Cisco router. You enter the commands shown in the following illustration. What will occur as a result of the entries you made in the routing table? (Choose all that apply.)

```
RouterA#config t
Enter configuration commands, one per line.  End with CNTL/Z.
RouterA(config)#ip route 172.19.20.0 255.255.255.0 172.19.10.2
RouterA(config)#ip route 172.19.30.0 255.255.255.0 172.19.10.2
RouterA(config)#^Z
RouterA#copy run star
```

A. The router will use the interface 172.19.20.0 as the next hop to reach the destination 172.19.10.2.

B. The router will use the interface 172.19.10.2 as the next hop to reach the destination 172.19.20.0.

C. The router will use the interface 172.19.10.2 as the next hop to reach the destination 172.19.30.0.

D. The router will use 255.255.255.0 as the next hop to reach destinations 172.19.20.0 and 172.19.30.0.

TEST YOURSELF OBJECTIVE 7.03

Default Routes

The default route is also referred to as the "router of last resort." It is impossible for the router to have the specific routes to every other internetwork accessible over the Internet. Every router should have a default route specified, so there will be a route to use when the router is unable to determine the route to a specific network. If there is no default route entered, and a Cisco router receives a packet whose subnet number isn't in the routing table, the default behavior of the IOS is to discard the packet.

- A default route is the one specified for data to follow if there is no explicit routing information for it to use in finding a direction.

- Every router should have a default route configured.

- The default route can be set in the same way as a static route, with the IP ROUTE command, using the network and subnet mask of all 0s.

exam
watch

A default route can be configured by using the IP ROUTE command. A second way to configure a default route is with the command IP DEFAULT-NETWORK <network number>. This command has a network number as the single parameter. Depending on the routing protocol, the router that owns this command does one of two things: automatically advertises the network number as the default route out of the internetwork, or advertises 0.0.0.0 as the default route. In any case, other routes in the internetwork dynamically discover a path out for unknown destinations.

QUESTIONS

7.03: Default Routes

7. Which of the following is the definition of a default route?

   A. A route that will override all other routes in the routing table and be used for routing of all packets

   B. A "route of last resort" that will be used if the router doesn't know the route to reach a specified destination network

   C. A route that is entered in the routing table by a dynamic routing protocol

   D. A route that is not to be used under any circumstances

8. You are a network administrator. You wish to set default routes on all your routers so that, if a packet's destination address has a network ID that does not match any route in the routers' routing tables, the routers will know what to do with the packet. You know that you can use the IP ROUTE command to set a default route, but you wish to use a different command that will allow the router to either advertise a single network number as the default route or advertise 0.0.0.0 as the default route (depending on the protocol used). Which of the following commands should you use?

   A. IP NETROUTE

   B. IP-NETWORK

   C. IP DEFAULT-NETWORK

   D. IP-DEFAULT NETWORK

9. If you have configured the routing table for Router A in the illustration on the following page as shown in the command-line entry, and a packet is addressed to a destination network with the network ID 174.32.3.0, for which there is no entry in the routing table, to which router will the packet be sent?

   ```
   RouterA(config)#ip route 0.0.0.0 0.0.0.0 203.21.20.2
   ```

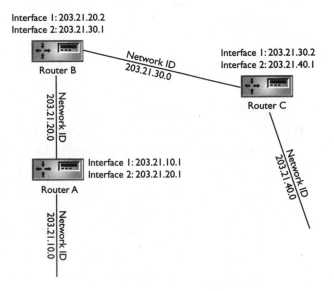

Interface 1: 203.21.20.2
Interface 2: 203.21.30.1

Router B

Network ID
203.21.30.0

Interface 1: 203.21.30.2
Interface 2: 203.21.40.1

Router C

Network ID
203.21.20.0

Interface 1: 203.21.10.1
Interface 2: 203.21.20.1

Router A

Network ID
203.21.40.0

Network ID
203.21.10.0

A. Router A.

B. Router B.

C. Router C.

D. The packet will be discarded.

TEST YOURSELF OBJECTIVE 7.04

Link State versus Distance Vector

Routing protocols can be categorized in several ways: first, as either interior or exterior routing protocols, then within each of those broad categories. They can be categorized by the type of routing algorithm they use. The two popular dynamic algorithms are link state (used by OSPF) and distance vector (used by RIP). Distance vector protocols create and maintain a database consisting of distances (hops) to specific destinations by exchanging routing tables between neighboring routers on a periodic basis. Link state protocols use Link State Advertisements and the Shortest Path First (SPF) algorithm to create a map of the network that contains more information than that maintained by the distance vector protocols. Cisco's IGRP combines advantages of link-state protocols with those of distance vector protocols, and is sometimes referred to as a balanced hybrid routing protocol.

- The two types of dynamic routing are link state and distance vector.
- A distance vector protocol router periodically sends its neighboring routers two pieces of information.
- Flash updates (also known as triggered updates) are sent whenever a router's routing information table is changed in a way that affects its updates.
- The purpose of the link state routing protocol is to map out the internetwork topology.
- Interior Gateway Protocols (IGPs) are also known as intra-domain because they work within the domain but not between domains. These protocols recognize that the routers they deal with are part of their system and freely exchange routing information with them.
- Exterior Gateway Protocols (EGPs) are known as inter-domain because they work between domains. These protocols recognize that they are on the edge of their system and only exchange the minimum of information necessary to maintain the capability to route information.

exam
⚠️atch

Distance vector protocols are vulnerable to routing loops, including a problem called count-to-infinity, wherein packets are continuously circulated around the network when the destination subnet is unreachable. Solutions include defining a maximum hop count (for example, RIP's maximum hop count is 15), and using the split horizon technique that prevents sending information about a route back to the router from which the information originally came. Hold-down timers, poison reverse, and triggered updates are other ways to prevent the count-to-infinity problem.

QUESTIONS

7.04: Link State versus Distance Vector

10. Your network uses a distance vector routing protocol. The protocol has detected that a connected network is currently unreachable. To speed up convergence time

so that other routers will not be susceptible to inaccurate updates, the protocol sets the routing table entry for the unreachable network at infinity, immediately making the route invalid for all neighboring routers. What is this technique called?

A. Split horizon

B. Triggered update

C. Poison reverse

D. ICMP

11. In the following illustration, the router to Network A fails. Prior to this failure, all routers had correct routing tables. Router 3's preferred path to Network A is by way of Router 2. Router 3's routing table shows a distance of 3 to Network A. When Network A fails, Router 5 sends an update to Router 1. Router 1 stops routing packets to network A, but Routers 2, 3, and 4 are unaware of the failure and continue to send packets to Network A. Router 1 sends an update, and Routers 2 and 4 stop sending packets to Network A. Router 3 has not been updated, and according to its tables, network A is still reachable via Router 2. Invalid information about Network A continues to loop until some process stops the looping. What is this condition called?

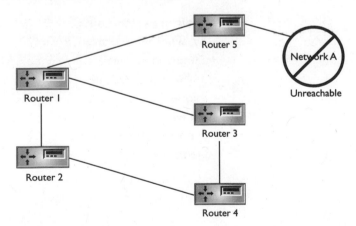

A. Split horizon

B. Count to infinity

C. Poison reverse

D. Link state looping

12. Which of the following is true of link state routing protocols? (Choose all that apply.)

    A. Link state protocols create a map of the entire network topology.

    B. Link state protocols obtain their view of the network by exchanging hello packets (LSPs) between routers.

    C. Link state protocols base routing decisions solely on hop count.

    D. Link state protocols include RIP for IP and RIP for IPX.

TEST YOURSELF OBJECTIVE 7.05

Routing Information Protocol (RIP)

RIP (Routing Information Protocol) is a distance vector routing protocol that uses classful routing and summarizes information, using network numbers instead of prefixes. Routers using RIP update their tables when they receive information about a better route. This information is then sent to neighboring routers. Updates are sent whenever the network topology changes, and at periodic intervals. RIP timers control the interval between periodic updates, the time that must pass without receiving updates from a route before the route is considered invalid, and the time between a route being marked as invalid and the removal of the route from the routing table.

■ RIP is a distance vector protocol for use intra-domain (on the interior of a gateway).

■ RIP uses classful routing and does not support prefix (classless) routing.

■ RIP routers send periodic updates to neighboring routers.

■ RIP routers send updates to neighboring routers whenever they enter a change to network topology into their routing tables.

■ RIP uses a metric of 1 to 15 to indicate the cost of a route.

■ RIP comes in two versions: RIP for IP and RIP for IPX. There are significant differences between the two.

exam
ⓦatch

RIP version 2 (RIPv2) for IP addresses some of the limitations of the original RIP protocol. Because RIP was developed prior to subnetting, it did not support complex subnetting. RIPv2 offers better flexibility in subnetted networks and those using CIDR (classless interdomain routing). RIPv2 also differs from version 1 in that it supports multicast announcements and simple password authentication. This latter allows for better security, in that RIP announcement packets that don't match the configured password are discarded. A RIPv2 router can be configured to send only RIPv2 message, or to respond to RIPv1 requests with a RIPv1 response. Cisco routers, when configured for IP RIP, default to accepting either RIPv1 or RIPv2 updates, but only sending RIPv1.

QUESTIONS

7.05: Routing Information Protocol (RIP)

Questions 13–15   This scenario and the following output should be used to answer questions 13, 14, and 15.

You are a network administrator, running RIP for IP on the routers on your network. You wish to obtain information regarding the protocol. You enter a command, which gives you the output shown in the following illustration:

```
Codes: C - connected, S - static, I - IGRP, R - RIP, M - mobile,
B - BGP, D - EIGRP, EX - EIGRP external, O - OSPF, IA - OSPF inter
area, E1 - OSPF external type 1, E2 - OSPF external type 2, E - EGP,
i - IS-IS, L1 - IS-IS level-1, L2 - IS-IS level-2, * - candidate
default

Gateway of last resort is not set

     181.16.0.0 255.255.255.0 is subnetted, 5 subnets
R    181.16.50.0 [120/2] via 181.16.20.2, 00:00:08, Serial0
R    181.16.40.0 [120/1] via 181.16.20.0, 00:00:08, Serial0
R    181.16.30.0 [120/1] via 181.16.20.0, 00:00:08, Serial0
C    181.16.20.0 is directly connected, Serial0
C    181.16.10.0 is directly connected, Ethernet0
```

13. What command did you enter to obtain the information shown?

    A. SHOW IP ROUTE

    B. SHOW IP PROTOCOL

    C. SHOW ROUTE RIP

    D. SHOW IP ROUTE RIP

14. Which value represents the administrative distance in the output example provided?

    A. 0

    B. 1

    C. 2

    D. 120

15. What does the 00:00:08 value in the output example provided represent?

    A. The time at which the next update will be sent

    B. The time since the router last received an advertisement for the route

    C. The hold-down time

    D. The time after which the information will be flushed

16. What routing metric is used by IP RIP to calculate the best path to a destination?

    A. Hop count

    B. Bandwidth availability

    C. Link congestion

    D. Link reliability

TEST YOURSELF OBJECTIVE 7.06

Interior Gateway Routing Protocol (IGRP)

In a large network like the Internet, it is not feasible to use just one routing protocol for the entire network. The network is divided into autonomous systems (ASs). Each

AS is generally administered separately, and each uses its own routing protocol. Routing protocols used inside an AS are called Interior Gateway Protocols (IGPs). Cisco's proprietary Interior Gateway Routing Protocol (IGRP) is a distance vector protocol designed for better efficiency and stability than RIP on large internetworks, with low overhead and fast responses to topology changes. IGRP can split traffic between two or more paths when the paths are equally good or, with some additional commands, when they are not equally good. A composite metric is calculated for each path that combines several metric components.

- IGRP is used in an autonomous system (AS) and includes the capability to advertise interior routes, exterior routes, and system routes.

- IGRP can be configured to a maximum hop count of 1 to 255, with a default of 100.

- IGRP uses delay and bandwidth by default when making routing decisions; reliability and load can be used as well (hop count and MTU information is sent but not used in determining best path).

- IGRP uses split horizon and poison reverse, along with hold-downs, to prevent and correct routing loops.

- IGRP advertises three route types: interior (routes between subnets), exterior (routes outside the AS), and system (routes to networks inside the AS).

- Enhanced IGRP (EIGRP) uses the same distance vector algorithm and distance information as IGRP. It has enhanced convergence properties and, effectively, the same efficiency.

exam
ⓌatcH

IGRP conserves bandwidth because it does not broadcast update messages to other routers at regular intervals as RIP does. The initial communication between an IGRP router and its neighboring routers involves an exchange of the complete routing table; subsequently, only changes to the routing table, not the entire routing table, are sent. The changes are sent only to the neighboring routers that are affected by the changes. The updates are sent as soon as changes in the network topology take place.

QUESTIONS

7.06: Interior Gateway Routing Protocol (IGRP)

17. IGRP can transmit one data stream in a round-robin manner with dual lines of equal bandwidth. What is this called?

   A. Multiprotocol routing

   B. Multipath routing

   C. Multistream routing

   D. Multilink PPP

18. In the following illustration, when a packet is sent from the source computer to the destination computer, what variables will IGRP use to determine the best route to the destination network?

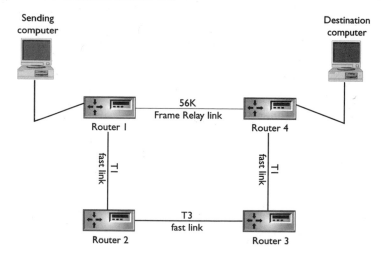

   A. Hop count

   B. Bandwidth available

   C. Reliability of the link

   D. A combined metric

LAB QUESTION
Objectives 7.01–7.06

You have been tasked with reconfiguring the network for your company, which has grown considerably over the past year. You have used only static routing in the past, but you do not wish to spend the administrative time required to maintain the routing tables now that the network has grown. You have recently experienced numerous inaccuracies in the routing table caused by entries you made when in a hurry. You would like to automate the entry and updating of routing information, but you are concerned about excessive memory and processor utilization if you implement dynamic routing protocols.

You also wish to minimize the use of network bandwidth. You prefer that the most efficient use of bandwidth be made so that packets will travel to their destinations over the truly shortest path, rather than just the path with the lowest number of hops. You have heard that routing loops can be a problem and wish to avoid them. However, you are concerned that if a link goes down, there should be redundancy so that traffic will go through. How can you accomplish your objectives, and what routing protocols and protocol features will you use to do so?

QUICK ANSWER KEY

Objective 7.01
1. **B** and **C**
2. **B**
3. **C**

Objective 7.02
4. **D**
5. **A** and **D**
6. **B** and **C**

Objective 7.03
7. **B**
8. **C**
9. **B**

Objective 7.04
10. **C**
11. **B**
12. **A** and **B**

Objective 7.05
13. **A**
14. **D**
15. **B**
16. **A**

Objective 7.06
17. **B**
18. **D**

IN-DEPTH ANSWERS
7.01: Why Routing Protocols?

1. ☑ **B** and **C** are correct. Because the dynamic routing protocol will automatically collect information from other routers, administration of the routing tables is easier. Updates are made more quickly because it is not necessary for an administrator to enter the new information manually.

   ☒ **A.** Network bandwidth is not reduced, but increased, by use of routing protocols, because distance vector routers periodically broadcast routing table information, and link state protocols flood the network with LSPs or hello packets when they come online. **D** is incorrect because static routing provides better control over routing table entries, because each entry is made manually by an administrator.

2. ☑ **B.** Installing a bridge will allow you to partition the collision domain for users transferring large files. In this way, traffic between users who transfer large files to each other will remain on one side of the bridge. The other users of the network will be located on the opposite side of the bridge, and will not be affected by the file transfers.

   ☒ **A** is incorrect. An active hub will not partition the collision domain. **C** and **D** are incorrect because the implementation of routing protocols will not improve performance; no routing is taking place within the single subnet.

3. ☑ **C.** Convergence is the process of all routers synchronizing their routing tables, or the time it takes for a single routing change to be reflected in all routers throughout the network.

   ☒ **A** is incorrect. A hop is the trip from one router to the next as a packet travels to its destination across the network. **B** is incorrect. Triggered updates are a means used by RIP to let neighboring routers know about changes to the network and avoid routing loops. **D** is also incorrect. Route filtering is a means of choosing which networks to announce or accept.

7.02: Static Routes and Dynamic Routes

4. ☑ **D.** The syntax for the IP ROUTE command on Cisco routers is IP ROUTE *<network ID> <subnet mask> <gateway (next hop router)> <administrative distance>*.

   ☒ **A**, **B**, and **C** are incorrect because the syntax is in the wrong order.

5. ☑ **A** and **D** are correct. Static routing is preferred for small networks, where it is feasible for the administrator to update the routing tables manually each time a change occurs in network topology. Static routing does not use routing protocols.

   ☒ **C** is incorrect. The dynamic routing protocols use more network bandwidth than static routing because they must exchange routing table information across the network. **B** is incorrect. Static routing does not provide automatic reconfiguration of routing tables when a router fails; the entries must be updated manually to reflect the failed router. Dynamic routing protocols will automatically update the routing tables when a router goes down.

6. ☑ **B** and **C** are correct. Using the IP ROUTE command with syntax IP ROUTE *<network ID (destination)> <subnet mask> <next hop router>*, the commands you entered will cause the router to use 172.19.10.2 as the next hop to reach both destination networks 172.19.20.0 and 172.19.30.0. 255.255.255.0 is the subnet mask.

   ☒ **A** and **D** are incorrect because they are not the valid results.

7.03: Default Routes

7. ☑ **B.** The default route is used by the router as a "route (or gateway) of last resort," in the event that the router does not have a route in its routing table for a specified destination network.

   ☒ **A** is incorrect. A default route does not override other routes in the routing table. **C** is incorrect because the default route may be entered as a static route. **D** is incorrect. The default route does not designate a route that is not to be used under any circumstances.

8. ☑ **C.** The correct command to set a single network number as the default route out of the network (or advertise 0.0.0.0 as the default route, depending on the protocol) is IP DEFAULT-NETWORK followed by the network number.

   ☒ **A**, **B**, and **D** are incorrect. The commands IP NETROUTE, IP-NETWORK, and IP-DEFAULT NETWORK do not use the correct syntax to make this configuration.

9. ☑ **B.** The IP ROUTE command with network number and subnet mask of all 0s sets the default route to the router interface specified in the command. In this case, Router B's interfaces are configured as 203.21.20.2 (connected to network 203.21.20.0) and 203.21.30.1 (connected to network 203.21.30.0). Router A is configured to send packets for which it does not have a network entry in its routing table to 203.21.20.2, the interface on Router B.

   ☒ **A**, **C**, and **D** are incorrect. The packet will be sent to Router B; it will not be discarded.

7.04: Link State versus Distance Vector

10. ☑ **C.** Poison reverse is the method of avoiding problems caused by inconsistent updates and slow convergence by setting the distance to a downed network to infinity (typically 16, when using RIP for IP).

    ☒ **A** is incorrect. Split horizon is a method of avoiding routing loops by adhering to a rule that routing table information is not sent back along the same path it came in. **B** is incorrect. Triggered updates reset the hold-down timers, to prevent regular update messages from reinstating a route that is now invalid. **D** is incorrect. ICMP is the Internet Control Message Protocol, used for message control and error reporting between a host server and an Internet gateway.

11. ☑ **B.** When invalid routing table information propagates in a circular fashion throughout the network until something (such as a maximum hop count) stops the process, it is called count to infinity. By setting a maximum hop count, when the metric value exceeds the maximum (or reaches infinity), the network is considered to be unreachable.

☒   **A** and **C** are both incorrect because split horizon and poison reverse are methods of preventing or solving routing loops. **D** is also incorrect. Looping is a problem associated with distance vector routing protocols.

12.   ☑   **A** and **B** are correct. Link state protocols create a map of the entire network, which is obtained by the exchange of hello packets (LSPs) between routers.

☒   **C** is incorrect. Distance vector protocols base routing decisions based solely on hop count, while link state protocols can analyze available bandwidth and the amount of congestion on each link to determine the best path to the destination. **D** is incorrect. RIP for IP and RIP for IPX are distance vector protocols. An example of a link state protocol is OSPF.

7.05: Routing Information Protocol (RIP)

13.   ☑   **A.** The SHOW IP ROUTE command will display the routing table as shown in the illustration.

☒   **B** is incorrect. The command SHOW IP PROTOCOL gives you information regarding the routing protocol in use (in this case RIP), the network to which RIP is assigned, routing information sources, and filter list information. **D** is incorrect. The SHOW IP ROUTE RIP command will display only the RIP connected networks. **C** is also incorrect. SHOW ROUTE RIP is not a valid command.

14.   ☑   **D.** The administrative distance is a value assigned to each routing protocol. The administrative distance for RIP is 120 (OSPF 110, IRGP 100, and EIGRP 90). The number following the slash mark is the metric.

☒   **A** is incorrect. A directly connected network has an administrative distance of 0. **B** is incorrect. A static route has an administrative distance of 1. **C** is incorrect because 2 is an incorrect administrative distance as well.

15.   ☑   **B.** The output shows the time since the last advertisement was received by the router for each route.

☒   **A**, **C**, and **D** are all incorrect. The hold-down timer information and time after which the information is flushed, as well as the number of seconds before the next update is due, can be displayed using the SHOW IP PROTOCOL command.

16. ☑ **A.** IP RIP, as a distance vector protocol, uses hop count to determine the best path to a destination, with the lowest hop count representing the best route.

    ☒ **B, C**, and **D** are incorrect. Link state protocols are able to consider other factors, such as bandwidth availability, link congestion and link reliability, in determining the shortest path. RIP for IPX uses both TICKs and hops (in that order).

7.06: Interior Gateway Routing Protocol (IGRP)

17. ☑ **B.** Multipath routing is the ability of IGRP to transmit a single data stream in round-robin manner over dual lines of equal bandwidth.

    ☒ **A** is incorrect because multiprotocol routing involves the routing of more than one routable protocol (for example, IP and IPX). **D** is incorrect. Multilink PPP involves consolidating two PPP links, such as two B channels of an ISDN line, to aggregate the bandwidth. **C** is incorrect because there is no such term as multistream routing.

18. ☑ **D.** IGRP uses a combined variable that includes several components, including bandwidth, delay, reliability, load, and maximum transmission unit (MTU).

    ☒ **A, B**, and **C** are incorrect. Unlike RIP, IGRP does not rely on hop count to determine the best path to a destination network. In the example in the figure, RIP would automatically send the packet from Router 1 to Router 4, due to the lower hop count. IGRP will take into account the transfer speed and reliability of the links, and would be likely to send the packet via the pathway from Router 1 to Router 2 to Router 3 to Router 4, over the fast T-carrier connections.

LAB ANSWER
Objectives 7.01–7.06

Because the network has grown, and maintaining the routing tables manually is no longer feasible, you should implement dynamic routing protocols on your routers. In determining which protocol will best suit your needs, you should consider memory, processor, and network bandwidth usage, since these are priority concerns of yours. Distance vector protocols use less resources and bandwidth than link state protocols; thus, you should consider implementing a distance vector protocol such as RIP or IGRP, rather than a link state protocol (which uses more bandwidth).

IGRP offers some improvements over RIP when used in large, autonomous systems. IGRP uses a combined metric to determine the best path to a destination, taking into account bandwidth availability, reliability, MTU, delay factors, and load factors. IGRP also uses split horizon, poison reverse updates, and hold-downs to avoid problems associated with routing loops. IGRP supports multipath routing, using dual lines that are equal in bandwidth to route a stream of traffic in round-robin manner, to provide for redundancy if a line fails. Although RIP can also provide load balancing when two equal hop-count paths exist, overall your best protocol choice in this situation is IGRP.

CISCO CERTIFIED NETWORK ASSOCIATE

8

IP Configuration

T his chapter addresses the use of IP parameters, services, and protocols to configure Cisco routers for internetworking and communication. In recent years, the Internet has expanded at an unequaled rate. This has contributed to many things, including the expansion of LANs and WANs, as well as the use of the Transmission Control Protocol/ Internet Protocol (TCP/IP) suite. Since the early 1990s, TCP/IP has become the defacto standard in personal and corporate networking.

Some of the more important areas to focus on for the IP Configuration portion of the CCNA exam are as follows:

- Configuring IP addresses on Cisco router interfaces, with the IP ADDRESS command, is an essential skill required for passing the CCNA exam.

- DNS is enabled by default on Cisco routers, but if disabled it can be enabled using the IP DOMAIN-LOOKUP command.

- After enabling DNS, you may add DNS servers to the router with the IP NAME-SERVER *server1 server2* command. You may add up to six DNS servers.

- To save on IP addresses, you may implement IP UNNUMBERED on a Serial interface.

- The IP ROUTE command builds static routes in the router table, but RIP and IGRP protocols build the same table dynamically. These two protocols must be enabled globally on the router. Once enabled, the administrator can modify the update interval with the TIMERS command.

- DHCP uses UDP broadcasts and requires, at a minimum, the configuration or the command IP HELPER-ADDRESS *address of dhcp server*.

- If there are multiple DHCP servers on a subnet, use the IP HELPER ADDRESS command where the address takes the form of network number.255, or a directed broadcast.

TEST YOURSELF OBJECTIVE 8.01

IP Configuration Commands

Each interface on a Cisco router must be configured to operate properly in an IP environment. Configuration of IP takes place on a per-interface basis. This means you will have to log onto the router, enter Privileged EXEC mode using the ENABLE command, enter Global Configuration mode using the command CONFIGURE

TERMINAL, and the use the INTERFACE *<interface>* command to enter the desired interface.

When configuring a WAN link, default configuration uses a full subnet to address the link. This makes valuable IP addresses and subnets unavailable for other uses. By using the IP UNNUMBERED command, a previously assigned IP address of another interface or the loop-back interface can be used for this purpose, thus freeing up the additional IP addresses.

- ■ There are some circumstances in which you might want to enable IP across an interface without having to assign an explicit IP address. This functionality is available exclusively on Cisco routers and is called IP UNNUMBERED.

- ■ IP UNNUMBERED allows communication across a link without having to allocate a whole subnet.

- ■ You cannot ping an unnumbered interface because of the lack of an IP address.

- ■ IP UNNUMBERED does not support Internet Protocol Security (IPSec) and cannot be used with X.25 or SMDS encapsulations.

There is the possibility that the Ethernet interface referenced may go down, disabling any communication with the router remotely. Because of this situation, use the loop-back interface as the reference point for the unnumbered interface. It is always up, because the loop-back adapter is a virtual device.

QUESTIONS

8.01: IP Configuration Commands

1. What is the proper syntax to configure serial port 0 with IP address 207.79.214.1 subnet mask 255.255.255.0?

   A. `Cisco # ip-config 207.79.214.1 255.255.255.0`

   B. `Cisco (config)# ip address 207.79.214.1 mask 255.255.255.0`

   C. `Cisco (config)#ip address 207.79.214.1`

   D. `Cisco (config-if)# ip address 207.79.214.1 255.255.255.0`

2. You have two routers and two subnets that must be connected. The routers have two serial ports and one Ethernet port each. All the IP addresses within each of these subnets are required for hosts on the two subnets. How should you configure the routers?

   A. Set up the serial ports on each router to use a single subnet and split the remaining subnet between the two Ethernet ports, providing IPs to each side of the connection.

   B. Configure the Ethernet ports using the two subnets. Then set up the serial ports to use IP unnumbered and the Ethernet ports as reference addresses, thereby eliminating the required dedicated subnet for the WAN link between the serial ports.

   C. Configure the Ethernet ports using the two subnets. Leave the serial ports alone; they will see each other because they are directly connected and need no IP address.

   D. Configure each of the serial ports using the two subnets and configure the Ethernet ports to use RIP routing protocol to configure the Ethernet portion of the connection.

TEST YOURSELF OBJECTIVE 8.02

Configuring Static Routes

We can configure a static route using the IP ROUTE command. To see and communicate with other interfaces and networks, routers require path descriptions. There are two methods used to deliver descriptions to routers. The first method is static routing. Static routing is manual configuration of the routing table, stating what interface a packet must be sent outbound to reach a desired destination network or individual IP address.

Static routes are best used in the following situations:

■ When the connected circuit is of an unreliable nature

■ When a dial-on-demand circuit is being used

- To map a single connection to an ISP or home office
- When a customer wishes not to share dynamic routing data
- When the router CPU usage could be significantly increased by use of a dynamic protocol

The IP ROUTE command is a global command with syntax as follows:

```
ip route address-[network or individual] netmask
address/interface
```

exam
Watch

Static routes have and administrative distance value of 1. Only directly connected networks have a superceding AD (AD value 0). The following chart shows the hierarchy a router uses to select the best path to a destination. In the dynamic routing protocols, these values can be modified using the DISTANCE ad network netmask command. This allows the administrator to create a preferred network link to which traffic will flow unless that particular interface is down. Watch for test questions comparing the static router precedence over other routes and make sure to evaluate this AD modifying command.

Protocol or Connection Type	Administrative Distance Value
Directly connected	0
Static	1
External EIGRP summary route	5
Internal EIGRP	90
IGRP	100
OSPF	110
RIP	120

QUESTIONS

8.02: Configuring Static Routes

3. Choose the proper command syntax to configure the first serial port, with an address of 207.79.12.1, to be the outbound interface for traffic destined for the 207.79.15.0 Class C network.

   A. `Cisco (config)# interface serial 1`
   `Cisco (config-if)# ip route 207.79.15.0 255.255.255.0`
   `207.79.12.1`

   B. `Cisco (config)# interface serial 0`
   `Cisco (config-if)# ip route 207.79.15.0 255.255.255.0`
   `207.79.12.1`

   C. `Cisco (config)# ip route 207.79.15.0 255.255.255.0`
   `207.79.12.1`

   D. `Cisco (config)# ip route 207.79.12.1 255.255.255.0`
   `207.79.15.0`

4. What advantages do static routes have over IGRP routes within the routing table? (Choose all that apply.)

   A. Static routes have a lower administrative distance value and therefore will be selected as a more reliable route.

   B. Static routes allow for modifying their default AD.

   C. Static routes use less CPU cycles on the router.

   D. Static routes are scalable and dynamically suit themselves to the network.

TEST YOURSELF OBJECTIVE 8.03

Configuring Default Routes

A router attempting to send packets to destinations first makes comparisons to the routing table to find destination networks. If a particular referenced network is not found, Cisco routers use the default route reference within the routing table. Default routes are used in situations where the network using the default route has a single connection to the referenced route. To set the default route, use the IP DEFAULT ROUTE IP ADDRESS command.

■ A default route specifies where to send packets when the routing information for the network in question is not found explicitly in the routing table. It is the responsibility of the next-hop router in the default route to forward or deliver the packet.

■ Default routes can be set statically or they can be configured for use by dynamic routing protocols.

exam
ⓦatch

Since Internet connections are so common today, many companies use default routes to offload the majority of routing CPU cycles to the backbone providers.

There are three different syntaxes available to implement a default route. To implement a default route using the reserved address 0.0.0.0 and a subnet mask of 0.0.0.0 through interface address 207.79.29.1 use this syntax:

```
Cisco (config)# ip route 0.0.0.0 0.0.0.0 207.79.29.1
```

To use the network address (for example 207.79.54.0) or a specific IP address (for example 207.79.25.1) use this syntax:

```
Cisco (config)# ip route 207.79.54.0 255.255.255.0 207.79.29.1
```

or

```
Cisco (config)# ip route 207.79.25.1 255.255.255.0 207.79.29.1
```

To use the fewest parameters use this syntax:

```
Cisco (config)# ip default-network 207.79.29.0
```

Note that this example refers to a network and not a specific IP. This same concept can be implemented in all three syntaxes.

QUESTIONS

8.03: Configuring Default Routes

5. What two commands are required to configure the default route for the networks comprised in 207.79.230.0/30 via interface 207.79.230.2?

   A.
   ```
   Cisco (config)# ip classless
   Cisco (config)# ip route 207.79.230.0 255.255.255.252
   207.79.230.2
   ```

   B.
   ```
   Cisco (config)# ip classless 207.79.230.0
   Cisco (config)# ip default-address 207.79.230.0
   255.255.255.252 207.79.230.2
   ```

   C.
   ```
   Cisco (config)# ip classless
   Cisco (config)# ip route 207.79.230.2 255.255.255.252
   207.79.230.0
   ```

   D.
   ```
   Cisco (config)# ip classless
   Cisco (config)# ip default-network 207.79.230.0
   ```

6. What is the purpose for the default route in configuring Cisco routers within complex networks? (Choose all that apply.)

   A. To give an administrator a router to which packets destined for unknown networks can be forwarded

   B. To provide a network to which all faulted packets can be sent

   C. To describe a non-local address or network to which packets may be sent

   D. To augment the IP ROUTING command once it is enabled

TEST YOURSELF OBJECTIVE 8.04

Configuring RIP Routing

RIP is configured on a global basis but has the capability to be configured per interface. Classless and prefix routing are not supported in RIPv1. RIP is enabled using the ROUTER RIP IOS command, followed by the NETWORK command to describe which networks will use the protocol. It is further defined using the VERSION and TIMERS attribute commands.

RIP uses a maximum of 15 hops between the source and destination node, as a metric to determine if a route is still valid. RIP uses timer sub attributes to determine if a route should be flushed from the routing table. The timers are, updates (typically 30 sec.), invalid (typically 90 sec.), hold-down (time allowed for suppressing new route) and flush (typically 240 sec.).

This is an example of the standard RIP configuration:

```
Cisco#configure terminal

Cisco (config)# router rip

Cisco (config-router)# version 2

Cisco (config-router)# network 207.79.214.0
```

■ Enabling RIP is performed at the global level, but a lot of the configuration can be performed on a per-interface basis.

■ You may advertise a directly connected network with RIP using the NETWORK ADDRESS command.

■ RIPv1 does not support classless IP addressing schemes.

exam
watch

RIP became a mainstream protocol when it was distributed within the UNIX BSD OS in the early 1980s. RIP is a distance vector protocol, meaning it uses distance between source and destination as a metric for routing decisions. RIP uses the UDP port 520 to broadcast route updates to other routers on the network. The NETWORK command in RIP sets that connected networks will receive these UDP broadcasts. If the connected network is not configured for broadcasts, neighbor routers can be set explicitly for unicast router updates using a NEIGHBOR IP-ADDRESS command.

QUESTIONS

8.04: Configuring RIP Routing

7. What Configuration mode must you use to configure a RIP network address of 207.79.35.0?

   A. `Cisco (config-rip)# network 207.79.35.0`

   B. `Cisco (config-if)# network 207.79.35.0`

   C. `Cisco (config-router)# network 207.79.35.0`

   D. `Cisco (config-if)# network 207.79.35.255`

8. The RIP broadcasts on network 131.251.0.0 are a large percentage of the traffic. Your MIS director has asked you to research the possibilities. Your proposed configuration change is required to eliminate router RIP broadcast traffic on the network. As an optional solution, you should provide an alternate configuration change that will reduce update traffic by a half. You use router cisco-2 and its WAN link neighbors 131.251.10.1 and 131.251.20.1 to show the proposed configuration commands.

   Required Configuration:

   ```
   Cisco-2 (config-router)# neighbor 131.251.10.1
   Cisco-2 (config-router)# neighbor 131.251.20.1
   ```

   Optional Configuration:

   ```
   Cisco-2 (config-router)# timers basic 60 180 190
   ```

   A. The proposed solution fulfills the required result and the optional result.

   B. The proposed solution does not fulfill the required result nor the optional result.

   C. The proposed solution fulfills the required result but not the optional result.

   D. The proposed solution does not fulfill the required result but does fulfill the optional result.

Configuring IGRP Routing

IGRP is Cisco's answer to the limitations of the RIP protocol. Instead of RIP's 15-hop count limitation, IGRP allows for 255 hops maximum (the default is 100). It is also important to realize that the hop count is not used to determine the best path to a destination. Instead, IGRP uses a complex metric based upon delay, bandwidth, reliability, and load criteria for more accurate router choice of the best path to a destination. IGRP has a faster convergence factor than RIP. IGRP uses timers similar to RIP.

To configure IGRP, use the global command ROUTER IGRP AUTONOMOUS-SYSTEM-ID. Next the NETWORK ADDRESS command should be executed. This should be a classful network address. Include only directly connected networks that are to participate in the route exchanges.

- The basic configuration of IGRP is a pretty straightforward process. First, you need to assign an autonomous system number to the IGRP process. The autonomous system number allows other routers that use the same number to exchange route information. Then you must tell the router which directly connected networks it should advertise its initial IGRP packet on.

- An autonomous system is a group of networks under a common administration that share a routing strategy.

- IGRP uses the same timers as RIP, except sleeptime. Sleeptime allows you to define an amount of time to delay a routing update after receiving a triggered update.

exam
ⓦatch

The split horizon feature within Cisco IOS enables the blocking of advertisement back out the interface through which they were originally learned. This prevents loops forming between two routers that constantly pass the same inaccurate information back and forth between themselves endlessly. Within non-broadcast environments, this feature may have to be explicitly disabled for proper operation. The split horizon syntax is as follows:

```
Cisco (config-if)# ip split horizon (to enable on the interface)
Cisco (config-if)# no ip split horizon (to disable on the
interface)
```

QUESTIONS

8.05: Configuring IGRP Routing

9. What are the default values for the update, invalid, and hold-down IGRP timers?

   A. Update 45, invalid 135, holddown 145

   B. Update 30, invalid 90, holddown 240

   C. Update 45, invalid 90, holddown 145

   D. Update 90, invalid 270, holddown 280

10. What is the series of commands used to configure the 207.79.214.0 network to participate in the AS 14 IGRP dynamic routing updates?

    A.
    ```
    Cisco#configure terminal
    Cisco (config)# igrp 14
    Cisco (config)# network 207.79.214.0
    ```

    B.
    ```
    Cisco#configure terminal
    Cisco (config)# router igrp 14
    Cisco (config-router)# network 207.79.214.0
    ```

    C.
    ```
    Cisco#configure terminal
    Cisco (config)# router network 207.79.214.0
    Cisco (config-router)# igrp 14
    ```

    D.
    ```
    Cisco#configure terminal
    Cisco (config)# router igrp 14 network 207.79.214.0
    ```

TEST YOURSELF OBJECTIVE 8.06

IP Host Tables

Cisco IOS software maintains a cache that contains host name-to-IP address mappings. These associations allow users on the Internet to use English names rather than have to memorize IP addresses for each of the sites to which they wish to connect. To configure the host name-to-address mapping use the IP HOST *name [tcp-port-number]* command in the global configuration state as exhibited in this example:

```
ip host widgets.com 23 207.79.214.52
```

To view the current cache entries use the SHOW HOSTS command. Having the host feature configured speeds the host name resolution for the local router.

- Cisco routers keep a table of host name-to-address mappings in their host cache.

- You can assign a port number to use when establishing a connection. The default is Telnet port 23.

- The IP HOST command must be used in the Global Configuration mode.

exam
ⓦatch

Host address resolution is a method of interpreting between human language and machine language. Machines (routers) speak in numbers, whereas humans prefer words. Whether it is DNS, ARP, or host name tables on the local router, they simply convert one language into another. The engine for this is the host table itself. These host tables can be built dynamically or configured manually, as is the case with the IP HOST command. When you enter IP HOST cisco router-1 207.79.51.1, you have made a permanent entry in the table to be used for future interpreting. A DNS entry is a temporary entry because it has been learned by the router and may change in the future or be purged.

QUESTIONS

8.06: IP Host Tables

11. Identify the configuration commands required to enter the following table into the host table on the router named cisco2500-1, so that while you are connecting from that router to the routers in the table, you will be able to use their names rather than their IP addresses.

Router Name	Interface IP Address	Port Number
Cisco2500-2	214.196.23.1	23
Cisco2500-3	214.196.25.2	23
Cisco7500-1	214.196.23.3	23

A.
```
Cisco2500-1# configure
Cisco2500-1 (config)# interface serial 0
Cisco2500-1 (config-if)# ip host cisco2500-2 23 214.196.23.1
Cisco2500-1 (config-if)# ip host cisco2500-3 23 214.196.25.2
Cisco2500-1 (config-if)# ip host cisco7500-2 23 214.196.23.3
```

B.
```
Cisco2500-1 (config)# ip host cisco2500-2 23 214.196.23.1
Cisco2500-1 (config)# ip host cisco2500-3 23 214.196.25.2
Cisco2500-1 (config)# ip host cisco7500-2 23 214.196.23.3
```

C.
```
Cisco2500-1 (config)# host cisco2500-2 23 214.196.23.1
Cisco2500-1 (config)# host cisco2500-3 23 214.196.25.2
Cisco2500-1 (config)# host cisco7500-2 23 214.196.23.3
```

D.
```
Cisco2500-1 (config)# ip host cisco2500-2 214.196.23.1
Cisco2500-1 (config)# ip host cisco2500-3 214.196.25.2
Cisco2500-1 (config)# ip host cisco7500-2 214.196.23.3
```

12. **Required Result:** You must configure the router cisco2500-2 to resolve host names cisco1 and cisco2 to IP addresses 215.31.2.2 and 215.31.2.1, respectively.

Optional Desired Result: You must configure host cisco1 to use the non-default Telnet port number 1302.

Proposed Solution:

```
Cisco2500-2# ip host cisco1 1302 215.31.2.2

Cisco2500-2# ip host cisco2 215.31.2.1
```

What results does the proposed solution produce?

A. The proposed solution fulfills the required result and the optional result.

B. The proposed solution does not fulfill the required result or the optional result.

C. The proposed solution fulfills the required result but not the optional result.

D. The proposed solution does not fulfill the required result but does fulfill the optional result.

TEST YOURSELF OBJECTIVE 8.07

DNS and DHCP Configuration

DNS is a service that maintains a central database of host name-to-address mapping. Similar to the IP host cache, only on a larger scale and accessible to all clients on the network, DNS is usually on a dedicated server. DNS is enabled by default in Cisco routers. If it has been disabled, you may use the IP DOMAIN-LOOKUP command to re-enable it. To add a DNS server to the Cisco router, you may use the following command syntax:

```
ip name-server server1 server2 etc.[up to 6 servers can be
configured]
```

DHCP is Dynamic Host Configuration Protocol. This network operating system feature dynamically allocates addresses to IP clients as they log on to the network. Clients use a UDP broadcast to find and request an IP lease as they log on to the network. We should configure the router using the following commands:

```
Interface E0

ip helper-address address
```

■ The dynamic capability to look up host name-to-address mappings is a feature of the Domain Name System (DNS).

- The Dynamic Host Configuration Protocol (DHCP) is used for the dynamic distribution of IP addresses to client machines. Cisco routers can forward DHCP requests across different subnets.

- DNS capability is enabled by default in the Cisco IOS.

- By default, Cisco routers (or any router for that matter) will not forward broadcast-based traffic.

e x a m
ⓦatch

Because DHCP uses UDP broadcasts, routers must use non-default configuration. Neither Cisco nor any other route forwards these broadcasts by default from the inbound interface to the outbound interface or subnet. Fortunately, Cisco provides the IP HELPER-ADDRESS command, allowing the router administrator to manually configure the forwarding of these critical broadcasts. Assume a Widgets 2500 series router exists with e0 with network address 207.79.214.1 255.255.255.0 and s0 with network address 207.79.215.1 255.255.255.0. On the 207.79.215.0 network exists multiple DHCP servers and on the 207.79.214.0 network is Mr. Smith trying to log on to the network. Upon starting up his machine he does not have an IP address and therefore his machine broadcasts a UDP packet to port 67. The DHCP server is on the other side of the router and by default inbound UDP broadcasts are discarded or not forwarded. Mr. Smith never receives an IP and cannot log on the network, nor does he communicate with any other hosts.

When enabled on an interface, IP HELPER-ADDRESS, by default, forwards the UDP protocols required for Mr. Smith to get an address. The ports involved are UDP port 67, for Mr. Smith's outbound IP request, and UDP port 68 for the DHCP servers' response and IP address lease data reply to his request. TFTP (port 69), DNS (port 53), Network Time Protocol (NTP) (port 37), Terminal Access Controller Access Control System (TACACS) (port 49), NetBIOS Name server (port 137) and NetBIOS Datagram server (port 138) are also forwarded by default when helper addressing is enabled.

```
Interface E0
ip helper-address 207.79.214.1
```

The IP FORWARD-PROTOCOL command can be used to configure the forwarding of other protocols not forwarded by default by IP HELPER-ADDRESS.

The command for forwarding these non-default protocols is

```
ip forward-protocol protocol port
```

QUESTIONS

8.07: DNS and DHCP Configuration

13. What is the default administrative distance for IGRP?

    A. 5

    B. 90

    C. 100

    D. 120

14. Your DHCP clients cannot obtain IP leases from the DHCP servers on another subnet.

    Required Result: Configure the Ethernet interface 0 (IP address 207.79.214.1) on the cisco-1 router, which already participates in the AS 51 in network 207.79.214.0, to forward DHCP traffic to the DHCP servers at address 207.79.215.11 and 207.79.215.12.

    Optional Desired Results:

    1. Set the update timer to 120.

    2. Make default adjustments to the invalid and hold-down timers to reflect this change.

    Proposed Solution:

    ```
    Cisco-1 (config)# interface ethernet 0

    Cisco-1 (config-if)# ip-helper 207.79.215.11

    Cisco-1 (config-if)# ip-helper 207.79.215.12

    Cisco-1 (config)# router igrp 51

    Cisco-1 (config-router)# timers basic 120 240 350
    ```

    What results does the proposed solution produce?

    A. The proposed solution fulfills the required result and of both the optional results.

B. The proposed solution fulfills the required result but none of the optional results.

C. The proposed solution fulfills the required result and one optional result.

D. The proposed solution does not fulfill the required result.

TEST YOURSELF OBJECTIVE 8.08

Secondary Addressing

Using the secondary addressing capabilities of the Cisco IOS will allow you to add another full subnet of IP addresses to an already configured interface with a full subnet. This allows for scalability to a limited extent. The command is as follows:

```
ip address ip-address mask secondary
```

If this option were not available, you would have to purchase hardware to add to your LAN and its additional administrative overhead.

Adding a secondary address requires that each and every interface that is directly connected to the newly configured interface also has a secondary address within the same subnet. If this were not the case, they would not be visible to the original router and therefore could not communicate.

- Along with the normal IP addressing you are familiar with, the Cisco IOS also supports adding multiple secondary addresses to single interfaces.

- When using secondary addressing with RIP or IGRP, a routing protocol update will be sent out on each subnet. In cases of low bandwidth availability, this can be a source of congestion.

exam
Watch

Using secondary IP addressing may be the ticket for your plans to make a single network of multiple WAN separated subnets. Subnets within the 131.242.0.0 network are separated by a backbone connection. To consolidate the two subnets, 131.242.2.0 and 131.245.3.0, into one logical address space, you implement this configuration:

```
cisco_subnet1 (config)# interface ethernet 1
cisco_subnet1 (config-if)# ip address 131.242.2.1 255.255.0.0
```

```
cisco_subnet1 (config-if)# ip address 131.245.3.2 255.255.0.0
secondary

cisco_subnet2 (config)# interface ethernet 2

cisco_subnet2 (config-if)# ip address 131.245.3.1 255.255.0.0

cisco_subnet2 (config-if)# ip address 131.242.2.2 255.255.0.0
secondary
```

Next, you perform the same operation on the BGP router to ensure that directly connected interfaces can see each subnet.

QUESTIONS

8.08: Secondary Addressing

15. How many secondary addresses are allowed per interface?

   A. 6

   B. 12

   C. 254

   D. Unlimited

16. There are two subnets in your network.

   ■ Subnet one, 207.79.59.0, has 214 addresses used including the router interface addresses. Its router interface addresses are e0 207.79.59.1, e1 207.79.59.2 and s0 207.79.59.3 s1 207.79.59.4.

   ■ Subnet two, 207.83.59.0, has 215 used addresses, including the router interface addresses. Its router interface addresses are e0 207.83.59.1, e1 207.83.59.2 and s0 207.83.59.3 s1 207.83.59.4. IP addresses below class C X.X.X.10 are reserved for routers.

   The Ethernet 1 addresses are directly connected via a backbone switch.

Subnets one and two use IGRP to learn routes. The AS is number 2. Interface e1 on subnet two also connects to a subnet that has external exposure beyond your network.

Required Result: Implement secondary addressing on interfaces that tie these subnets into one logical network.

Optional Desired Result: Configure the interface not to advertise IGRP routes to external hosts via the subnet two router's serial 0 interface, beyond your intranet.

Proposed Solution:

```
cisco_subnet1 (config)# interface ethernet 1

cisco_subnet1 (config-if)# ip address 207.79.59.2 255.255.255.0

cisco_subnet1 (config-if)# ip address 207.83.59.3 255.255.255.0
secondary

cisco_subnet2 (config)# interface ethernet 1

cisco_subnet2 (config-if)# ip address 207.83.59.2 255.255.255.0

cisco_subnet2 (config-if)# ip address 207.79.59.3 255.255.255.0
secondary

cisco_subnet2 (config)# router igrp 2

cisco_subnet2 (config-router)# network 207.83.59.2

cisco_subnet2 (config-router)# passive-interface serial 0
```

Which of the required and optional results does the proposed solution fulfill?

A. The proposed solution fulfills the required result and the optional result.

B. The proposed solution does not fulfill the required result or the optional result.

C. The proposed solution fulfills the required result but not the optional result.

D. The proposed solution does not fulfill the required result but does fulfill the optional result.

17. Which of the following configuration commands properly configures the e0 interface with IP address 212.12.243.1 and the secondary IP address of 207.79.28.3?

A. ```
Cisco1 (config)# interface ethernet 1
Cisco1 (config-if)# ip address 212.12.243.1 255.255.255.0
Cisco1 (config-if)# ip address 207.79.28.3 255.255.255.0
secondary
```

B. ```
Cisco1 (config)# interface ethernet 0
Cisco1 (config-if)# ip address 207.79.28.3 255.255.255.0
Cisco1 (config-if)# ip address 212.12.243.1 255.255.255.0
secondary
```

C. ```
Cisco1 (config)# interface ethernet 0
Cisco1 (config-if)# ip address 212.12.243.1 255.255.255.0
Cisco1 (config-if)# ip address 207.79.28.3 255.255.255.0
secondary
```

D. ```
Cisco1 (config)# ethernet 0
Cisco1 (config)# ip address 212.12.243.1 255.255.255.0
Cisco1 (config)# ip address 207.79.28.3 255.255.255.0
secondary
```

LAB QUESTION

Objectives 8.01–8.08

Your company, Widgets, Inc., has decided that they will create a new subnet on which they will test the Windows 2000 Advanced Server Active Directory. This will require you to set up the internal interface, Ethernet 0, on a Cisco 2500 router that will provide WAN/Internet connections to the isolated LAN segment. The WAN access filters and security will be assigned to the appropriate team.

This LAN will eventually be integrated into the current network, which uses IGRP as a dynamic routing protocol. You must use AS number 69 and there should be no advertising of routes outside the test LAN.

Your assigned subnet numbers are 10.169.32.0 255.255.255.0 with the internal router interface being IP address 10.169.32.2. You will have the internal DNS server at IP addresses 10.169.32.24 and 10.169.32.25. Because these are all servers and very few workstations, you will not be configuring DHCP for clients. IPs will be assigned to each workstation.

1. Configure the router with name win2k_rtr1 with its basic IP address and subnet mask on the Ethernet port 0. (Assume that the router has been configured by the networking team with the host name using the system configuration dialog.)

2. Next, configure the DNS servers (assume basic configuration defaults).

3. Lastly, create a configuration that will cause win2k_rtr to participate in the local IGRP AS 69. The router should learn routes but not pass them to the external routers (external to the test subnet).

A QUICK ANSWER KEY

Objective 8.01
1. D
2. B

Objective 8.02
3. C
4. A and C

Objective 8.03
5. A and D
6. A and C

Objective 8.04
7. C
8. A

Objective 8.05
9. D
10. B

Objective 8.06
11. B and D
12. B

Objective 8.07
13. C
14. C

Objective 8.08
15. D
16. A
17. C

IN-DEPTH ANSWERS
8.01: IP Configuration Commands

1. ☑ **D.** Is the proper answer because it is in the per-interface mode, which is required to assigning an IP address to an interface.

   ☒ **A** is not correct because it does not use a valid command line. **B** and **C** are not correct because they are not in the proper Configuration mode (per interface) and also B uses improper syntax. (The word *mask* is unnecessary.)

2. ☑ **B.** By configuring the Ethernet ports first with their individual addresses and the subnet masks, they are now available to be used as reference addresses in the IP UNNUMBERED configuration of the serial ports.

   ☒ **A** is incorrect because even though the serial ports are configured correctly, the Ethernet ports will be unable to communicate without infinite looping unless there is further subnetting of the remaining subnet used for the Ethernet ports (there will be the same subnet reference on both sides of the connection). **C** is incorrect because for communication to take place there must be an address to communicate with at each end of the connection. **D** is incorrect because RIP cannot be used in this fashion to provide IP addressing. Addressing must be set prior starting RIP so that the address may be broadcast and learned by neighboring routers.

8.02: Configuring Static Routes

3. ☑ **C.** The routes are configured in a global mode because all the interfaces must use them to evaluate incoming traffic requests.

   ☒ **A** is incorrect because it attempts to configure the second interface with the route. **B** is incorrect because it again attempts to configure the serial interface, although the port was requested. **D** is incorrect because it configures the 207.79.12.1 host to be routed through the 207.79.15.0 network. This could be a correct configuration if a static route to that host was requested and the 207.79.15.0 were replaced with the interface name.

4. ☑ **A** and **C** are correct. The main advantages to static routes are that, relative to the dynamic protocol routes, they are preferred and seen as more reliable. Also they do not have the metrics that IGRP has, which require CPU cycles to be expended.

☒ **B** is not correct because both IGRP and Static route AD can be modified. **D** is incorrect because static routes are just that—static—and do not deal with change well.

8.03: Configuring Default Routes

5. ☑ **A** and **D** are correct. There are two different methods of providing a default route to a classless address space although both must have the IP CLASSLESS feature enabled prior to configuration of the route.

☒ **B** is not correct because it uses an IP CLASSLESS command with an invalid parameter and it uses a non-existent command IP DEFAULT-ADDRESS. The proper command syntax is IP DEFAULT-NETWORK. **C** is incorrect because the IP ADDRESS parameter is misplaced and should have been reversed with the NETWORK ADDRESS parameter.

6. ☑ **A** and **C** are correct. All routers in complex networks do not know all other routers and connected networks. They rely on a hierarchical querying of this information and forwarding of packets via the default route.

☒ **B** is not correct. Faulted packets are handled by Transport layer protocols such as TCP. **D** is incorrect because default routing specifically cannot be configured on a router that has IP routing enabled.

8.04: Configuring RIP Routing

7. ☑ **C.** The router must be in Configuration mode and use the proper syntax and input variables.

☒ **A** is incorrect because the config-rip mode is a non-existent mode. **B** is wrong because it attempts to configure the interface for this parameter. Route summarization, RIP version, authentication chain and mode, and split horizon are parameters that can be configured on a per interface basis. **D** is also wrong because it attempts to configure the interface for this parameter. In addition, it attempts to configure a multicast address for the network.

8. ☑ **A.** By using the NEIGHBOR command, the router is configured to unicast directly to routers explicit in the command and not use the default broadcast method to exchange routes. By resetting the update, invalid, and hold-down timers to twice their default values, you have essentially reduced the current broadcast traffic by half.

☒ **B**, **C**, and **D** are incorrect.

8.05: Configuring IGRP Routing

9. ☑ **D.** Update 90, invalid 270, (update × 3 = 90 × 3) and holddown 280, (invalid +10 = 270 + 10).

☒ **A** and **C** are invalid for any protocols values. **B** is the value of the RIP times value defaults.

10. ☑ **B.** The router must be in Router Configuration mode and the IGRP command must be followed by the AS number. Finally, the network participation must be stated.

☒ **A** is not correct. The router must be in Router Configuration mode and that mode attribute must be set to IGRP. **C** is not correct. NETWORK is not a valid Router Configuration mode value. **D** is not correct. The command NETWORK must be performed after entering CONFIG-ROUTER mode and the AS number parameter, not simultaneously.

8.06: IP Host Tables

11. ☑ **B** and **D** are correct. Because the port of 23 is the default port for Telnet, it is not a required parameter. If the default Telnet had been disabled for security reasons, and an alternate Telnet port set, then B and D both would be incorrect.

☒ **A** is incorrect. IP HOST is a command that must be executed from within a Global Configuration mode and not on a per interface basis. **C** is incorrect. It is missing the IP from IP HOST in the command.

12. ☑ **B.** The configuration syntax is correct but the mode is in exec status. This command must be executed in a Global Configuration mode.

☒ **A**, **C**, and **D** are incorrect in that they state that one or more objectives have been met.

8.07: DNS and DHCP Configuration

13. ☑ **C.** 100 is the default AD for IGRP but it can be customized by the administrator to adjust its preference over another IGRP route or within the routing table.

    ☒ **A** is incorrect. This is the default AD value for the Enhanced IGRP summary route. **B** is incorrect. This is the default AD value for Internal Enhanced IGRP. **D** is incorrect. This is the default AD value for a RIP route within the table.

14. ☑ **C.** The IP-HELPER command is executed properly and the TIMERS BASIC update timer is set properly, but the invalid and hold-down timers are not set to the defaults based on the new update timer. They should be 360 and 370, respectively.

    ☒ **A, B**, and **D** are incorrect.

8.08: Secondary Addressing

15. ☑ **D.** There is no limit to the secondary addresses that can be configured on an interface.

    ☒ **A** is incorrect. This is the number limit placed upon the name-server entry. **B** is incorrect. **C** is incorrect. This is a limit placed on hosts on a Class C network.

16. ☑ **A.** The configuring is done in the proper mode throughout and to the proper interfaces and in the proper order.

    ☒ **B, C**, and **D** are incorrect because these all have too few options fulfilled to represent what has occurred through this configuration session.

17. ☑ **C.** The Configuration mode is appropriate, and the proper addresses are assigned as primary and secondary as ordered.

    ☒ **A** is incorrect. The wrong interface is configured. **B** is incorrect. The IP address assignments are reversed but the remainder is correct. **D** is incorrect. The first command is non-existent and fails to put the interface into Configuration mode.

LAB ANSWER
Objective 8.01–8.08

To answer the question configurations, perform the following steps:

1. ```
   Win2k_rtr1# configure
   Win2k_rtr1 (config)# interface ethernet 0
   Win2k_rtr1 (config-if)# ip address 10.169.32.2 255.255.255.0
   ```

   This has the router in the Interface Configuration mode and includes the IP address as well as the proper subnet mask.

2. ```
   Win2k_rtr1 (config)#ip domain-lookup
   Win2k_rtr1 (config)# ip domain-name widgets.com
   Win2k_rtr1 (config)# ip name-server 10.169.32.25 10.169.32.24
   ```

   Or you could configure the DNS servers with the following commands:

   ```
   Win2k_rtr1 (config)# ip domain-name widgets.com

   Win2k_rtr1 (config)# ip name-server 10.169.32.25 10.169.32.24
   ```

   The Configuration mode is correct and the syntax is without flaw. How can both be correct? The default for Cisco is to have the IP domain-lookup enabled.

3. ```
   Win2k_rtr1 (config)# router igrp 69
   Win2k_rtr1 (config-router)# network 10.169.32.0
   Win2k_rtr1 (config-router)# passive-interface ethernet 0
   ```

   It is set in the Router Configuration mode and applies the passive-interface attribute to the proper Ethernet port.
   ```

CCNA
CISCO CERTIFIED NETWORK ASSOCIATE

9

Virtual Local Area Networks (VLANs)

TEST YOURSELF OBJECTIVES

This chapter will cover a summary of information and self-test questions on virtual local area networks (VLANs) to test your knowledge on this exam topic. This chapter is divided into seven sections covering the basic operations of VLANs, the default VLAN settings for a Catalyst 1900, static and dynamic VLANs, extending VLANs across multiple switches, configuring VLAN trunks, VLAN trunking protocol, and VLAN security.

Some of the more important areas to focus on for the VLAN portion of the CCNA exam are the segmentation of LANs, how to configure VLANs on a Catalyst 1900, the difference between static and dynamic VLAN membership, VTP concepts, and VLAN security. It is also important to understand Spanning-Tree Protocol, trunking states, and trunking encapsulation.

TEST YOURSELF OBJECTIVE 9.01

VLAN Operations

VLANs provide a means for logically segmenting a switched network into several different broadcast domains. These different broadcast domains can span multiple switches, and one switch can contain multiple VLANs. Cisco Catalyst switches assign VLANs either on port configuration or dynamically via MAC address. The advantages of using VLANs include: the simplification of moves, adds, or changes; reduction of administrative costs; removal of physical boundaries; tightening of network security; distribution of traffic load; relocation of servers into secured locations; and better control of broadcasts. The following list highlights what is important to remember:

- VLANs provide a means for segmenting the network.
- VLANs logically segment the physical LAN into different broadcast domains so that broadcast frames get switched only between ports within the same VLAN. To a router, a broadcast domain is a subnet.
- In a Cisco switch, the segmentation of VLANs can be based on the port ID or the MAC address.

Do not forget that switching occurs at the second layer of the OSI model, thus VLANs also operate at Layer 2. VLANs cannot be configured on hubs because a hub functions at the Physical layer. A hub can be a member of a VLAN only if it connects to a switch port. In this case, the VLAN membership of a hub is determined by the switch port to which it is connected.

QUESTIONS

9.01: VLAN Operations

1. How do Cisco Catalyst switches segment a VLAN? (Choose all that apply.)

   A. MAC address

   B. Protocol

   C. Port

   D. Application

2. **Current Situation:** Your company has a large LAN connected with 10-Mbps hubs. IP subnet is currently 10.1.0.0/16 for all 3000 workstations on the LAN. Recently, several new network-enabled applications have been installed on the workstations, and broadcast storms are becoming frequent. There are six departments in your company.

   Required Result: Eliminate the corporate-wide broadcast storms.

   Optional Desired Results:

   1. Increase the speed of the LAN

   2. Keep the cost of the solution low.

   Proposed Solution: Replace all hubs with 10/100 switches and implement departmental VLANs.

   What results does the proposed solution produce?

   A. The proposed solution produces the required result and both of the optional results.

   B. The proposed solution produces the required result and only one of the optional results.

   C. The proposed solution produces the required result but does not meet either of the optional results.

   D. The proposed solution does not meet the required results.

Catalyst 1900 Default VLAN Configuration

The Catalyst 1900 complies with the IEEE 802.1d Spanning-Tree Protocol (STP) guidelines and can work in conjunction with bridges and switches from other vendors. By default, all of the ports on a Catalyst 1900 belong to VLAN 1, which is also the default management VLAN. Cisco recommends that VLAN 1 never be used for user data if you decide to keep it as your management VLAN. The 1900 can be managed by Simple Network Management Protocol (SNMP) and by default can monitor statistics, history, alarms and events via Remote Monitoring (RMON).

- A maximum of 64 VLANs may be configured simultaneously on the Catalyst 1900. The VLAN numbers may range from 2 through 1005 (VLAN 1 is a default VLAN and cannot be removed or modified).

- Switch ports are originally configured on VLAN 1.

- There are several steps to define a VLAN in a Catalyst 1900. From the Main menu, select option [V] for VLAN configuration, enter the VLAN number, and select option [C] to configure.

If you connect a hub or a cascade of hubs to a switch port, that hub segment can only be assigned to one VLAN. Therefore, even if you still have old hubs in your network (for example, during a migration to a switched LAN), you can still gain the benefits of VLANs.

QUESTIONS

9.02: Catalyst 1900 Default VLAN Configuration

3. What protocol is used to avoid loops in switches and VLANs?

   A. Virtual Trunking Protocol (VTP)

    B.   Open Shortest Path First (OSPF)

    C.   Loop Tree Protocol (LTP)

    D.   Spanning-Tree Protocol (STP)

4.   **Current Situation:** You are the senior network manager of a large company, in which you are responsible for the entire network from LAN to WAN. Currently you are in the process of designing and engineering replacement LANs for the entire enterprise. Your 12 existing LANs all consist of 10-Mbps Ethernet hubs running over CAT5 cable.

    Required Results: The new LAN should be faster, scalable, and allow for the use of Virtual LANs.

    Optional Desired Results:

    1.   The LAN should be capable of being managed by SNMP.

    2.   The LAN should provide 100 Mbps in bandwidth to the desktop.

    Proposed Solution: You have selected the Catalyst 1900 switch to replace all of your hubs. This new LAN will utilize VLANs.

    What results does the proposed solution produce?

    A.   The proposed solution produces the required results and both of the optional results.

    B.   The proposed solution produces the required results and only one of the optional results.

    C.   The proposed solution produces the required result but does not meet either of the optional results.

    D.   The proposed solution does not meet the required result.

TEST YOURSELF OBJECTIVE 9.03

Static Versus Dynamic VLAN Membership

There are two methods of assigning ports to VLANs: static and dynamic. Static VLAN membership requires that ports be manually assigned to a particular VLAN. Static

VLAN membership is more secure and easier to manage. It is also useful in networks that require managed moves. Filtering and end-station MAC address tables are not needed for static VLAN membership. Dynamic VLAN membership is automatically determined using a VLAN Membership Policy Server (VMPS). A VMPS contains a table of MAC addresses and determines which VLAN a node belongs to. The following details are important to remember:

■ Static VLAN configuration requires the use of the CLI.

■ Dynamic VLAN membership requires the use of a VMPS.

exam **!**
ⓦatch

Spanning-Tree Protocol is used in order to avoid and eliminate loops in a switched network. In other words, STP ensures that there is only one active path to every destination in a VLAN/broadcast domain so that bridging loops never occur. If a loop does occur, STP eliminates the loop via port states. STP defines five states for ports: Blocking, Listening, Learning, Forwarding, and Disabled. The root of the Spanning-Tree finds redundant links and automatically selects the appropriate state for each port of the entire switched network.

QUESTIONS

9.03: Static Versus Dynamic VLAN Membership

5. You have your switches configured for dynamic VLANs, and they access a VLAN Membership Policy Server (VMPS) database configuration file on a TFTP server. The address table within the VMPS database is as follows:

```
address 0a2e.2341.e9a9 vlan-name acct

address a8ca.d98e.f345 vlan-name hr

address aa34.34ef.291e vlan-name acct

address 879f.ea78.97fd vlan-name it
```

```
address 1e59.3da7.a78e vlan-name acct

address 035d.98ed.789a vlan-name hr
```

What configuration changes do you need to make to your VMPS database and your switches when you replace the computer with the MAC address of aa34.34ef.291e with a brand new computer? (The user at the desktop location will not change, nor will the VLAN membership.) (Choose all that apply.)

A. No changes necessary; it will be dynamically changed.

B. Change the MAC address in the VMPS database.

C. Change the MAC address settings on the switch port configuration.

D. Change the MAC address in the VMPS database, and then issued the DOWNLOAD VMPS command on the switch.

6. What potential problem exists in the following switching configuration diagram, and what protocol is used in this situation to fix the potential problem?

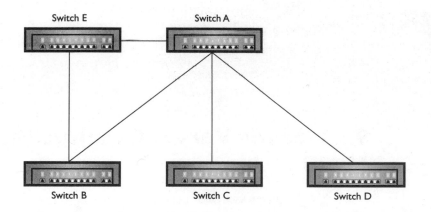

A. Routing loop, Spanning-Tree Protocol

B. ISL loop, VMPS

C. Switching loop, VTP

D. Bridging loop, Spanning-Tree Protocol

TEST YOURSELF OBJECTIVE 9.04

Extending VLANs Across Multiple Switches

Using VLAN Trunking Protocol (VTP), it is possible to advertise VLANs across multiple switches. Inter-Switch Link (ISL), 802.1Q, 802.10, and LANE are supported trunking encapsulations. Delivery methods such as frame filtering and frame tagging are used by switches to forward packets.

■ Two methods of data delivery are frame filtering and frame tagging.

■ Catalyst 5000 series switches do not support frame tagging.

■ ISL was developed by Cisco to exchange VLAN information and can only be used by Cisco devices.

■ Spanning-Tree PortFast should only be used on end node devices.

It is important to note that extending VLANs across multiple switches is hardware dependent. Some only support certain types of trunking encapsulation. Before extending VLANs across switches of different models, make sure to check the switch documentation or use the SHOW PORT CAPABILITIES command to determine which trunking encapsulations are supported.

QUESTIONS

9.04: Extending VLANs Across Multiple Switches

7. You have seven switches connected and divided into three VLANs (10, 20, and 30), as shown in the following illustration. What method is used to figure out which VLAN a given packet belongs to?

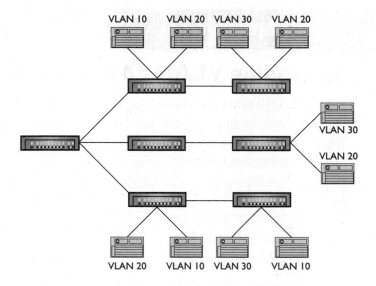

A. Filtering

B. Identification

C. Tagging

D. Aggregation

8. What method does the 802.1Q trunking standard use for identifying VLANs?

A. Encapsulation

B. Frame tagging

C. VTP

D. Frame filtering

9. What standard method is used to transport VLANs over ATM networks?

A. ISL

B. 802.1Q

C. LANE

D. 802.10

TEST YOURSELF OBJECTIVE 9.05

Configuring VLAN Trunks

All Ethernet ports are non-trunk ports by default, and all Fast Ethernet ports are set to auto and are willing to become a trunk port. It is suggested that only 100-Mbps or 1-Gbps lines be used as trunks. Inter-Switch Link was developed by Cisco to encapsulate Ethernet frames of any VLAN and send them between switches. It can only be used between Cisco devices. IEEE 802.1Q is a standard encapsulation for allowing multiple VLANs to pass between switches across a single port.

- The command SET TRUNK defines the trunking state for each switch.
- Trunking may be configured as four different states: on, off, auto, and desirable.

exam
ⓦatch

The SET TRUNK command automatically transports VLANs 1 through 1005 regardless of whether you specify a range or not. If you do not want any of these VLANs on the trunk, you must explicitly clear those VLANs from the trunk.

QUESTIONS

9.05: Configuring VLAN Trunks

10. How does ISL use encapsulation, as shown in the following illustration, to interconnect multiple switches and maintain VLAN information between switches as the traffic is passed on the trunk links?

ISL header 26 bytes	Encapsulated frame 1–24.5KB	CRC 4 bytes

A. It tags each frame with identification criteria.

B. It encapsulates each frame with an ISL header.

    C. It filters each frame based on header information.

    D. It is proprietary, and Cisco does not disclose how ISL works.

11. What are the four trunk states?

    A. Active, inactive, auto, and disabled

    B. On, off, auto, and desirable

    C. Blocking, listening, learning, and forwarding

    D. Enabled, disabled, auto, and desirable

TEST YOURSELF OBJECTIVE 9.06

VLAN Trunking Protocol (VTP)

VLAN Trunking Protocol (VTP) provides a method for distributing VLAN information. The benefits of using VTP include: minimal configuration required for new devices, new switches dynamically learning from VTP advertisements, consistent configuration, and improved security. A VTP domain is used for the control and configuration of VLANs using VTP on one or more interconnected switches. There are three VTP modes: Server, Client, and Transparent. VLAN changes in a VTP domain can only be made on a switch that is in VTP Server mode. VTP pruning increases available bandwidth by restricting unnecessary flooded traffic.

- ■ VTP is the method by which Cisco switches can distribute VLAN information.
- ■ VTP can only be configured on trunk ports.
- ■ VTP domains must be consistent between switches for VLANs to be advertised.
- ■ There are three VTP modes: Client, Server, and Transparent.

exam
ⓦatch

You can assign passwords to your VTP domains to prevent unauthorized switches being added to the domain. All switches configured in the same VTP domain must use the same domain password for the VLAN tables to be advertised between switches. If a VTP password is not used and an unauthorized switch is added to a VTP domain, incorrect VLAN information could be passed to your VTP domain, causing a network outage.

QUESTIONS

9.06: VLAN Trunking Protocol (VTP)

12. In what mode must a VTP member switch be for configuration changes to be made?

    A. Server

    B. Client

    C. Auto

    D. Transparent

13. How does VTP pruning increase available bandwidth?

    A. Compresses frames to allow more bandwidth

    B. Eliminates all frames outside of the VTP domain

    C. Eliminates broadcast and multicast packets

    D. Eliminates broadcast, multicast, unknown, and flooded unicast packets

14. The senior network administrator has asked you to configure a Catalyst 5000 switch as a VTP domain server. The VTP domain name should be "accounting," and the password for the domain is "money." What command(s) must you issue to make the configuration change?

    A. SET VTP *accounting server money*

    B. SET VTP DOMAIN *accounting* MODE *server* PASSWORD *money*

    C. VTP DOMAIN *accounting* MODE *server* PASSWORD *money*

    D. VTP: *accounting server money*

TEST YOURSELF OBJECTIVE 9.07

VLAN Security

Secure port filtering is used to provide port security for VLANs. Secure port filtering allows an administrator to block input on switch ports based on MAC addresses. If the MAC address of the device attached to the port does not match the MAC address specified, the port is disabled, the link LED for that port turns orange, and a link-down trap is sent to the SNMP manager. The SET PORT SECURITY command is used to configure a port for secure port filtering.

- A port on a switch may be configured for optimum security.
- The command SET PORT SECURITY may be enabled for source port filtering.

Trunk ports cannot be configured to use port security. One of the reasons for this is that addresses learned on trunk ports might change frequently. It is also important to remember that not all Cisco Catalyst switches support port security and documentation should be checked for certainty.

QUESTIONS

9.07: VLAN Security

Questions 15–16   This scenario should be used to answer questions 15 and 16.

You are responsible for a LAN consisting of Catalyst 5000 switches using six VLANs in one VTP domain. There are approximately 1,000 workstations on your network. Your company is preparing to bring 30 consultants in for a major project, and you have been asked to tighten security in the network. The company wants to make sure that only company-approved workstations and laptops are allowed to access the LAN. They do not want a contractor to be able to plug any computer into a wall jack and connect into the network.

15. The port security on all of your switches is still set to the factory default setting. What command should you use to configure port security on your switches?

 A. PORT SECURE [MAX-MAC-COUNT *maximum_mac_count*]

 B. SET PORT SECURITY *mod_num/port_num* ENABLE *mac address*

 C. PORT SECURITY *mod_num/port_num* ENABLE *mac address*

 D. SET PORT MAC *mac-address*

16. Your contractors arrived last week, and as you were checking your network, you noticed that several port LEDs had turned orange. You have never seen a port LED turn orange before. What is causing this?

 A. Ports that have port security enabled on them turn orange.

 B. The orange port LED indicates a hardware failure.

 C. The ports with orange LEDs are disabled because a device tried to plug into the port that did not match the assigned MAC address.

 D. The orange port LED indicates a software configuration error.

LAB QUESTION
Objectives 9.01–9.07

A local company is expecting rapid growth and is currently occupying the bottom four floors of a high-rise building. Last year they expanded into the fourth floor and will continue to occupy an additional floor each year for the foreseeable future. The building supports approximately 150 people per floor, and the company has nine departments that are interspersed throughout the four floors. Each floor has a network equipment closet, and one floor houses the network operations center where the WAN equipment and servers reside.

The Director of IT for this company wants a high-speed, flexible, securable, and scalable LAN that will meet their business needs for the next several years. He has asked you, a consultant, to submit a network design proposal, upgrade their LAN, and plan for its future growth.

Currently, the company is using 10-Mbps hubs that are several years old and use CAT5 standard cabling throughout the building. What kind of equipment would you recommend, and what would be the general configuration of it?

A QUICK ANSWER KEY

Objective 9.01
1. **A** and **C**
2. **B**

Objective 9.02
3. **D**
4. **B**

Objective 9.03
5. **B** and **D**
6. **D**

Objective 9.04
7. **B**
8. **B**
9. **C**

Objective 9.05
10. **B**
11. **B**

Objective 9.06
12. **A**
13. **D**
14. **B**

Objective 9.07
15. **B**
16. **C**

IN-DEPTH ANSWERS
9.01: VLAN Operations

1. ☑ **A** and **C** are correct. Cisco Catalyst switches segment VLANs based on switch ports or MAC address.

   ☒ **B** is incorrect because Cisco Catalyst Switches do not segment based on a protocol. **D** is incorrect because Cisco Catalyst Switches do not segment based on applications.

2. ☑ **B.** The required result is met because implementing VLANs with fewer workstations than the previous LAN will eliminate the corporate-wide broadcast storms. The first optional result is met because a switch provides for a faster LAN, especially if a workstation is connected at 100 Mbps. The second optional result is not met because switches are fairly expensive, and the proposed solution would not be as inexpensive as keeping the hubs.

   ☒ **A** is incorrect because only the first optional result was met. **C** is not correct because the required result was met and one of the optional results was met by the proposed solution. **D** is incorrect because the required result was met.

9.02: Catalyst 1900 Default VLAN Configuration

3. ☑ **D.** STP is used to prevent loops in switches and VLANs.

   ☒ **A** is not correct because VTP is used to distribute VLAN information. **B** is incorrect because OSPF is a routing protocol. **C** is incorrect because LTP is not a valid protocol.

4. ☑ **B.** The required result is met because the Catalyst 1900 switches offer faster and more scalable service than the previous hubs and they are able to utilize VLANs. The first optional result is met because the Catalyst 1900 switch supports SNMP. The second optional result is not met because the

Catalyst 1900 only offers 10-Mbps user ports (although there are two 100-Mbps ports, they are typically used for uplinks).

☒ **A** is not correct because the second optional result is not met. The Catalyst 1900 only offers 10-Mbps user ports. **C** is incorrect because the first optional result was met. The Catalyst 1900 switch supports SNMP. **D** is incorrect because the required result was met.

9.03: **Static Versus Dynamic VLAN Membership**

5. ☑ **B** and **D** are correct. You need to update the VMPS database file with the correct MAC address. The VMPS server is queried every few minutes by the switch and the switch will automatically get the new MAC address mapping. If you want to speed up this process, you can issue the DOWNLOAD VMPS command to make the configuration changes effective immediately on the switch.

   ☒ **A** is incorrect because the client MAC address has changed. Dynamic changes only take place if the device with the MAC address is moved to a new port location and needs to stay in the same VLAN. **C** is incorrect because the VMPS database cannot be altered on the switch; it must be changed on the TFTP server and then downloaded to the switch(s).

6. ☑ **D.** Routing loop, Spanning-Tree Protocol. Without the Spanning-Tree Protocol there would be multiple active links between switches A, B, and E.

   ☒ **A** is incorrect because the potential loop is with switches, not routers. **B** is incorrect because ISL is not used in this scenario and VMPS would not correct a switching/bridging loop. **C** is incorrect because VTP would not correct a switching loop

9.04: **Extending VLANs Across Multiple Switches**

7. ☑ **B.** Identification. VLAN frame identification methods, such as 802.1Q and ISL, logically identify which packet belongs to which VLAN.

   ☒   **A** is incorrect because filtering is a method that allows administrators to define attributes on switches that require certain actions to be taken on frames meeting the criteria. **C** is incorrect because tagging assigns a user-defined ID to each frame as it is passed through the switch. **D** is incorrect because aggregation is not a method used in switch-to-switch configurations.

8.   ☑   **B.** The 802.1Q standard uses frame tagging to identify VLANs by inserting identifiers into the frame header.

   ☒   **A** is not correct because encapsulation is used by the ISL identification method. **C** is incorrect because VTP is not a method of identification. **D** is incorrect because frame filtering is a method in which particular user-defined offsets are examined.

9.   ☑   **C.** ATM networks can transport VLANs using LANE (LAN Emulation).

   ☒   **A** is incorrect because ISL is only used on Ethernet networks. **B** is not correct because 802.1Q is also only used on Ethernet networks. **D** is incorrect because the 802.10 method is used on FDDI networks.

9.05: Configuring VLAN Trunks

10.   ☑   **B.** ISL encapsulates each Ethernet frame with an ISL header that transports VLAN IDs between switches and routers.

   ☒   **A** is incorrect because 802.1Q uses frame tagging, not ISL. **C** is incorrect because frame filtering is not used by ISL. **D** is not correct because Cisco does disclose how ISL works, even though ISL is a Cisco proprietary protocol.

11.   ☑   **B.** The four trunk states are on, off, auto, and desirable.

   ☒   **A** is incorrect because the four trunk states are on, off, auto, and desirable. **C** is incorrect because the answer lists four of the modes of STP. **D** is incorrect because the four trunk states are on, off, auto, and desirable.

9.06: VLAN Trunking Protocol (VTP)

12.   ☑   **A.** Configuration changes can only be made to a VTP domain on VTP server switch.

☒ **B** is incorrect because a switch in VTP Client mode cannot create, change, or delete VLANs in a VTP domain. **C** is incorrect because it is not a valid VTP mode. **D** is incorrect because a switch configured in VTP Transparent mode does not participate in a VTP domain, and therefore cannot create, change, or delete VLANs in a VTP domain.

13. ☑ **D.** VTP Pruning eliminates broadcast, multicast, unknown, and flooded unicast packets.

☒ **A** and **B** are incorrect because VTP pruning only eliminates unnecessary flooded traffic. **C** is not the best answer because VTP pruning also eliminates unknown and flooded unicast packets.

14. ☑ **B.** The correct syntax for the command is SET VTP [DOMAIN *domain-name*] [MODE *mode*] [PASSWORD *password*].

☒ **A, B,** and **D** are incorrect because they do not follow the correct syntax.

9.07: VLAN Security

15. ☑ **B.** The SET PORT SECURITY command is used to enable port security on a Catalyst 5000 switch.

☒ **A** is incorrect because the PORT SECURE command is used for IOS-based switches. **C** is incorrect because the initial SET command is missing. **D** is not correct because it is not a valid command.

16. ☑ **C.** A port with security enables checking the MAC address of every received frame. If the MAC address does not match the port setting, the port is disabled, and the port LED turns orange.

☒ **A, B,** and **D** are incorrect because a port LED turns orange when it is disabled.

LAB ANSWER
Objectives 9.01–9.07

In this situation it would be best to replace all 10-Mbps hubs with Catalyst 5509s for each floor and a Catalyst 5500 with Route Switch Module (RSM) or Route Switch Feature Card (RSFC) to aggregate the floor Catalyst 5509 switches. The Catalyst 5509 switches would each be populated with a supervisor engine and seven 24-port RJ-45 10/100-Mbps Fast Ethernet switching modules.

A general configuration that would best fit this company would be a single VTP domain with nine VLANS (one for each department). This network would be flexible, scalable, and fast, and would allow them to enable port security if required. By using the modular Catalyst 5500 series switches, the network will be able to change as technology improves. The Fast Ethernet modules will provide a high-speed network infrastructure. The Catalyst 5500 series switch also provides the capability to utilize port security.

10

Configuring
Novell IPX

T he questions in this chapter pertain to the architecture and properties of IP's distant cousin, IPX (Internetworking Packet Exchange). Both protocols were developed from Xerox's XNS protocol, and they share a very similar-looking protocol stack model and datagram pattern. However, Novell implements IPX over several different data-link frame formats, and the CCNA candidate must be able to distinguish between them and understand the "gotchas" inherent in implementing one data link type over another.

We will then look at two fundamental IPX protocols, RIP and SAP, and their function in the IPX protocol architecture. Finally, we will look at some examples of configuring IPX on a Cisco router.

TEST YOURSELF OBJECTIVE 10.01

IPX Protocol Stack

Like IP (also developed from the XNS protocol), IPX is a suite of protocols that maps to the OSI reference model with a fair degree of accuracy. IPX and RIP both work at the Network layer (Layer 3) protocol, SPX is a Transport layer (Layer 4) protocol, SAP is a Session layer (Layer 5) protocol, and NCP (NetWare Core Protocol) is an Application layer (Layer 7) protocol.

It is important to remember the function of each protocol, and how each works hand-in-hand with the others. It is also important to keep in mind the differences between the RIP protocol used in IPX, and the RIP protocol used in IP: while they share the same name, lineage, and purpose, their operations are quite different.

- The Internetwork Packet Exchange (IPX) protocol is the native networking protocol for Novell NetWare.

- IPX provides the basis for the stack of protocols designed by Novell to support NetWare.

exam
ⓦatch

While IPX has gone the way of the dodo with NetWare version 5, there are still thousands of networks out there that run IPX to a greater or lesser degree. The adage says, "If it isn't broken, don't fix it," and this one of the major reasons why IPX will continue to be covered in technical training classes and on certification tests—it's out there, and it's working. NetWare version 5 is IP-based but is also backward compatible with IPX. Don't make the mistake of glossing over IPX. If you already have a solid foundation in TCP/IP, IPX won't be much trouble to pick up.

QUESTIONS

10.01: IPX Protocol Stack

1. The IPX protocol provides _____ services to upper-layer protocols.

    A. Connection-oriented

    B. Connectionless

    C. Congestion notification

    D. Beaconing

2. **Current Situation:** Connie is installing a large multiprotocol network consisting of IP, IPX, and IP-based Macintosh clients. Despite having offices in many locations nationwide, the IPX clients are located solely in Boston, Massachusetts, and Flint, Michigan. The IPX clients are in the middle of an upgrade, so some clients are running NetWare version 5, while others are still running NetWare version 4.12. Connie is pushing for an IP-only environment and wants to keep the overhead on her routers to a minimum.

    Required Result: All IPX clients, regardless of version, must be able to talk to all other IPX clients. All IP and Macintosh clients must be able to communicate.

    Optional Desired Result: Keep router overhead to a minimum by running only IP on this network.

    Proposed Solution: Enable IP and IPX on all routers connecting Boston and Flint.

    Which of the following results does the proposed solution produce?

    A. The proposed solution produces the required result and the optional result.

    B. The proposed solution produces the required result but not the optional result.

    C. The proposed solution produces neither the required result, nor the optional result.

    D. The proposed solution produces the optional result, but not the required result.

3. IPX can run over which data-link protocols? (Choose all that apply.)

   A. Ethernet v2

   B. Token ring

   C. FDDI

   D. PPP

TEST YOURSELF OBJECTIVE 10.02

IPX Datagram

The important fields to keep in mind in an IPX datagram are the Packet Type and Source/Destination Address fields. The Packet Type identifies the upper-layer protocol in the data field and becomes invaluable as we start looking at filtering IPX packets, especially on WAN interfaces. Keep in mind the format of an IPX address: 32-dot-48 (32 bits for the network portion of the address, and 48 bits for the host portion). These values are fixed, meaning no subnet mask is needed (whew!). The 32 bits of the network portion are statically assigned by the network administrator, while the 48 bits for the host portion are simply copied from the host's adapter card MAC address.

- An IPX datagram consists of a 30-byte header followed by the user data.

- Each IPX network is given a 32-bit network number. These numbers are generated by network administrators and must be unique throughout the IPX internetwork.

exam
Ⓦatch

Here's a quick and easy way to assign IPX network addresses: steal them from your existing IP networks! Let's assume you've got an IP subnet, 192.168.13.0/24. Since IP subnets must be unique throughout your network, and since IPX subnets also must be unique throughout your network, simply converting the 32-bit decimal IP network address into a 32-bit hexadecimal IPX network address will guarantee global uniqueness for each of your IPX networks. This is also good practice of your binary math skills.

Try to convert that address, 192.168.13.0/24, into hexadecimal. If you end up with C0A80D00, you know your stuff (or at least your calculator does).

QUESTIONS

10.02: IPX Datagram

4. The Transport Control field in the IPX header holds what information?

   A. The age of the packet

   B. Protocol type

   C. Router hop count

   D. Level of service required

5. What is the length of an IPX network number?

   A. 16 bits

   B. Variable

   C. 48 bits

   D. 32 bits

6. The Checksum field in the IPX header is normally set to:

   A. A checksum of the entire IPX packet

   B. A checksum of the IPX header fields only

   C. 0xFFFF

   D. 0

TEST YOURSELF OBJECTIVE 10.03

IPX Encapsulation Types

One of the most fundamental yet often overlooked factors in implementing an IPX-based network is the issue of encapsulation types. While 90 percent of all Ethernet networks in the world today are Ethernet v. 2, Novell NetWare requires network administrators to support varying Ethernet frame formats, depending on which version of NetWare is being implemented. Not only do network administrators need to ensure that all NetWare clients and servers are using the correct encapsulation type, they also need to make sure that all the network routers use the same Ethernet frame format(s).

- What Novell refers to as a frame type, Cisco calls an encapsulation.

- The Cisco IOS configuration commands also use different names for the Novell frame types.

- The Ethernet_802.3 frame is also called 802.3 raw in some documentation. This is the default encapsulation for NetWare versions up to (and including) 3.11.

- The Ethernet_802.2 frame type uses the same base frame format as Ethernet_802.3 but includes the LLC (802.2) information as well. This is the default encapsulation for NetWare 3.12 and 4.*x*.

- SNAP was devised to allow protocols to continue to use the Ethernet_II packet type numbers.

- Multiple frame types can be in use on one physical network segment.

- RIP is a distance vector protocol, which means that it bases its choice of the best route to a given destination on the distance to the destination via the route.

exam
Watch

Think managing a NetWare environment is a no-brainer? Think again. When Novell introduced version 3.12 of NetWare, the company issued all the documentation necessary for network administrators to perform a smooth upgrade of all clients and servers...except for one little thing. They didn't document the fact that they changed the default data link encapsulation type! Any clients running version 3.11 or lower were running one type, while those upgraded to 3.12 were running a second frame type. With no translation mechanism in place (for example, a router with two subinterfaces, each running a different encapsulation type), the 3.11 clients couldn't talk to the 3.12 clients. The moral of the story is this: Walk the layers when troubleshooting, and when in doubt, sniff it out.

QUESTIONS

10.03: IPX Encapsulation Types

7. Each of these Novell frame types (on the left) corresponds to a Cisco encapsulation name (on the right).

    a. Ethernet_II   1. SNAP

    b. Ethernet_802.2   2. novell-ether

    c. Ethernet_802.3   3. arpa

    d. Ethernet_SNAP   4. SAP

    Which of the following represents the correctly matched pairs?

    A. a-3, b-4, c-2, d-1

    B. a-1, b-4, c-3, d-2

    C. a-3, b-2, c-4, d-1

    D. a-4, b-1, c-2, d-3

8. Identify the format of the following frame:

Dest. MAC 6 bytes	Source MAC 6 bytes	Type 2 bytes	Data 46–1500 bytes	FCS 4 bytes

    A. SAP

    B. SNAP

    C. Novell-ether

    D. Arpa

9. What is the default encapsulation type for Novell NetWare version 3.12 and 4.x?

    A. Ethernet_II

    B. Ethernet_802.3

    C. Ethernet_802.2

    D. Ethernet_SNAP

RIP and SAP

IPX RIP (Routing Information Protocol) and SAP (Service Advertising Protocol) answer two questions in a NetWare network: where else can I go, and what will I find when I get there? Routers use IP RIP to teach one another how to get to the various IP subnetworks in the network. IPX RIP does exactly the same thing, but in slightly different ways and with slightly different ramifications. IPX SAP, which has no counterpart in IP, allows routers to teach one another what NetWare services are available to clients (for example, print servers or file servers).

- When an IPX node wishes to send a packet to a remote network, it must locate an IPX router that knows of a route to the network.

- NetWare file servers have an internal virtual IPX network.

- Before an IPX packet can be transmitted onto a network, it must be placed inside a MAC frame.

- SAP allows servers to advertise the services they provide on the network.

- There are three types of SAP packets defined: periodic updates, service queries, and service responses.

- To provide information on the topology of the network and the services available on it, IPX servers, routers, and clients use two protocols: Service Advertising Protocol (SAP) and Routing Information Protocol (RIP). Both these protocols use IPX broadcasts to propagate information around the network.

- SAP advertises and distributes service information, and RIP is used to propagate IPX routing information.

- RIP is the default routing protocol when IPX routing is enabled.

- NetWare Link Services Protocol (NLSP) is a link-state protocol similar to the OSPF protocol used with TCP/IP.

- Enhanced Interior Gateway Routing Protocol (EIGRP) is a distance vector protocol, but it has been designed to cause less overhead on the network than RIP.

Why do we network engineers need to know about all of this? Because IPX support protocols (RIP and SAP) will soak up valuable network bandwidth if they're not monitored and tamed. From a LAN perspective: When a NetWare client boots up, it's like a lost sheep. It sends out a GNS (Get Nearest Server) query in order to find its way back to the fold. We can configure our routers to respond to GNS queries locally (since GNS queries are broadcasts, which routers will not forward), or to forward them on to specified NetWare servers. From a WAN perspective: Users on the east coast generally do not need to know about services on the west coast (for example, a print server). By default, IPX SAP will advertise every service to every IPX network. However, we can implement filtering on our WAN interfaces to prevent certain SAP entries from being advertised over a slow WAN link, soaking up expensive bandwidth.

QUESTIONS

10.04: RIP and SAP

10. Brooke is a network administrator of an IPX network that spans a slow WAN link. She wants to block a print server on the Boston LAN from being advertised to the Santa Clara end of the WAN link. However, that same server also is a file server that she does want to have advertised over the link. On what field in the IPX packet will she filter?

   A. Source Address

   B. Destination Address

   C. Packet Type

   D. Service Type

11. What prevents service loops in the SAP protocol?

   A. Time ticks

   B. Spanning-Tree

   C. Split horizon

   D. Subinterfaces

12. How many SAP packets does a router send out over a 56-Kbps WAN link over a five-minute period if its SAP table contains 49 entries and no filtering is being applied?

   A. 7

   B. 21

   C. 35

   D. 42

TEST YOURSELF OBJECTIVE 10.05

IPX Configuration

Now that we have an understanding of the various protocols in the IPX suite, we can turn our attention to the Cisco router commands used to configure IPX. For the CCNA exam, the commands are fairly simple and they mimic those used in IP configuration. One of the major differences is the inclusion of the IPX ROUTING command, which is essential to making IPX work on a Cisco router. The IPX ADDRESS command enables IPX on individual interfaces (like the IP ADDRESS command). Once IPX is up and running, we can verify its operation using several SHOW and DEBUG scripts: SHOW IPX INTERFACE, SHOW IPX TRAFFIC, SHOW IPX SERVERS, SHOW IPX ROUTES, and DEBUG IPX ROUTING ACTIVITY.

- Before you start to configure IPX, you must either obtain or generate a plan for the network.

- The first step in configuration is to enable IPX routing using the IOS command IPX ROUTING.

- Once you have IPX enabled, you can configure the router interfaces.

- Use subinterfaces to configure multiple frame encapsulations. Remember that secondary interfaces are no longer supported in future releases of the IOS.

- The SHOW IPX INTERFACE command allows you to check the configuration of the interface.

- Once you know that the interfaces are configured correctly, you can use the SHOW IPX TRAFFIC command to look at the amount of activity on the network.
- The SHOW IPX SERVERS command shows the SAP database in the router.
- The SHOW IPX ROUTE command will display the IPX routing table.
- The DEBUG IPX ROUTING ACTIVITY command allows you to see the routing updates as they are being sent and received.

exam
ⓦatch

There's a little "gotcha" when configuring IPX on a Cisco router. By default, the router will assume that you want IP to be routed, and therefore you can sit down and start configuring routers with IP addresses and routing protocols. However, if you try to do that with IPX, you'll find out sooner or later that no routing is occurring. There's an extra command needed to initialize IPX on a Cisco router: IPX ROUTING. This command tells the router that you're doing more than just the standard IP routing on your network.

QUESTIONS

10.05: IPX Configuration

13. What is the default encapsulation type on an Ethernet interface configured with IPX?

   A. Arpa

   B. SAP

   C. SNAP

   D. Novell-ether

14. **Current Situation:** You need to configure a brand new Cisco router to route IPX for a new subnet you're creating. The stations on this subnet are running NetWare version 4.12.

Required Result: All NetWare clients on the new subnet (0xA on interface e0) must be able to communicate with their default gateway (the new router), as well as with existing NetWare 4.12 clients on the other side of the router (on subnet 0xB, interface e1).

Optional Desired Result: Clients on network 0xA must be able to talk with other clients on network 0xA.

Proposed Solution: You sit down at the router and type in the following commands:

```
Router (config)# int e0

Router (config)# ipx network A

Router (config)# int e1

Router (config)# ipx network B encaps SAP
```

Which of the following results does the proposed solution produce?

A. The proposed solution produces the required result and the optional result.

B. The proposed solution produces the required result but not the optional result.

C. The proposed solution produces the optional result but not the required result.

D. The proposed solution produces neither the required result nor the optional result.

15. Which IPX routing protocol sends updates every 60 seconds by default?

A. IPX RIP

B. NLSP

C. OSPF

D. EIGRP

LAB QUESTION

Objectives 10.01–10.05

You are the network administrator for the following IPX network, which stretches between Santa Clara and Boston:

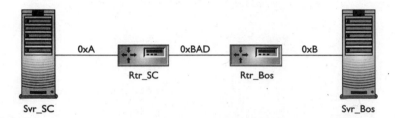

In Santa Clara you have a server, Svr_SC, which is running NetWare 3.11, and whose gateway is the Cisco router Rtr_SC. Rtr_SC also serves several IPX clients on the same network, 0xA. The clients are also running NetWare 3.11. Rtr_SC is connected via a point-to-point 56-Kbps link (IPX network number 0xBAD) to the Cisco router Rtr_Bos, located in Boston. Off of Boston is an IPX network, 0xB, which has several IPX clients running NetWare 3.12, as well as a server running NetWare 3.12, Svr_Bos.

You need to make sure that the IPX clients in Boston can talk to the clients in Santa Clara, and vice versa. At the same time, you'd like to keep GNS queries from crossing the WAN. To further minimize WAN bandwidth usage, you'd like to prevent the print server on Svr_SC from being advertised over the WAN link, but you still need to have the print server on Svr_Bos be advertised to Santa Clara. What steps will you take to make sure all of these criteria are met in your network?

A QUICK ANSWER KEY

Objective 10.01

1. **B**
2. **B**
3. **A, B, C** and **D**

Objective 10.02

4. **C**
5. **D**
6. **C**

Objective 10.03

7. **A**
8. **D**
9. **C**

Objective 10.04

10. **D**
11. **C**
12. **C**

Objective 10.05

13. **D**
14. **C**
15. **A**

IN-DEPTH ANSWERS
10.01: IPX Protocol Stack

1. ☑ **B.** IPX is a connectionless protocol.

   ☒ **A** is incorrect. because connection-oriented services are implemented at Layer 4 with the SPX protocol. **C** is incorrect because congestion notification is commonly a Frame Relay feature. **D** is incorrect, as beaconing is a token ring process.

2. ☑ **B.** IPX must be enabled in order for the older NetWare clients to communicate with each other, and with the NetWare 5 clients. Keep in mind that NetWare 5 is backward compatible with IPX-based versions of NetWare. However, this does not minimize the overhead on the router. Once all of the NetWare clients have been upgraded to version 5 and become IP-based, IPX can be disabled on all routers.

   ☒ **A, C,** and **D** are incorrect because the proposed solution produces the required result but not the optional result.

3. ☑ **A, B, C,** and **D** are correct. IPX is a Network layer (Layer 3) protocol, compatible with any Data-Link layer (Layer 2) protocol found in modern networks (Frame Relay, PPP, SMDS, or X.25)

10.02: IPX Datagram

4. ☑ **C.** The Transport Control field in the IPX header holds router hop count information. The Transport Control field is initialized to zero when the packet is generated, and incremented each time it travels through a router.

   ☒ **A** is incorrect because the age of the packet is not recorded. **B** is also incorrect. The protocol type is recorded in the Packet Type field of the IPX header. **D** is incorrect, as the level of service is nonexistent in IPX, but there is a Service Type field in the header of a SAP packet.

5. ☑ **D.** The Network Number is a fixed-length, 32-bit number, although it is normally written with leading zeros omitted. An IPX network that is numbered 0x32 is, in actuality, network 0x00000032.

    ☒ **B** is incorrect because there is no subnet mask used in IPX. **A** and **C** are incorrect because the length of an IPX network number is always 32 bits.

6. ☑ **C.** The Checksum field in the IPX header is not used by default. It is set to 0xFFFF when the packet is generated.

    ☒ **A, B,** and **D** are the incorrect settings.

10.03: IPX Encapsulation Types

7. ☑ **A.** This represents the correct pair matchings: Ethernet II with arpa; Ethernet 802.2 with SAP; Ethernet 802.3 with novell-ether; and Ethernet SNAP with SNAP.

    ☒ **B, C,** and **D** are all incorrect matchings.

8. ☑ **D.** The frame shown is Ethernet v. 2, called arpa in Cisco terminology.

    ☒ **C** is incorrect. The novell-ether frame type is denoted by a Length field instead of the Type field shown here. **A** and **B** are also incorrect. The SAP and SNAP formats both contain DSAP and SSAP fields, which are not shown here.

9. ☑ **C.** With the release of NetWare 3.12, Novell changed the default encapsulation type from 802.3 to 802.2.

    ☒ **B** is incorrect. With NetWare 3.11, the default encapsulation type is 802.3. **A** and **D** are also incorrect because Ethernet II and Ethernet SNAP formats have never been the default encapsulation types for NetWare.

10.04: RIP and SAP

10. ☑ **D.** Service type would be used to look specifically for the print server service and block only that service from being advertised.

    ☒ **A** and **B** are incorrect. While filtering on the Source Address and Destination Address fields would work to block the print server, it would also block the file server. **C** is incorrect, as the packet type would potentially block all SAP advertisements.

11. ☑ **C.** Split horizon dictates that anything learned on a particular interface will not be advertised out that same interface, which helps avoid loops in IPX RIP and IPX SAP.

    ☒ **A** is incorrect. Time ticks are a measure of link delay in IPX RIP. **B** is incorrect, as Spanning-Tree is a Layer 2 protocol used in bridged environments and not applicable to IPX. **D** is incorrect because subinterfaces are a Cisco Layer 1 feature.

12. ☑ **C.** SAP advertisements can contain a maximum of seven services per packet. 49 services will therefore require seven SAP packets. SAP advertisements go out once every 60 seconds, regardless of the speed of the link. Therefore, a total of 35 packets will go out in this scenario.

    ☒ **A**, **B**, and **D** are the incorrect number of SAP packets.

10.05: IPX Configuration

13. ☑ **D.** Novell-ether is the default encapsulation type for any Ethernet interface on a Cisco router. Note that novell-ether is the default encapsulation type for NetWare version 3.11 and lower, which means that if you're installing a newer version of NetWare, you will need to use a non-default encapsulation type.

    ☒ **A**, **B**, and **C** are not the correct default encapsulation types.

14. ☑ **C.** While the configuration commands shown are all necessary, there is one essential command missing: IPX ROUTING. Without this command, the router will not be able to route IPX packets between NetWare clients on either side of the router. However, the router is not necessary for clients on the 0xA network to speak with one another, so the optional result has been achieved.

    ☒ **A**, **B**, and **D** are incorrect. The proposed solution produces the optional result but not the required result.

15. ☑ **A.** IPX RIP sends out routing updates every 60 seconds.

    ☒ **B** is incorrect. NLSP is a link state protocol that uses triggered updates. **C** is incorrect because OSPF is an IP routing protocol, not an IPX routing protocol. **D** is incorrect because EIGRP is a hybrid protocol that supports IPX, but uses triggered updates.

LAB ANSWER
Objectives 10.01–10.05

First, identify the issues at hand in this network:

- Provide basic IPX communication between Boston and Santa Clara.

- Keep GNS queries local to each LAN.

- Block the print server in Santa Clara from being advertised to Boston.

- Allow the print server in Boston to be advertised to Santa Clara.

Providing basic IPX communication between Boston and Santa Clara is the most fundamental challenge. If you don't solve this, nothing else will work. The clients on each LAN are already physically connected to their gateway, so the next issue we need to look at is whether they are all using the same data-link protocol. Over on the Santa Clara side, the clients and server are all running NetWare 3.11, which uses the novell-ether type encapsulation, which also happens to be the default encapsulation type on the Cisco router. In Boston, however, the clients and server are running NetWare 3.12, which uses a different frame type, SAP. The Boston router, Rtr_Bos, will need to be configured to support this frame type on its Ethernet interface leading to 0xB (the command IPX NETWORK 0xB ENCAPS SAP should do the trick). What about over the WAN? IPX over WAN technologies is not covered in the CCNA exam, but is covered in more depth in the CCNP exams. Suffice it to say, at this point the default IPX configuration should work over the 56-Kbps point-to-point circuit, so we will assume that it is functioning properly. Since all the stations on each LAN are using the same framing type, no subinterfaces are necessary.

Keeping GNS queries local to each LAN is the easiest issue to deal with for two reasons: First, GNS queries are broadcasts, and broadcasts stop dead at a router interface. Second, there is a server local to each of our LANs, which means GNS queries will be responded to locally (assuming the servers are functional). The bottom line is that this problem takes care of itself, with no configuration changes necessary.

The problem of blocking the print server in Santa Clara from being advertised to Boston requires us to have intimate knowledge of the SAP packet format, and the ability to configure access lists. We will set up an outbound packet filter on Rtr_SC's

WAN interface to search for 0x0047 in the SAP Service Type field. This will make Rtr_SC suppress the advertisement of this service out the WAN, and Boston will have no knowledge of the print server in Santa Clara.

The problem of allowing the print server in Boston to be advertised to Santa Clara is easy to solve: Do nothing. Rtr_Bos will have no access list configured on its WAN interface, and will therefore advertise everything in its SAP table over the WAN, including the print server on the Boston side. Rtr_SC has no inbound SAP filter and will accept the SAP advertisement from Rtr_Bos.

CCNA

CISCO CERTIFIED NETWORK ASSOCIATE

11

Basic Traffic Management with Access Lists

T his chapter will concentrate on the proper use and configuration of access lists. Access lists give the administrator control over the traffic in a network. Limiting access from a user or device to a part of the network, and managing traffic flows, are both possible with access lists. When you place access lists on a router, the network can be more efficiently utilized by eliminating unnecessary protocol traffic, which consumes valuable network bandwidth. Security policies can be implemented to restrict which users, devices, and services may be available for use on the network.

Access lists are applied to the inbound or outbound traffic on any interface. Once the access list is in place, packets are inspected by the router and a decision is made to either drop or forward the packets. "Permit" is the term in an access list that instructs the router to forward the packet if a match is made. "Deny" is the term in an access list that instructs the router to drop the packet. A packet is compared against each line of an access list in sequential order. Once a match is made, the router will forward or drop the packet according to the rule, and no further comparisons against the access list are made. Each access list has an implied "Deny All" statement at the end, so that if no matches are made against the access list, the packet is dropped.

TEST YOURSELF OBJECTIVE 11.01

Standard IP Access Lists

Cisco routers use access list numbers 1 to 99 for the use of standard IP access lists. IOS 12.0 also introduced an expanded range for standard IP access lists of 1300 to 1999. This new range does not change the old range; it merely adds an additional range for more lists. These access lists have a very specific function: they examine the bits in the source IP address of the packet. By using a wildcard mask, the administrator can tell the router how many of the 32 bits of the source address are necessary for making a match. The access list is not concerned with the actual netmask of the IP address it is examining. Its only concern is the parts of the source address that match against the access list itself.

■ Packet filtering is performed on Cisco routers through the use of access lists. Access lists can be used to control the transmission of packets across an interface, to restrict traffic across virtual terminal lines, or to restrict routing updates.

- An IP access list is a collection of permit and deny rules that are applied to IP addresses.

- There are three basic types of IP access lists: standard, extended, and dynamic extended.

- The basic format for adding a standard access list is

```
ACCESS-LIST access-list-number DENY|PERMIT
SOURCE[source-wildcard]|ANY
```

Understanding the wildcard mask is essential to understanding access lists on the CCNA exam. Do not confuse the wildcard mask with a netmask. The wildcard mask is used to match either an entire IP address, or a subset of the IP address. Mask bits that have a value of 0 imply that the corresponding bits in the IP address must match exactly. Mask bits that have a value of 1 are referred to as "don't care" bits, and the corresponding bits in the IP address do not have to match. Many CCNA candidates find it more difficult to look at a wildcard mask than a netmask and make sense of it. For this reason, do not hesitate to use the paper and pencil provided during the test to write out the address and mask in binary and make a clear comparison.

QUESTIONS

11.01: Standard IP Access Lists

1. Which of the following lists would block all traffic from 192.168.1.5 and allow everything else?

   A. `access-list 12 deny 192.168.1.5 255.255.255.255`
      `access-list 12 permit any`

   B. `access-list 12 deny 192.168.1.5 0.0.0.0`
      `access-list 12 permit any`

   C. `access-list 100 deny 192.169.1.5 255.255.255.255`
      `access-list 100 permit any`

   D. `access-list 100 deny 192.168.1.5 0.0.0.0`
      `access-list 100 permit any`

2. Steve is a network administrator for a large corporation. He has been tasked with developing a single access list that will block traffic from both the engineering and marketing subnets, within the company he works for, from entering the subnet the Accounting Department is on. Which of the following statements is correct?

   A. A standard IP access list would be a bad choice because standard IP access lists only allow the filtering of one source address, and Steve needs to filter multiple addresses.

   B. A standard IP access list would be a bad choice because standard IP access lists can only block outgoing traffic, not incoming.

   C. A standard IP access list would be a good choice because standard IP access lists can block traffic from a specific source or set of sources from entering your network.

   D. A standard IP access list would be a good choice because standard IP access lists can block traffic to a specific destination, such as the accounting subnet.

3. **Current Situation:** Your client has made you aware that they are concerned about the possibility of the competition being able to access files on their network. They have asked that you develop a solution, so that traffic coming from their competition cannot get into their network. The competition uses networks 10.1.100.0/24, 10.1.1.0/24 and 172.16.1.0/24 and are reachable through the company's serial 0 WAN link.

   Required Result: Traffic coming from the competition's three networks must not be allowed into the serial 0 interface.

   Optional Desired Results:

   1. Still allow users from within the company to visit the competition's Web site.

   2. Still allow the competition to visit your client's Web site.

   Proposed Solution: Create the following access list and apply it to the client's serial 0 WAN interface using the command IP ACCESS-GROUP 10 IN.

   ```
   ip access-list 25 deny 10.1.100.0 0.0.0.255

   ip access-list 25 deny 10.1.1.0 0.0.0.255

   ip access-list 25 deny 172.16.1.0 0.0.0.255

   ip access-list 25 permit any
   ```

A. The proposed solution produces the required result and both of the optional results.

B. The proposed solution produces the required result and only one of the optional results.

C. The proposed solution produces the required result and none of the optional results.

D. The proposed solution doesn't produce the required result.

TEST YOURSELF OBJECTIVE 11.02

Extended IP Access Lists

Extended access lists provide the administrator with additional flexibility when compared with standard access lists. Whereas standard access lists only take the source IP address into consideration when making a match, extended access lists allow for much greater control. An extended access list allows a match to be made on the source address, destination address, IP protocol, and port information. To be successful on the CCNA test, you must remember all the items that each type of list can check to make a match. Extended access lists use access list number 100 to 199. Cisco IOS 12.0 added an expanded range of 2000 to 2699, which can also be used for extended IP access lists in addition to 100 to 199.

- Extended IP uses both the source and destination address when it tries to match up packets to your list, and you can optionally use protocol type information for even finer control.

- The syntax for adding and removing access lists is

    ```
    NO ACCESS-LIST access-list-number DENY | PERMIT protocol
    source source-wildcard

    destination destination-wildcard
    ```

It is important to pay attention to which level filtering is taking place with an extended access list. This can be found by looking at the protocol type that follows the Permit or Deny directive. Extended access lists of protocol type IP cannot have source or destination ports associated with them because ports are not a part of the IP header. For this same reason, if an access list is to be constructed to examine the port number of all packets, there would need to be a minimum of two rules to accomplish this: one for protocol type TCP and one for protocol UDP. Other protocols can be filtered on in addition to IP, TCP, and UDP. Some of these include routing protocols such as OSPF and IGRP, and protocols such as ICMP and IGMP.

QUESTIONS

11.02: Extended IP Access Lists

Questions 4–6   The illustration that follows should be used to answer questions 4, 5, and 6.

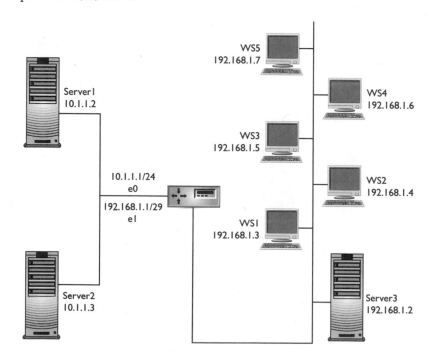

4. What access list rule, when applied to e1's input, would allow Server3 to reach 10.1.1.0/24, but deny all other addresses in 192.168.1.0/29?

    A. `access-list 101 permit ip 192.168.1.2 0.0.0.0 any`

    B. `access-list 101 permit ip 192.168.1.2 0.0.0.7 any`

    C. `access-list 101 permit ip any 192.168.1.2 0.0.0.0`

    D. `access-list 101 permit ip any 192.168.1.2 0.0.0.7`

5. **Current Situation:** Management has contacted you because they would like to institute some changes to the security policies on the network. They would like for the workstations in network 192.168.1.0/29 to be able to access only Web services on Server1, but would not like them to be able to access anything on Server2. Although Server3 will need to be able to access both Server1 and Server2 at a later date, it is not a firm requirement at this time.

    Required Result: An access list must be constructed and applied to the input of e1, which will allow the workstations to access Web services only on Server1 and deny any access at all to Server2.

    Optional Desired Results:

    1. Allow Server3 to continue to access all services on Server1 and Server2.

    2. WS5 is used by interns and should not be able to access 10.1.1.0/24.

    Proposed Solution: Apply the following access list to e1 using the command IP ACCESS-GROUP 101 IN.

    `access-list 101 deny ip 192.168.1.7 0.0.0.0 10.1.1.0 0.0.0.255`

    `access-list 101 permit tcp 192.168.1.0 0.0.0.7 10.1.1.2 0.0.0.0 eq 80`

    `access-list 101 permit tcp 192.168.1.2 0.0.0.0 10.1.1.0 0.0.0.255`

    A. The proposed solution produces the required result and both of the optional results.

    B. The proposed solution produces the required result and only one of the optional results.

    C. The proposed solution produces the required result and none of the optional results.

    D. The proposed solution doesn't produce the required result.

6. Which of the following commands would block only traffic from WS1 from reaching port 1000 of Server1?

A. `ip access-list 99 deny ip 192.168.1.3 0.0.0.0 10.1.1.2 0.0.0.0 eq 1000`

   `ip access-list 99 permit ip any any`
   `int e1`
   `ip access-group 99 in`

B. `ip access-list 100 deny ip 192.168.1.3 0.0.0.0 10.1.1.2 0.0.0.0 eq 1000`

   `ip access-list 100 permit ip any any`
   `int e1`
   `ip access-group 100 in`

C. `ip access-list 99 deny tcp 192.168.1.3 0.0.0.0 10.1.1.2 0.0.0.0 eq 1000`

   `ip access-list 99 deny udp 192.168.1.3 0.0.0.0 10.1.1.2 0.0.0.0 eq 1000`

   `ip access-list 99 permit ip any any`
   `int e1`
   `ip access-group 99 in`

D. `ip access-list 100 deny tcp 192.168.1.3 0.0.0.0 10.1.1.2 0.0.0.0 eq 1000`

   `ip access-list 100 deny udp 192.168.1.3 0.0.0.0 10.1.1.2 0.0.0.0 eq 1000`

   `ip access-list 100 permit ip any any`
   `int e1`
   `ip access-group 100 in`

TEST YOURSELF OBJECTIVE 11.03

Named Access Lists

Named access lists are fundamentally the same as standard and extended access lists, but they allow the list to be referenced by name rather than number. Named access lists allow you to create more access lists than numbered access lists. Recall that with numbered access lists you are limited to 99 standard (1 to 99) and 100 extended (100 to 199). The names of named access lists must be unique for each list on an individual router. You can, however, duplicate names of lists across routers. One of the benefits of named access lists is that you are able to delete individual statements from the list. Recall that with numbered access lists, the entire list must be deleted and re-created. With named access lists, inserting new statements requires the deletion and re-addition of the new statement and all later statements in the list.

■ With named lists, you can identify IP access lists, whether standard or extended, with an alphanumeric name instead of a number.

■ You can verify your IP access lists with the SHOW ACCESS-LISTS command and the SHOW IP INTERFACES command.

exam
ⓦatch

When answering questions on the exam about named access lists, it's important to understand that, although they behave fundamentally the same as their numbered counterparts, when it comes to editing the list, they are different. An individual line of a named access list can be deleted, but insertions of new lines always go to the end of the list. Because the ordering of the lines within an access list is key to its operation, you must usually delete not only the line that you wish to modify, but also all the lines that come afterwards. You would then insert the newly modified line and follow it with the lines that followed before the change. Although some may see this as not a great improvement over numbered lists, which usually involve the re-insertion of the entire list, it can save considerable amount of time when dealing with very large access lists.

QUESTIONS

11.03: Named Access Lists

7. What command should you use to apply the following access list to the input of a router's interface?

```
stargate#show ip access-lists jupiter

Extended IP access list jupiter
```

```
permit tcp host 192.168.1.1 any eq www

permit udp host 192.168.1.1 any eq domain

deny ip 10.1.0.0 0.0.255.255 any

deny ip host 192.168.1.1 any

permit ip any any
```

A. IP ACCESS-LIST JUPITER IN

B. IP NAMED ACCESS-GROUP JUPITER IN

C. IP ACCESS-GROUP JUPITER EXTENDED IN

D. IP ACCESS-GROUP JUPITER IN

8. You wish to edit a standard named IP access list that contains five statements. You type a NO version of the third statement and immediately add a new statement to the list. Which answer best describes the state of the access list at this time?

A. The access list contains only the newly added statement.

B. The access list contains five statements, with the newly added statement at the end.

C. The access list contains five statements, with the newly added statement as the third statement in the list, taking the place of the deleted statement.

D. The access list contains three statements, with the newly added statement at the end.

9. Which of the following statements is not true about named IP access lists?

A. Named IP access lists are more intuitive because the name of the list can be associated with the function.

B. Named IP access lists allow for more lists than numbered access lists.

C. Named IP access lists allow for individual statements to be deleted.

D. Named IP access lists cannot be used at the same time as numbered access lists on the same router.

TEST YOURSELF OBJECTIVE 11.04

Standard IPX Access Lists

Standard IPX access lists are used to filter IPX packets on the network. Recall that an IPX address is 80 bits, with the first 32 bits used for the network portion of the address and the last 48 bits used for the node portion of the address. The node portion is normally the MAC (hardware) address of the host. With a standard IPX access list, the source and destination network numbers can be examined. Additionally, the node portion of the source and destination addresses can be examined, with or without a wildcard mask. IPX uses the keyword −1 to denote any and all network numbers. Wildcard masks in IPX access lists are configured much the same as with IP access lists, except they are configured as hexadecimal numbers.

■ IPX access lists permit or deny traffic across interfaces based on either specified network nodes or messages sent using particular protocols and services.

■ IPX standard access lists use the access list range of 800 to 899.

exam
Ⓦatch

Although standard IPX access lists support wildcard masks on both the source and the destination node numbers, this feature is very rarely used. Recall that with IP addressing, the host portion of the address is assigned out of a subnet. The subnet is a logical range of addresses. Because it is a logical range, a wildcard mask can be applied, which applies to a useful range of host addresses. With IPX addressing, the node portion of the address normally comes from the MAC address of the network interface of the host. This address follows no logical grouping within a network, and consequently you will almost never have a wildcard mask that would allow you to aggregate or summarize entries on IPX access lists.

QUESTIONS

11.04: Standard IPX Access Lists

Questions 10–11   The illustration to follow should be used to answer questions 10 and 11.

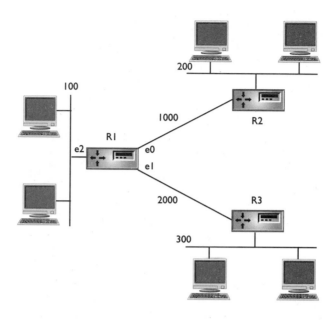

10. What commands, when applied to the input of e0 on router R1, would block traffic from network 200 from getting to network 100, yet still allow traffic from network 200 to get to network 300?

    A. ```
       access-list 820 permit -1
            access-list 820 deny 200 100
       ```

    B. ```
       access-list 820 deny ipx 200 100
            access-list 820 permit ipx -1
       ```

    C. ```
       access-list 820 deny 200 100
            access-list 820 permit -1
       ```

    D. ```
       access-list 820 permit ipx -1
            access-list 820 deny ipx 200 100
       ```

11. Your client has asked that you apply standard IPX access list 800 to interface serial0 on their router. You apply the access list in Interface Configuration mode by typing **ipx access-group 800**. Which of the following statements is correct?

    A. You have enabled the access list in the incoming direction only.

    B. You have enabled the access list in the outgoing direction only.

C. You have enabled the access list for both inbound and outbound traffic.

D. The command is incomplete. The IPX ACCESS-GROUP command must be followed by either IN or OUT to specify the direction to check traffic. (Choose all that apply.)

12. Which of the following commands would block traffic from a network designated as network 5 to any destination?

A. ACCESS-LIST 800 DENY 5 0

B. ACCESS-LIST 800 DENY 5 -1

C. ACCESS-LIST 800 DENY 5 ANY

D. ACCESS LIST 800 DENY 5

TEST YOURSELF OBJECTIVE 11.05

IPX SAP Filters

IPX SAP packets are used to advertise services on an IPX network. By creating outbound SAP filters, you can stop information from reaching a router's neighboring IPX servers and routers. By creating inbound SAP filters, you can stop SAP packets from being added to a router's SAP table. Because SAP packets contain the actual service information, they must be opened by the router and examined. SAP packets are never forwarded by the router; instead, they are advertised to its directly connected IPX networks. SAP updates can use up a lot of valuable bandwidth. This is especially important in NBMA networks such as Frame Relay. In many cases, SAP filters are used instead of IPX filters. By blocking the advertisements in the first place, unnecessary or unwanted IPX traffic is never initiated.

- All servers on a NetWare-type network can dynamically advertise their services and addresses using the Service Advertising Protocol (SAP).

- SHOW IPX INTERFACES allows you to view all the various types of filters that can be set for IPX packets, routes, routers, SAPs, and NetBIOS packets.

- SHOW ACCESS-LISTS will show all access lists, not just IP or IPX.

e x a m
Watch

Because clients can only connect to servers in the SAP table of their GNS server, filtering SAP packets is very important in IPX networks. It is much more common to implement an SAP filter than an IPX filter. With an IPX filter, every IPX packet must be checked against the IPX access list. Since SAP packets are sent only once every 60 seconds, there is much less filtering to do. Once the SAP packets are filtered, they don't reside in the GNS server's SAP table, and the client therefore cannot begin an IPX conversation. SAP filters are more popular than IPX access lists and, as a result, will probably be touched on more in the exam.

QUESTIONS

11.05: IPX SAP Filters

13. Your client has asked you to place SAP filter 1002 on the input of Serial0. To accomplish this, you should use which command in the interface configuration mode of Serial0?

   A. IPX SAP-FILTER 1002 IN

   B. IPX SAP-FILTER-IN 1002

   C. IPX-SAP-FILTER 1002 IN

   D. IPX INPUT-SAP-FILTER 1002

14. The IPX SAP access list shown here would deny which of the following packets?

   ```
   access-list 1010 deny 2000 0000000F
   access-list 1010 permit -1
   ```

   A. Packets with a source network of 2000 and a destination network of 0000000F

   B. Packets with a source network of 2000 and a service type of 0000000F

   C. Packets with services in networks 2000 to 200F

   D. Packets with a source network of 2000 and a node number of 0000000F

15. Which is the correct number range for IPX SAP filters?

    A. 900 to 999

    B. 1000 to 1099

    C. 800 to 899

    D. 1100 to 1199

LAB QUESTION
Objectives 11.01–11.05

Your client is running a mixed IP and IPX network, shown in the following illustration.

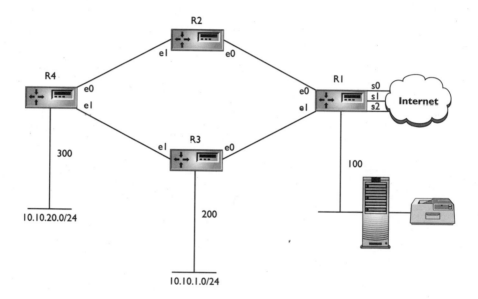

Your client is running IP on all routers. IPX is being run (along with IP) only between routers R1 and R3, and between routers R3 and R4.

The client would like to deploy a comprehensive system of access lists on their network to improve efficiency and security. There are several objectives they would like you to accomplish using the best method to solve each issue.

- The border router R1 to the Internet should only allow traffic out of its serial interfaces originating from the client's network space of 10.10.0.0/16, but they should be free to use any services they would like such as Web, FTP, or mail.

- The only traffic that should be allowed to originate on the Internet and enter the client's network is HTTP traffic destined for the company's Web server 10.10.20.2/32.

- All four of the client's routers should only allow Telnet from the administrative segment of 10.10.1.0/24.

- The network printer on IPX network 100 should not be usable by users on IPX networks 200 and 300.

Suggest a solution that addresses each of these issues.

QUICK ANSWER KEY

Objective 11.01
1. B
2. C
3. C

Objective 11.02
4. A
5. B
6. D

Objective 11.03
7. D
8. B
9. D

Objective 11.04
10. C
11. B
12. B and D

Objective 11.05
13. D
14. C
15. B

IN-DEPTH ANSWERS
11.01: Standard IP Access Lists

1. ☑ **B.** This rule has an access list number 12, which is between 1 and 99, the allowable range of a standard IP access list. The access list has the Deny directive specifying that once the match is made, the packet should be dropped and no further processing of the list should take place. The rule also has a wildcard mask of 0.0.0.0, which means that each octet in the source address of the packet being checked must match exactly with the source address listed in the access list.

   ☒ **A** is incorrect because the wildcard bits specify that none of the bits in the source address matter (all of them are "don't care" bits), and because of this, all packets will be dropped regardless of source address. **C** has an access list number of 100, which is outside the allowable range of a standard IP access list. The wildcard bits are also incorrect for the same reason as answer A. **D** is incorrect because it has an access list number of 100. Standard IP access lists must have an access list number in the range of 1 to 99.

2. ☑ **C.** A standard IP access list can examine only the source address and make a match against all or part of it, depending on the wildcard mask that is set. Multiple lines can exist in a standard IP access list, to match multiple separate networks if needed. Because the traffic Steve is trying to block is coming from two known subnets, Steve can construct a standard IP access list that will block those two subnets from entering the interface the accounting subnet is on.

   ☒ **A** is incorrect because a standard IP access list allows you to create multiple entries on a single access list, each with its own address and wildcard mask pair for the packet to be matched against. **B** is incorrect because the direction of traffic is not dependent on, nor specified in, the access list itself. The direction of traffic is specified when applying the access-list to an interface using the IP ACCESS-GROUP command. **D** is incorrect because standard IP access lists cannot block based on the destination of a packet, only the source.

3. ☑ **C.** The proposed solution produces the required result and none of the optional results. The access list will correctly block all traffic with a source address of the competition's network from entering the client's network. The Permit rule at the end of the list will allow all other traffic to enter the network. The company would not be able to view the competition's Web site with this access list, because data coming back from the Web site would have a source address of the competition's network and be blocked, regardless of the fact that the request was made from the company's own network. The competition would also not be able to view the client's Web site, because standard IP access lists do not allow traffic to be distinguished by protocol or service, only source address. Because of this, all traffic from the source addresses listed in the access list is blocked.

    ☒ **D** is incorrect because the required result is met. **A** and **B** are both incorrect because neither the competition nor the company itself can view each other's Web sites after the access list is in place.

11.02: Extended IP Access Lists

4. ☑ **A.** This rule allows only the host address of 192.168.1.2 0.0.0.0 to access any host through e1. Another way this could have been written is to use the HOST directive, which implies a single host as in IP ACCESS-LIST 101 PERMIT IP HOST 192.168.1.2 ANY.

    ☒ **B** is incorrect because the wildcard mask specified would allow not only Server3's traffic, but the other hosts in Server3's subnet as well. **C** is incorrect because this rule would allow any packet with a destination of 192.168.1.2. **D** is incorrect because this rule would allow any packet with a destination of 192.168.1.0/29.

5. ☑ **B.** The first rule of the access list will block all traffic from 192.168.1.7 from being able to reach any destination on 10.1.1.0/24, satisfying one of the optional requirements. The second rule of the access list will allow all hosts in 192.168.1.0/29 to be able to reach TCP Web services on Server1. The third line in the access list permits all TCP packets from 192.168.1.1 to reach 10.1.1.0/24. Because the optional requirement was to allow all services and not just TCP, the requirement is not met. The final rule of the list is the implicit Deny Any rule, which all access lists have at the end. This ensures that no other traffic is allowed into e1.

☒   **A** is incorrect because the third line of the list used the TCP protocol type instead of IP. **C** is incorrect because the optional result of denying all traffic from 192.168.1.7 from reaching 10.1.1.0/24 was met. **D** is incorrect because the required result was met.

6.   ☑   **D.** Since a protocol type was not specifically mentioned, two deny rules are needed to block both UDP and TCP traffic. You cannot block UDP and TCP traffic to a specific port with a single list rule. A PERMIT IP ANY ANY must follow so that all other traffic is allowed. This access list could have been applied to either the outbound of interface e0 or the inbound of e1. It is typical for security filters to be applied to the input of interfaces rather than the output.

☒   **A** is incorrect because the access list is numbered 99 and yet shows an extended access list format. Furthermore the protocol type specified is ip, but a port number 1000 is referenced. The format for an extended IP access list utilizing protocol type ip does not include a port reference. Ports are a quality of transport layer protocol such as TCP and UDP. **B** is incorrect because extended IP access lists of protocol type "ip" do not include port numbers in them. In order to block TCP and UDP traffic from a particular source, two access list rules are needed. **C** is incorrect because extended IP access lists are numbered 100 to 199. Extended IP access lists can also use the range of 2000 to 2699 in IOS 12.0 and above.

11.03: Named Access Lists

7.   ☑   **D.** Named access lists are added to interfaces the same way as numbered access lists, but instead of specifying a number, you specify the name of the list.

☒   **A** is incorrect because IP ACCESS-LIST is the command used to create an access list when in global configuration mode. IP ACCESS-GROUP is the command used to apply created access lists to interfaces. **B** is incorrect because the word NAMED does not follow IP when applying an access list to an interface. The IP ACCESS-GROUP command knows you are talking about a named access list when you specify the name of an access list rather than a number. **C** is incorrect because the IP ACCESS-GROUP command does not have the EXTENDED or STANDARD references in it. All you need to do is specify the name of the list. Because the list itself is configured as either "extended" or "standard" in the configuration, the IP ACESS-GROUP command does not need to know this.

8. ☑ **B.** When you delete a statement from a named IP access list, only the statement you are removing gets removed. Newly added statements are placed at the end of the list.

   ☒ **A** is incorrect because when you delete a named IP access list, the entire list is not removed, only the statement you wish to delete. **C** is incorrect because newly added statements to a named IP access list are added to the end of the list. **D** is incorrect because statements following the one being deleted are not removed; only the statement specified to be removed is deleted.

9. ☑ **D.** Named access lists can be used at the same time as numbered access lists. Each interface on a router can have one access list per interface, per direction. Those access lists can be any combination of named and numbered access lists.

   ☒ **A** is incorrect because one of the many benefits of a named IP access list is that its name can give insight to its function. **B** is incorrect because named IP access lists can have more lists than their numbered counterparts. **C** is incorrect because named IP access lists do in fact allow you to delete individual statements.

11.04: Standard IPX Access Lists

10. ☑ **C.** This access list rule would deny any packets with a source of network 200 from getting to the destination network 100. The second line uses the IPX access list keyword –1, which is a wildcard for "any and all network numbers."

    ☒ **A** is incorrect because the first line would match every packet, and thus no packets would ever make it to the second line in the access list. Once packets match a line in an access list, no further processing of the list is done for that packet. **B** is incorrect because standard IPX access lists do not contain the word IPX. They are distinguished as being standard IPX access lists by being numbered in the range of 800 to 899. **D** is incorrect for the same reasons as B.

11. ☑ **B.** When you do not specify a direction when using the IPX ACCESS-GROUP command, the default behavior is to apply the access list to the outbound traffic.

    ☒ **A** is incorrect because in order for traffic to be checked in the incoming direction, you must use the IN keyword at the end of the command. **C** is incorrect because you must use a separate line to configure an access list for each direction. **D** is incorrect because the direction is optional when using the IPX ACCESS-GROUP command. If it is not specified, then it will apply the access list to the output of the interface.

12. **B** and **D** are correct. This standard IPX access list would block all traffic with a source network of 5 going to any destination. Recall that –1 is a keyword when used in IPX access lists, which specifies "any and all" network numbers. **D** is correct because with a standard IPX access list, if you only specify the source network, that implies "any and all" destinations.

☒ **A** is incorrect because this standard IPX access list would block traffic from network 5 destined for network 0 only. **C** is incorrect because standard IPX access lists do not use the keyword ANY.

11.05: IPX SAP Filters

13. ☑ **D.** IPX SAP filters are created using the commands IPX INPUT-SAP-FILTER and IPX OUTPUT-SAP-FILTER.

☒ **A, B,** and **C** are incorrect because these commands do not exist.

14. ☑ **C.** Remember that SAP packets represent service advertisements. Packets with services from networks 2000 to 200F will be filtered, because the first part of the access list is the network and the second part is the mask. The 0s in the mask represent bits that must match exactly, and the 1s represent "do not care," or "throwaway" bits, and match any value. Notice how the network is four digits, yet the mask is eight digits. Don't let this throw you off. The first four zeros do not need to be expressed since they have no value.

☒ **A** is incorrect because the access list is showing a network and a wildcard mask. **B** is incorrect because although IPX SAP access lists can be made to filter by service type, the second part of the access list shown here is a wildcard mask. **D** is incorrect because the second part of the access list shown is the wildcard mask.

15. ☑ **B.** The range assigned for IPX SAP filters is 1000 to 1099.

☒ **A** is incorrect. 900 to 999 is the range for IPX extended access lists. **C** is incorrect. 800 to 899 is the range for IPX standard access lists. **D** is incorrect. 1100 to 1199 is the range for bridge extended access lists.

LAB ANSWER
Objectives 11.01–11.05

The first step is to identify clearly the issues that need resolution. They are listed here with solutions.

- Only allow traffic that originates in 10.10.0.0/16 out of R1 to the Internet.

  This issue can be addressed by using a standard IP access list applied to the outbound traffic on each of R1's three serial interfaces. An extended IP access list could also be used, but is unnecessary since all that is being examined is the source IP address. The access list would look like this:

  ```
  access-list 10 permit 10.10.0.0 0.0.255.255
  ```

  It should be applied to R1's s0, s1, and s2 interfaces with the IP ACCESS-GROUP 10 OUT command.

- Only allow traffic into R1 that originated from the Internet with a destination of 10.10.20.2/32.

  To allow only data that originated from the Internet to come into the Web server, you must use an extended IP access list. You need to examine not only the IP header to get the destination IP address, but also the TCP packets that are inside of the IP packets, and you must check them for a destination port of 80. You also must make sure that traffic that originated within 10.10.0.0/16 is allowed back in. The access list would look like this:

  ```
  access-list 101 permit tcp any any established
  access-list 101 permit tcp any host 10.10.20.2 eq 80
  ```

  It should be applied to R1's s0, s1, and s2 interfaces with the IP ACCESS-GROUP 101 IN command.

■ Only allow Telnet to each router from the administrative network of 10.10.1.0/24.

There are several possible solutions to this issue, but we are looking for the best one. One may think to put extended IP access lists on every router interface, but this can make for a very messy configuration throughout the network. Instead, the best choice is to use a standard IP access list and apply it to the VTY line interfaces using the ACCESS-CLASS command. The access list would look like this:

```
access-list 12 permit 10.10.1.0 0.0.0.255
```

It would be applied to the VTY's in-line Interface Configuration mode with the ACCESS-CLASS 12 IN command.

■ Block users on IPX networks 200 and 300 from using printers on IPX network 100.

This could be done with IPX access lists or IPX SAP filters. SAP filters are usually the preferred method for stopping users from using network services. IPX SAP filters would be a good choice here as well. An IPX SAP filter could be created that looks like this:

```
access-list 1001 deny 100 7
access-list 1001 permit -1
```

This IPX SAP filter would block any SAP packets of service type 7 (printer services) from network 100. Applying this filter to R3's e0 would block the traffic from being seen at networks 200 and 300. Since only IP is run on the links between routers R1 and R2, and between routers R2 and R4, no filtering is necessary there.

12

Configuring ISDN

T his chapter will cover a summary of information and self-test questions on Integrated Services Digital Network (ISDN) to build and verify your knowledge on this exam topic. This chapter is divided into three sections: an overview of ISDN, the components that make it up, and dial-on-demand routing (DDR). In order to pass the exam, you will need to have a solid understanding of setting up Basic Rate Interface (BRI) ISDN services using Cisco equipment and the terminology and protocols associated with ISDN.

Some of the more important details to remember for the exam are why ISDN is replacing analog service, the types of ISDN service available, Q.921 signaling, and Q.931 signaling. Understanding and knowing the basics of ISDN terminal equipment, network termination devices, reference points, ISDN protocols, and ISDN switch types are essential to passing the CCNA exam. One of the most difficult aspects of the exam is understanding DDR and knowing how to configure legacy DDR.

TEST YOURSELF OBJECTIVE 12.01

ISDN Overview

There is a lot of basic information you need to be familiar with before sitting down for this exam. You will also need to know what makes ISDN better than traditional analog service. Make sure you understand that B channels carry the users' network traffic and D channels carry the call control and signaling information. Know that the two main types of ISDN are BRI and PRI, what they are comprised of, and their differences. It is important to know that some service providers use Service Profile Identifiers (SPIDs) to identify each B channel, but they are not required and are only used in North America. You also need to know what the Q.921 and Q.931 protocols do and at what OSI layer they function. The following points are important to remember:

- ISDN can support voice, video, and data, and offers a much higher bandwidth than traditional analog telephone services.

- ISDN BRI is comprised of two B channels of 64 Kbps each and one 16-Kbps channel and is often referred to as 2B+D.

- For North America and Japan, PRIs are channelized as a T1 of 24 channels. In a T1 PRI, the first 23 channels are B channels, each running at 64 Kbps, and the 24th channel is the D channel, running at 64 Kbps. The T1 PRI is commonly referred to as 23B+D, and it gives a T1 PRI a total bit rate of 1.544 Mbps.

- Outside North America and Japan, PRIs are channelized as an e1 of 32 channels. In an e1 PRI there are 30 B channels, each running at 64 Kbps, one D channel running at 64 Kbps, and one channel reserved for the service provider. The e1 PRI is commonly referred to as 30B+D, and gives an e1 PRI a total bit rate of 2.0484 Mbps.

- Link Access Procedure on the D channel (LAPD) is the data-link control protocol used by ISDN. This protocol is also known as Q.921, according to the ITU-T.

- The ITU Q.931 signaling protocol is used for all handshaking required for establishing, monitoring, and terminating connections across an ISDN circuit. This protocol is also known as DSS1 (Digital Signaling System 1) in European ISDN networks, and it operates at Layer 3 of the OSI model.

exam
ⓦatch

The two Q signaling protocols can be easy to confuse and difficult to grasp. It is easy to remember at which OSI layer the Q protocols function by looking at the second numeric digit of the Q protocol; for example, the Q.921 protocol functions at the second layer. Another key thing to remember is that the term Link Access Procedure on the D channel and the term Q.921 can be used interchangeably in the exam.

QUESTIONS

12.01: ISDN Overview

1. A manager in your company dials into your network from home on an analog phone line using a 56-Kbps modem and experiences sudden disconnections and slow connection speeds. She connects to the corporate network for one or two hours almost every evening. What would be the best solution for this problem?

   A. Have a Frame Relay circuit installed from her house to the corporate network.

   B. Inform the manager that there is not a cost-effective solution and that she should just stay later at the office to finish up her work there.

    C. Install ISDN BRI circuits and the necessary equipment at the corporate office and her home for a DDR solution.

    D. Have a new analog phone line installed by the telephone company on the basis that the old line is susceptible to interference.

2. A friend of yours told you that he had an ISDN BRI connection installed at his house and is now connecting to his Internet service provider (ISP) at 144 Kbps. You tell him this is impossible, but he informs you that his ISP has it specially configured so that he can use his D channel to transmit data. Is your friend really connecting at 144 Kbps?

    A. Yes. By combining the two B channels of 64 Kbps each and one D channel, you get 144 Kbps. The D channel is only used during call setup and termination, and therefore can be used, during the connection, to transmit data.

    B. No. The D channel can never be used to transmit data. It is only used for call control and signaling.

    C. No. While it is possible to use part of the D channel on a BRI to transmit user data, it is not possible to use the full 16 Kbps. On a BRI, the ISDN switch does not require the full 16 Kbps of the D channel, and it is possible in some cases to use up to 9.6 Kbps to transmit user data. This gives a maximum of 137.6 Kbps for a connection.

    D. Yes. On a BRI, the ISDN switch does not require the full 64 Kbps of the D channel, and it is possible in some cases to use up to 16 Kbps to transmit user data. In this case, the ISP has configured the connection to use this "extra" 16 Kbps, thus providing a connection speed of 144 Kbps.

3. Which of the following are true regarding Q.921 signaling? (Choose all that apply.)

    A. It is more commonly referred to as Link Access Procedure of the D channel (LAPD).

    B. It is used for all handshaking required for establishing, monitoring, and terminating connections across an ISDN circuit.

    C. It ensures that control and signaling information is transmitted and received properly.

    D. It functions at the Network layer of the OSI reference model.

4. **Current Situation:** You've been hired as a network consultant for a company. They have three locations, with the two remote locations connected to the company headquarters via two Frame Relay connections. The three locations have Cisco 2600 series routers. Over the past few months, they have experienced two circuit outages at critical times, causing the company to lose a substantial amount of money in profits. There are two years left on a three-year term agreement the company signed for their Frame Relay connections.

   Required Result: The company has hired you to find a low-cost solution that will provide redundancy and prevent network outages from affecting their business. This solution should also be transparent during an outage.

   Optional Desired Results:

   1. The company does not want to break its term agreement on the Frame Relay connections and end up paying penalties.

   2. The company also would like a backup solution that will work if both Frame Relay circuits go down at the same time.

   Proposed Solution: Have ISDN BRI lines installed at each location, install BRI WAN Interface Cards in each 2600 series router, and configure the routers to use ISDN circuits as a backup link with use of PPP multilink.

   What results does the proposed solution produce?

   A. The proposed solution produces the required results and both of the optional results.

   B. The proposed solution produces the required results and only one of the optional results.

   C. The proposed solution produces the required results and both of the optional results.

   D. The proposed solution does not produce the required results.

5. What protocol is used for all handshaking required for establishing, monitoring, and terminating connections across an ISDN circuit?

   A. Q.921

   B. I.120

   C. Q.931

   D. HDLC

TEST YOURSELF OBJECTIVE 12.02

ISDN Components

This part of the chapter contains an overview of what ISDN components you will need to know for this exam. You will be expected to know and understand terminal equipment (TE1 and TE2), network termination devices (NT1, NT2, and NT1/2), reference points, and ISDN protocols. Besides knowing what each of these components is, you will need to know how they all fit together.

- TE1 devices are specialized ISDN terminals that connect to the ISDN network through a four-wire, twisted-pair digital link.

- TE2 devices are non-ISDN terminals that connect to the ISDN network.

- The NT1 is the ISDN device responsible for terminating the ISDN connection at the customer premises.

- The NT2 is the active switching or call distribution equipment on the customer premises (for example, PBX, LAN, host computer, and router).

- The ISDN reference points are R (between TE2 and TA), S (between TE1 or TA and NT2), T (between NT1 and NT2), and U (between NT1 and the carrier network).

- The ISDN protocol categories defined by the ITU are E (Existing Telephone Network), I (Concepts and Terminology), and Q (Switching and Signaling).

- When configuring ISDN, it is important that you know what kind of ISDN switch you are connecting to.

exam
ⓦatch

The ISDN components are probably one of the most difficult parts on the exam. The reason for this is because you have to know the components and their associated terminology. In other words, you need to memorize the components and what they are used for. You can use memorization techniques such as forming the acronym Real Secure Telephone Unit (RSTU) to help yourself remember the order of ISDN reference points. Create your own mnemonics that you will remember while you are taking the exam.

QUESTIONS

12.02: ISDN Components

6. You are installing a router that connects to a four-wire S/T interface. What type of terminal equipment is this?

    A. NT1

    B. TE1

    C. TE2

    D. S/T

7. Your company has sent you to Europe to install some ISDN routers. You take some Cisco 802 routers with you, but when you attach them to the ISDN network, it doesn't work. Why not?

    A. ISDN in Europe uses different signaling and requires a special ISDN router.

    B. The Cisco 802 router you brought with you has an NT1 interface built in and does not provide an S/T interface.

    C. The Cisco 802 router you brought with you provides a U interface.

    D. The Cisco 802 router requires a TA to interface with the European ISDN network.

8. You are trying to connect an older, non-ISDN device to the ISDN network. What type of equipment will you need to make this connection possible?

    A. TE2

    B. ISDN U adapter

    C. TA

    D. TA2

9. What category of International Telecommunication Union (ITU) ISDN Protocols define the concepts and terminology of ISDN?

   A. I

   B. Q

   C. T

   D. E

10. What type of network termination device performs Layer 2 and 3 protocol functions and concentration services?

    A. Q.921/Q.931

    B. TE2

    C. TE1

    D. NT2

11. **Current Situation:** You were hired as a consultant for a manufacturing company that consists of a large central manufacturing plant and four smaller remote manufacturing plants. This company has not upgraded its data network for the past several years and currently has the remote plants connected to the central plant via analog 56-Kbps switched circuits. The 56-Kbps switched circuits are used for replicating the manufacturing databases three times a day, after each shift is over. This replication takes about thirty minutes to complete, and the new shift cannot start until the replication process is finished. Also, there is an analog modem pool of 15 modems that service the sales force on the road and managers who dial in from home.

    Required Results:

    1. The manufacturing company wants you to provide them with a faster and better network without spending a lot of money.

    2. They want the database replication time cut in half at a minimum, and down to ten minutes if possible. This way, less time is wasted between shifts and more money can be made.

    Optional Desired Results:

    1. The company does not want to pay for full-time data circuits that they only use three times a day.

    2. They want faster dial-in connections for their sales force.

Proposed Solution: Install a PRI circuit and a Cisco 3620 router at the central manufacturing plant with a PRI interface module and a 24-port digital MICA modem module. At the remote sites, install BRI circuits and Cisco 802 ISDN routers. Configure a hub-spoke DDR solution, and configure the digital modems to accept analog modem calls via the PRI. Ensure that the sales force is equipped with V.90-compliant modems for their laptops.

What results does the proposed solution produce?

A. The proposed solution produces the required results and both of the optional results.

B. The proposed solution produces the required results and only one of the optional results.

C. The proposed solution produces the required results and both of the optional results.

D. The proposed solution does not produce the required results.

TEST YOURSELF OBJECTIVE 12.03

Dial-on-Demand Routing

This part of the chapter covers dial-on-demand routing (DDR), which has become more important with the release of the second edition of the CCNA exam. DDR is a method of creating a dial-up route that connects only when interesting traffic is received. There are two types of DDR: Legacy DDR and Dialer Profiles. In order to set up DDR, you need to specify the ISDN switch type, configure the interface, define the static route(s), and specify the interesting traffic. To verify your configuration, you can use various SHOW and DEBUG commands.

- Dial-on-demand routing is a method of creating a dial-up route that connects only when interesting traffic is received.

- With Legacy DDR, the call destinations are directly associated with a physical interface.

- DDR Dialer Profiles were introduced with IOS version 11.2, and this new type of DDR essentially separates the dial configuration and the physical interface.

- The DIALER-GROUP command enables a dialer list on the interface, logically connecting the DDR interface to a dialer-list.

- In order to set up DDR, you need to specify the ISDN switch type, configure the interface, define the static route(s), and specify the interesting traffic

- Once you have your ISDN DDR configured, you need to verify that your configuration works. To do this, there are several SHOW and DEBUG commands you can use.

exam
Watch

Make sure you understand what spoofing is and how you specify interesting traffic for an interface that is spoofed. Spoofing is a method that makes the router think that an interface is up at all times, even though it is not. This is important for ISDN configured for DDR, because you only want to pay the connection fee of the ISDN circuit if it is passing interesting traffic; otherwise, you want the circuit to disconnect. Spoofing keeps "chatty" protocols from keeping the link open all the time. The DIALER-LIST command is used to specify interesting traffic.

QUESTIONS

12.03: Dial-on-Demand Routing

12. What Cisco IOS command is used to specify interesting traffic?
    A. DIALER-GROUP
    B. DIALER-STRING
    C. DIALER-LIST
    D. DIALER-MAP

13. What DEBUG command displays all call setup and teardown messages?
    A. DEBUG ISDN Q921
    B. DEBUG ISDN Q931
    C. DEBUG DIALER EVENTS
    D. DEBUG DIALER PACKETS

Questions 14–15　This scenario should be used to answer questions 14 and 15.

Your company has ordered a new ISDN connection to your Internet service provider. On your end, you have a Cisco 2610 router with a BRI interface configured to use DDR to your ISP. You configured your router as follows:

```
InternetRouter(config)#username ispuser password isppassword
InternetRouter(config)#dialer-list 1 protocol ip permit
InternetRouter(config)#router eigrp 25000
InternetRouter(config-router)#network 10.0.0.0
InternetRouter(config-router)#exit
InternetRouter(config)#interface BRI0
InternetRouter(config-if)#isdn switch-type basic-5ess
InternetRouter(config-if)#ip address 10.1.1.1 255.255.255.255
InternetRouter(config-if)#isdn spid1 111222123401
InternetRouter(config-if)#isdn spid2 111222234502
InternetRouter(config-if)#encapsulation ppp
InternetRouter(config-if)#ppp authentication pap
InternetRouter(config-if)#dialer-group 1
```

14. When you plugged everything in, your link did not connect as it should, so you logged on the router, issued the SHOW ISDN STATUS IOS command, and received the following output. What possible problem(s) might be causing the ISDN circuit to not connect? (Choose all that apply.)

```
The current ISDN Switchtype = basic-5ess
ISDN BRI0 interface
      Layer 1 Status:
          DEACTIVATED
      Layer 2 Status:
          Layer 2 NOT Activated
      Layer 3 Status:
          No Active Layer 3 Call(s)
      Activated dsl 0 CCBs = 0
      Total Allocated ISDN CCBs = 0
```

A. Faulty cable

B. Authentication problem

C. Wrong switch type or SPID(s)

D. Faulty ISDN line

15. After using all the SHOW commands, you think you have narrowed the problem down to the dialer, so you decide to use the DEBUG DIALER command. You get the following output. What is the most likely cause of the problem?

```
BRI0: Dialing cause: BRI0: ip PERMIT

BRI0: No dialer string defined. Dialing cannot occur..

BRI0: Dialing cause: BRI0: ip PERMIT

BRI0: No dialer string defined. Dialing cannot occur..

BRI0: Dialing cause: BRI0: ip PERMIT

BRI0: No dialer string defined. Dialing cannot occur..

BRI0: Dialing cause: BRI0: ip PERMIT
```

A. The ISP did not configure their end of the link.

B. You did not define a dialer string or dialer map.

C. Your router is configured to dial the wrong number.

D. Your router is defective.

16. You finally got your ISDN working and for the past month, everything has been great. You just received the first phone bill since the ISDN circuit was ordered and have noticed that the ISDN circuit was connected almost all the time and the bill was astronomically high. When you configured DDR on the BRI interface, you chose to use the EIGRP routing protocol so that the routing table would be updated automatically. What is the most likely cause of the high ISDN phone bill?

A. The phone company messed up the bill.

B. The idle-timeout is set too high.

C. EIGRP.

D. Your users are using the new circuit constantly.

LAB QUESTION

Objectives 12.01–12.03

You were recently hired for an Internet service provider as network engineer, and you have been tasked to perform your first solo installation for a client. The client's request for service states that they are currently dialing into your network with analog modems and want a BRI ISDN connection to your network backbone. This client has three computers that will be connecting to the network.

You will be configuring a BRI ISDN router to connect to an existing and pre-configured router with a PRI interface. The telephone company has already installed an ISDN line at the client's business. They are providing a U interface and using a National ISDN-1 Switch. A senior network engineer has given you the following information for the configuration:

- User name: client_a
- User password: letmein
- Encapsulation: PPP
- Authentication type: CHAP
- SPID1: 91955511110100
- SPID2: 91955511121010
- ISP telephone number: 5551234
- Remote IP address: 10.10.10.2
- Client IP address: 10.10.10.1
- Subnet mask: 255.255.255.0

You need to decide which type of Cisco router to use for this installation, install it, configure it, and then test it. What router do you choose and why? How do you configure that router, and how do you test it?

A QUICK ANSWER KEY

Objective 12.01

1. **C**
2. **C**
3. **A** and **C**
4. **B**
5. **C**

Objective 12.02

6. **B**
7. **B**
8. **C**
9. **A**
10. **D**
11. **A**

Objective 12.03

12. **C**
13. **B**
14. **A** and **D**
15. **B**
16. **C**

IN-DEPTH ANSWERS
12.01: ISDN Overview

1. ☑ **C.** By installing a DDR ISDN solution using BRI, you make her connection between her house and the corporate office more reliable and faster. The digital solution offered by ISDN will alleviate any interference problems and offers a significantly lower error rate. Using ISDN will more than double the connection speed the manager was getting before. Another consideration would be using a PRI interface at the corporate office so that other employees could use the same solution.

   ☒ **A** is not the best solution because the manager does not need a full-time connection and this solution would not be cost-effective. **B** is not correct because ISDN is a cost-effective solution. **D** is not the best solution because installing a new analog phone line may not necessarily fix the problem that is causing the frequent disconnects and it will not offer the manager a faster connection either.

2. ☑ **C.** Although in some cases it is possible to use part of the D channel on a BRI to transmit user data, it is not possible to use the full 16 Kbps. On a BRI, the ISDN switch does not require the full 16 Kbps of the D channel, and it is possible in some cases to use up to 9.6 Kbps to transmit user data. This gives a maximum of 137.6 Kbps for a connection, not 144 Kbps.

   ☒ **A** is incorrect because the ISDN switch constantly needs a portion of the D channel, thus it is impossible to have a 144-Kbps connection for user data on a single ISDN BRI circuit. **B** is not correct, because in some cases, you can configure the D channel, on a BRI circuit, to transmit up to 9.6 Kbps of user data. This is not possible at all on the D channel of a PRI. **D** is incorrect because the D channel on a BRI is only 16 Kbps, not 64 Kbps as it is for PRI.

3. ☑ **A** and **C** are correct. Q.921 is more commonly referred to as LAPD, and does ensure that control and signaling information is transmitted and received properly.

☒ **B** is incorrect because the handshaking is a function of Q.931 signaling. **D** is incorrect because Q.921 functions at the Data-Link layer of the OSI reference model.

4. ☑ **B.** The required result is met because using ISDN as a backup link is very low cost. This is because the ISDN circuit will only connect if one of the Frame Relay circuits goes down. This proposed solution also provides a transparent redundancy that will allow the company's business to go unaffected should a Frame Relay circuit go down. Only the first optional result is met with the proposed solution. Using ISDN as a backup would leave the Frame Relay circuits in place, and the term agreements would not be affected. The second optional result would be met only if another BRI line and interface card were installed at the headquarters location. If both Frame Relay links go down at the same time, only one of the remote sites will be able to connect to the headquarters site. This is because the ISDN link will bring up both B channels, since PPP multilink is in use.

☒ **A** is incorrect because only the first optional result was met. The second optional result would only be met it another BRI line and interface card were installed at the headquarters location. If both Frame Relay links go down at the same time, only one of the remote sites will be able to connect to the headquarters site. **C** is not correct because the required result was met and one of the optional results was met by the proposed solution. **D** is incorrect because the required result was met.

5. ☑ **C.** Q.931 is used for all handshaking required for establishing, monitoring, and terminating connections across an ISDN circuit.

☒ **A** is incorrect because Q.921 ensures that control and signaling information is transmitted and received properly. **B** is not correct because a protocol that starts with the letter I refers to ISDN concepts and terminology, not signaling. **D** is incorrect because HDLC is a method of encapsulation and is not a signaling protocol.

12.02: ISDN Components

6. ☑ **B.** A Cisco 760 ISDN router is Terminal Equipment type 1 (TE1).

☒ **A** is incorrect because NT1 is a network termination device type. The Cisco 760 ISDN router has the NT1 built into the device. **C** is incorrect because Terminal Equipment type 2 (TE2) are non-ISDN terminals. The Cisco 760 ISDN router is an ISDN device. **D** is incorrect because S/T is the interface that the Cisco 760 provides and is not a type of terminal equipment.

7. ☑ **B.** Outside North America, the NT1 is part of the ISDN network, therefore, you will need a non-North American router without the NT1 and one that provides an S interface.

☒ **A** is incorrect because the ISDN signaling is standard throughout the world. The only difference is that you would have to specify the switch type used. **C** is incorrect because the Cisco 802 router does not provide a U interface; it provides a S/T interface. **D** is not correct because a TA is only used for non-ISDN equipment, which is not the case for the Cisco 802 router.

8. ☑ **C.** You will need a Terminal Adapter (TA) in order to connect a non-ISDN device (TE2) to the ISDN network.

☒ **A** is incorrect because that is the type of equipment you are trying to connect. **B** and **D** are incorrect because they are not valid types of ISDN equipment and do not exist.

9. ☑ **A.** The I category defines the concepts and terminology of ISDN, such as the I.120 protocol, which initially defined ISDN in 1984.

☒ **B** is incorrect because the Q category defines switching and signaling. **C** is incorrect because it is not an ITU category for ISDN protocols. **D** is not correct because the E category defines the protocols for the existing telephone network.

10. ☑ **D.** The NT2 device performs Layer 2 and 3 protocol functions and concentration services. It is the active switching or call distribution equipment on the customer premises.

☒ **A** is not correct because the Q protocols are not network termination devices, although they do function at Layers 2 and 3. **B** and **C** are incorrect because they are terminal equipment types and not network termination devices.

11. ☑ **A.** The proposed solution produces the required results and both of the optional results. The ISDN BRI circuits provide over twice the speed of the analog 56-Kbps switched circuits, which will cut the database replication time by more than half. The first optional result is met because as DDR is configured, the circuits will only be active when the databases are replicated. The second

optional result is met because the sales force will now be able to connect with the V.90 protocol, thus giving them 53.3 Kbps downstream and 36.6 Kbps upstream connectivity.

☒ **B, C,** and **D** are incorrect because both optional results were met.

12.03: Dial-on-Demand Routing

12. ☑ **C.** The DIALER-LIST command is used to specify interesting traffic.

☒ **A** is incorrect because the DIALER-GROUP command is used to associate the dialer-list to the interface. **B** is incorrect because the DIALER-STRING command is used to specify a single call destination. **D** is not correct because the DIALER-MAP command is used for specifying multiple call destinations.

13. ☑ **B.** The DEBUG ISDN Q931 command displays all call setup and teardown messages.

☒ **A** is incorrect because the DEBUG ISDN Q921 command verifies that a connection exists with an ISDN switch. **C** is not correct because the DEBUG DIALER EVENTS command displays debugging information about the packets received on a dialer interface. **D** is incorrect because the DEBUG DIALER PACKETS command shows when a packet is interesting and is being sent out a dialer interface.

14. ☑ **A** and **D** are correct. Try replacing the cable from the router to the ISDN jack. If that does not work, verify your switch type and SPID with your phone company and in your router configuration. If the problem is still not resolved, you can plug an analog phone into the ISDN jack and listen for either a light static or a clicking noise. If you don't hear either, the ISDN line is not active.

☒ **B** is incorrect because the output of the SHOW command does not indicate an authentication error. **C** could be a problem, but that would not give the same results as shown in the trap. SPIDs are used at Layer 2; if Layer 1 is down then Layer 2 will also be down.

15. ☑ **B.** If you look back at the configuration, you will notice that a dialer string or dialer map is not defined.

☒ **A** is incorrect because, while this is possible, in this case no dialer destination was specified in the configuration. **C** is not the best answer because the ISP number was specified in the configuration. **D** is not correct because your SHOW and DEBUG commands indicate that the router is fine.

16. ☑ **C.** Using any routing protocol, such as EIGRP, on a DDR link will cause that link to be up almost constantly for routing table updates and requests. For this reason, it is imperative that the DDR be configured with static routes.

☒ **A** is not correct because it is not the most likely cause, although telephone companies are notorious for sending out incorrect bills. **B** is incorrect because it also is not the most likely cause. Even if you had set the idle-timeout fairly high, it would still drop the circuit after that period of time. **D** is not correct because it is the least likely of the possible answers. It would be highly unlikely that users would be transmitting data all the time.

LAB ANSWER
Objectives 12.01–12.03

The best router for this situation is a Cisco 804 ISDN router. This router has an integrated NT1 and interfaces with a U interface, allowing you to plug it directly into the jack provided by the telephone company. It also has a built-in, four-port 10BaseT hub, allowing the client to connect all three of his computers directly to the router. Configure the router with the following configuration:

```
ClientRouter#config terminal

ClientRouter(config)#username client_a password letmein

ClientRouter(config)#dialer-list 1 protocol ip permit

ClientRouter(config)#ip route 10.10.10.2 255.255.255.0
10.10.10.1

ClientRouter(config)#interface BRI0

ClientRouter(config-if)#isdn switch-type basic-ni1

ClientRouter(config-if)#ip address 10.10.10.1 255.255.255.0

ClientRouter(config-if)#isdn spid1 91955511110100

ClientRouter(config-if)#isdn spid2 91955511121010

ClientRouter(config-if)#encapsulation ppp

ClientRouter(config-if)#ppp authentication chap

ClientRouter(config-if)#dialer-group 1

ClientRouter(config-if)#dialer string 5551234

ClientRouter(config-if)#^Z

ClientRouter#copy running-config startup-config
```

You will also need to configure the hub portion of the Cisco 804 to use Network Address Translation (NAT) and DHCP for the clients as outlined in the documentation that came with the router.

Once the configuration is complete, you will need to test it. To establish the link, ping the remote IP address. When you get five replies, you know the link is working. To be sure the link is up, use SHOW INT BRI0 or SHOW ISDN STATUS.

CISCO CERTIFIED NETWORK ASSOCIATE

13

Configuring Point-to-Point Protocol

W ithin this chapter, the focus of the questions will be on WAN communications, particularly on PPP. The WAN overview is designed to give you some knowledge about what type of questions can be asked about specific equipment configuration and technology. This chapter is geared to test your knowledge about WAN technology, PPP specification, configuration, and troubleshooting. Make sure that you not only check your answers, but also that you understand why the answers are right or wrong.

TEST YOURSELF OBJECTIVE 13.01

Wide Area Network (WAN) Overview

In WAN technology, there are three types of connections to be aware of: dedicated, circuit switched, and packet switched. T1 is and example of a dedicated (Point-to-Point) type of a connection. ISDN is a good representation of circuit switched, and Frame Relay is a packet-switched WAN technology. You must be familiar with all of these things, as well as how they work and at what speeds are typically available.

It is also a good idea to know the equipment associated with each technology. For instance, ISDN uses Network Terminator Type 1 (NT1) and Terminal Adapters (TAs), T1 uses CSU/DSUs with DTE and/or DCE interfaces, and Frame Relay generally uses CSUs and Frame Relay Access Devices (FRADs).

- Data Communications Equipment (DCE) provides a physical connection to the network, forwards traffic and provides a clocking signal used to synchronize data transmission between DCE and Data Terminating Equipment (DTE) devices. A Channel Service Unit (CSU) or a modem is an example of a DCE.

- Circuit-switched networks are most commonly used as a backup to a faster, packet-switched or leased-line connection. This occurs when a low volume of traffic needs to be sent between two locations, or when a single location needs to send small amounts of data to many locations.

- The ISDN service can be comprised of two B channels for BRI service, or 23 B channels for PRI service, with each running at 64 Kbps. BRI and PRI both have one D channel, but the difference is that BRIs D channel is 16 Kbps, whereas PRI's D channel is 64 Kbps.

■ T1 consists of 24 channels or DS0s. Originally designed to allow the transmission of multiple-voice calls over the same two-pair circuit, it employs a technology known as Time Division Multiplexing (TDM) for processing of the data.

■ Two important items to T1 technology are Framing and Line Coding. Framing comes in two basic flavors: Super Frame (SF) and Extended Super Frame (ESF). SF consists of 12 T1 frames, whereas ESF consists of 24 T1 frames. ESF is the preferred framing in modern T1, and allows for added benefits like the Facility Data Link (FDL). The FDL adds functionality for testing and other purposes. T1 frames are 193 bits each.

■ Line Coding comes in two basic types: Alternate Mark Inversion (AMI) and Binary 8 Zero Substitution (B8ZS). AMI is susceptible to loss of timing through 1s-density violations and thus steals the least significant bit to maintain timing. This means that in the event of eight consecutive 0s, it will change the last 0 to a 1. It is because of this that AMI DS0s only run at 56 Kbps. B8ZS, on the other hand, will insert a unique bipolar violation in the event of eight consecutive 0s. This allows B8ZS T1s to run at a full 64 Kbps per DS0.

■ E1 technology is a bit different from T1, and is used by most of the rest of the world. There are several differences between E1 and T1, with the most basic being the number of channels carried. E1 technology uses 32 DS0s. 30 DS0s are used for customer data, DS0 slot 0 is used for synchronization, and DS0 slot 16 is used for call control (on and off hook type functions). The extra DS0s allow E1 to carry 2.048 Mbps of data with a 256-bit frame. The framing and line coding are also different in E1 technology. E1 uses CRC4 or NON-CRC4 framing, and AMI or HDB3 line coding. Unlike T1, E1 technology does not use RBS (Robbed Bit Signaling) for voice functions.

■ Frame Relay was designed as a cost-saving alternative to the often expensive Dedicated Circuit market and is offered anywhere from 56 Kbps to 1.544 Mbps.

■ Frame Relay employs packet-switching technology as its primary mode of data transportation, and it uses Permanent Virtual Circuits (PVCs), Switched Virtual Circuits (SVCs), and Data-Link Connection Identifiers (DLCIs) for end-to-end packet transfer and addressing. It is important to remember that Frame Relay is a Layer 2 function and can run over most digital technologies, from DDS up through T1.

exam

Watch

There is so much to remember with WAN communications today that it is difficult to keep up with it all. Of the WAN technologies you need to know, it is probably most difficult to remember all of the speeds available. Be sure you know all of these specifications, as you will definitely be tested on them in the exam.

QUESTIONS

13.01: Wide Area Network (WAN) Overview

1. In ISDN, what is the D channel used for?

    A. Transmission of user data, whether it is voice, data, or video.

    B. Inserting a unique bipolar violation in the event of eight consecutive 0s online.

    C. Call setup and teardown. This also includes signaling such as Q.921 and Q.931.

    D. Connecting ISDN-ready equipment to the ISDN network.

2. As the Network Administrator for ACME, Inc., you have been asked to select the most appropriate technology for your company's WAN and Internet access. There are two major factors to keep in mind when selecting the technology: lowest cost is a priority, and the technology must be able to support ACME users at your location. Your office has 100 users, of which 50 will need WAN access to remote locations and to the Internet. Most users will not need to use the WAN connection often, but it needs to have enough available bandwidth for any type of transmission, high or low. From this scenario, which technology would you select and why?

    A. BRI ISDN, because it is less expensive than most other technologies and it will allow you to support up to 128 Kbps of bandwidth. ISDN will allow you to use one B channel for one function and one B channel for another (one for voice and one for data, for example).

B. Frame Relay, because it is not as expensive as a dedicated T1, but it can provide more bandwidth than a BRI ISDN circuit. Frame Relay will also allow you to support bursty traffic from the CIR up to wire speed.

C. T1, because it provides a larger amount of bandwidth for your corporate site, and it will allow you to support any of the needs that your users have. Anytime users need to access the Internet, they can download at speeds of up to 1.544 Mbps.

D. Fractional T1, because you can decide how much of a T1 connection you need, but still make sure that you are not wasting money. Depending on how much traffic you need to support, you can get a fractional T1 in speeds such as 384 Kbps, 512 Kbps, and 768 Kbps.

3. What does the acronym SPID stand for?

A. Special Information Date

B. Service Performance Indication Digit

C. Support Program Initiation Data

D. Selected Profile Identification

E. None of the above

4. With which technology was Frame Relay designed to compete?

A. X.25

B. RS-232

C. V.42

D. X.400

TEST YOURSELF OBJECTIVE 13.02

Point-to-Point Protocol (PPP) Overview

The Point-to-Point Protocol (PPP) has emerged as a popular standard in the communication world. It was developed to simplify point-to-point communications, and it offers several enhancements over its predecessor, Serial Line Internet Protocol (SLIP).

Several things including compression, authentication, encryption, and the support for synchronous and asynchronous communication were added to allow for a more robust set of supportable features. Something to keep in mind, though, is that SLIP is still the default for Cisco asynchronous serial interfaces, and HDLC is the default for synchronous interfaces.

- PPP will work over any DTE/DCE interface. PPP does not care what the transmission rate is, so the line speed is not a significant factor.

- PPP will run on any synchronous or asynchronous WAN interface, including ISDN BRI or PRI.

exam
ⓦatch

When thinking about PPP, realize that it was designed as a serial communications transport. What this means is that when we are planning where we are to configure it, we should consider serial interfaces. When most people connect to the Internet, they are using PPP and probably don't even know it. Most analog modems are nothing more than asynchronous serial communications equipment (DCE). So when taking the exam, pay close attention to the interfaces being used and what they are being used for.

QUESTIONS

13.02: Point-to-Point Protocol (PPP) Overview

5. What does the acronym SLIP stand for?

   A. Serial Line Interface Protocol

   B. Serial Link Information Packet

   C. Serial Line Internet Protocol

   D. Serial Line Integration Protocol

6. You need to implement a security model for your remote users. You suspect that passwords may have gotten into the wrong hands and would like to ensure that only those individuals from Locations 1, 2, and 3 (shown in the following

illustration) can log in remotely. All of your remote users are using PPP to connect into the corporate network. How would you ensure secure connections if the passwords may be a security concern?

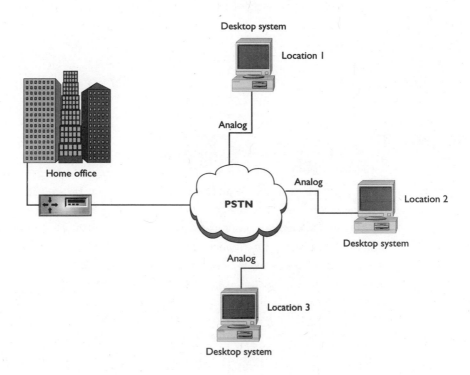

A. Do not allow connections from anywhere other than the home office.

B. Replace the users' passwords on their accounts.

C. Force your remote users to get a digital access service such as ISDN.

D. Utilize the PPP-callback security feature of the Access Router.

E. Rely on your users to keep their passwords secure.

7. Name the two main components of PPP.

A. TCP and UDP

B. IP and Frame Relay

C. NCP and LCP

D. SSAP and DSAP

8. What are some of the improvements PPP makes upon its predecessor, SLIP? (Choose all that apply.)

    A. Authentication

    B. Encryption

    C. Layer 3 support

    D. Filtering

    E. Compression

TEST YOURSELF OBJECTIVE 13.03

Configuring Point-to-Point Protocol

For the CCNA exam, you not only need to know what PPP can do, but you must also know how to configure it. The most important thing to remember about PPP is that it is configured on an interface and not in Privileged EXEC or Global Configuration modes. To get to this mode, you must go into Global Configuration and then select the interface that you want with the interface command:

```
Router(config)#interface S0
```

■ Other than assigning an IP address, the only configuration commands that are required to enable PPP on an interface are ENCAPSULATION PPP and NO SHUTDOWN.

■ The three most commonly configured PPP options are authentication, compression, and multilink.

When configuring PPP, there are several extra options that you may set, including authentication. The PPP command set accepts both PAP and CHAP authentication types. Password Authentication Protocol (PAP) is initiated one-way by sending a clear-text username and password, but Challenge Handshake Authentication Protocol (CHAP) is initiated by the called party and can challenge at any time throughout the active session. CHAP also employs encryption of the passwords sent during authentication. This gives added security functionality to CHAP.

QUESTIONS

13.03: Configuring Point-to-Point Protocol

9. You have configured PPP encapsulation on a WAN interface and you need to set up authentication. Which of the following command modes is correct?

   A. `Router>`

   B. `Router(config-if)#`

   C. `Router#`

   D. `Router(config-ppp)#`

   E. `Router-if#`

10. What is the proper syntax for configuring multilink PPP?

    A. `Router(config-if)#`**`ppp multilink`**

    B. `Router(config)#`**`ppp multilink interface s0`**

    C. `Router#`**`ppp multilink`**

    D. `Router (config-if)#`**`multilink`**

11. You are the Administrator of ACME Networks, Inc., and you have been asked to select and configure their WAN. You are given the following task requirements:

    ■ The connection must be able to support at least 300 users during the day. They will be using the line heavily.

    ■ The WAN selection must have inherent redundancy.

    ■ You must set up a PPP connection to the Los Angeles office.

    ■ Your corporate office has ten remote users. You must allow access into the corporate network.

You have chosen Frame Relay as your WAN connection. You have also selected DDS as your access line. You have set up the DLCI to Los Angeles as 300, and you have created a PPP subinterface on that PVC. You have also set up a RAS with CHAP authentication and PPP callback. Which of your requirements have you fulfilled? (Choose all that apply.)

A. The connection must be able to support at least 300 users during the day. They will be using the line heavily.

B. The WAN selection must have inherent redundancy.

C. You must set up a PPP connection to the Los Angeles office.

D. You must allow access by ten remote users into the corporate network.

E. All of the above.

TEST YOURSELF OBJECTIVE 13.04

Verification of Point-to-Point Protocol

Once you have PPP set up, there are many different ways to check your configuration. Within this section, you will drill down into several different modes of checking settings. For the exam, remember that you can show the running configuration, show interfaces, and show protocol statistics. Something to remember as a tip is to COPY RUN START when you have made significant modifications to your device. If you don't and you lose power or reload, you could be reconfiguring for quite some time.

■ When you look at the output of a SHOW RUNNING-CONFIGURATION, you should look for the interface that you have just configured and check for the ENCAPSULATION PPP command. Be sure that you have assigned an IP address, as well as taken the interface out of shutdown mode.

■ When you look at the output of SHOW INTERFACES, you should look for two things to verify your configuration. First, look at the top line to make sure that your interface and line protocol are both up. Second, look for the line ENCAPSULATION PPP.

An easy way for you to do preliminary verification is to type show running-configuration *from the Privileged EXEC mode prompt. This will give you most of the information you need to verify systems and interface configuration. Something else that you should remember is that your show commands will need to be run from the Privileged EXEC mode interface, denoted as follows:*

```
Router#
```

QUESTIONS

13.04: Verification of Point-to-Point Protocol

Here is a helpful tip configuring for Cisco routers. You can use it if you have multiple Cisco devices with the same hardware and they need to be configured similarly. You can either copy the configurations to a TFTP server and then back out to a router, or simply cut and paste. Note that bangs (!) signify the end of a set of configuration commands. There is one after each interface to notify the IOS to move on to the next interface. The basic idea here is that you can copy one AS5300's configuration from the version line to the end and paste it in another AS5300's terminal session. This must be done in Global Configuration mode, and you should make sure that they are configured the same or you will get errors on the paste.

Questions 12–14   This scenario should be used to answer questions 12, 13, and 14.

You are a Network Engineer and you work for a small systems integrator. You have been assigned a trouble call for a printing firm in your area, E-Z Graphic Printing Plus. The call information for the company is as follows.

"We have been experiencing serious problems getting connected to our ISP. We need to be able to upload our images to a remote press station so that they can be printed in the following morning's edition of the Local Star. We have attached what little documentation we have on this network setup and would like someone to come out and fix it. Thank you for your assistance."

You also find out that they should be using PAP authentication for the PPP link to the Remote Press Station.

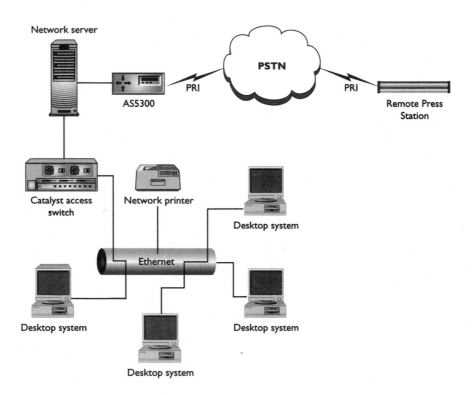

```
controller T1 0

  framing esf

  clock source line primary

  linecode b8zs

  cablelength short 133

  pri-group timeslots 1-24

  description Network PRI connection to Remote Press Station.


interface Loopback0

  ip address 88.1.0.2 255.255.255.0
```

```
no ip directed-broadcast


interface Serial0:23
 no ip address
 no ip directed-broadcast
 shutdown
 encapsulation ppp
 no logging event link-status
 dialer-group 1
 isdn switch-type primary-ni
 isdn protocol-emulate user
 isdn incoming-voice modem
 fair-queue 64 256 0
 ppp authentication chap
```

12. As soon as you get on site, you begin to hunt for the cause of the issues. You have lost the printed information, but still have the image of the network. How can you reproduce the output previously shown?

    A. `Router(config-if)#`**`show all statistics`**

    B. `Router(config)#`**`show devices configuration`**

    C. `Router#`**`show running-config`**

    D. `Router#`**`show ppp multilink`**

    E. `Router#`**`show all`**

13. After you have reproduced the running router configuration onscreen, you would like to check the ISDN status on s0:23. How do you check this information?

    A. `Router#`**`show isdn`**

    B. `Router#`**`show isdn status serial 0:23`**

    C. `Router#`**`show isdn link state serial 0:23`**

    D. `Router#`**`show isdn serial 0:23`**

14. The last output shows that the ISDN line is in service. Now you would like to check on the method of authentication being used. How do you check the method of authentication being used on serial interface 0:23?

   A. `Router#`**`show ppp authentication`**

   B. `Router#`**`show ppp config`**

   C. `Router#`**`show interface serial 0:23`**

   D. `Router#`**`show running-config`**

15. You have set up a Frame Relay WAN connection with PPP subinterfaces. Which of the following commands would allow you to verify that PPP has been configured on a Frame Relay PVC?

   A. `Router#`**`show frame-relay map`**

   B. `Router#`**`show frame-relay ppp configuration`**

   C. `Router#`**`show ppp frame-relay`**

   D. `Router#`**`show serial ppp encapsulation`**

TEST YOURSELF OBJECTIVE 13.05

Troubleshooting Point-to-Point Protocol

While troubleshooting any problem with Cisco devices, your two best friends will be SHOW commands and DEBUG commands. SHOW commands will give you the configuration information about the desired router or interface, and DEBUG commands will let you see very detailed information about the requested protocol.

■ Using the DEBUG PPP PACKET command is a good place to start when troubleshooting PPP because it will give you a very low-level summary of the PPP traffic on the router.

■ The table that follows is a quick list of some of the more useful DEBUG commands associated with the WAN portion of the CCNA exam and the function of each command.

Command	Function
Router#**debug dialer**	Debug dial-on-demand.
Router#**debug ethernet-interface**	Debug of the Ethernet interface.
Router#**debug frame-relay end-to-end**	Debug Frame Relay VC end-to-end.
Router#**debug frame-relay events**	Debug important Frame Relay packet events.
Router#**debug frame-relay lmi**	Debug LMI packet exchanges with service provider.
Router#**debug frame-relay packet**	Debug Frame Relay packets.
Router#**debug ip nat**	Debug NAT events.
Router#**debug ip rip**	Debug RIP protocol transactions.
Router#**debug ip tcp**	Debug TCP information.
Router#**debug ip udp**	Debug UDP-based transactions.
Router#**debug isdn q921**	Debug ISDN q921 (Layer 2) packets. This is D-channel information.
Router#**debug isdn q931**	Debug ISDN q931 (Layer 3) packets. This is D-channel information.
Router#**debug ppp authentication**	Debug CHAP and PAP authentication.
Router#**debug ppp cbcp**	Debug callback control protocol negotiation.
Router#**debug ppp compression**	Debug PPP compression.
Router#**debug ppp error**	Debug protocol errors and error statistics.
Router#**debug ppp multilink**	Debug multilink activity.
Router#**debug ppp negotiation**	Debug protocol parameter negotiation.
Router#**debug ppp packet**	Debug low-level PPP packet dump.

exam
ⓦatch

While there may not be a huge amount of debugging on the CCNA exam, you never know what will be asked, and it's a good idea to know how to do it.

QUESTIONS

13.05: Troubleshooting Point-to-Point Protocol

16. Debugging is great for problem resolution, but what problem might it cause?

    A. It can cause the router to lose its configuration.

    B. It deactivates the router while running.

    C. It can cause the router to overheat.

    D. It will not allow you to make configuration changes to the router.

    E. None of the above.

17. How can you show what debugging features are turned on?

    A. `Router#show debugging`

    B. `Router(config)#show debugging`

    C. `Router>show all debugging`

    D. `Router#show all debugging`

LAB QUESTION
Objectives 13.01–13.05

In this chapter, we have reviewed how to configure, verify, and troubleshoot PPP and its features. In this lab, you must use all of this knowledge to complete the objective.

Objective: Use what you have learned to configure your router as shown in the following illustration. Please make sure that you verify the configuration with the proper SHOW commands. The interface to be used on the New York router is serial 1.

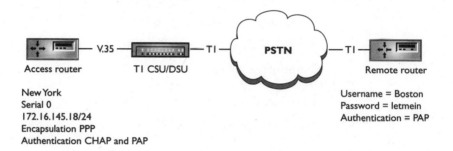

Access router   TI CSU/DSU   Remote router

New York   Username = Boston
Serial 0   Password = letmein
172.16.145.18/24   Authentication = PAP
Encapsulation PPP
Authentication CHAP and PAP

A QUICK ANSWER KEY

Objective 13.01
1. **C**
2. **B**
3. **E**
4. **A**

Objective 13.02
5. **C**
6. **D**
7. **C**
8. **A, B,** and **E**

Objective 13.03
9. **B**
10. **A**
11. **B, C,** and **D**

Objective 13.04
12. **C**
13. **B**
14. **D**
15. **A**

Objective 13.05
16. **E**
17. **A**

IN-DEPTH ANSWERS

13.01: Wide Area Network (WAN) Overview

1. ☑ **C.** This D-channel is used for ISDN signaling. Some of the associated protocols are LAPD, otherwise specified in Q.921, and I.451 (Q.931).

   ☒ **A** is incorrect because transmission of user data is the purpose of the customer equipment as well as the B channels. **B** is incorrect because it is the description of B8ZS, a popular T1 line-coding scheme. **D** incorrect because this is the definition of the function of the NT-1 with TE type 1 (TE1).

2. ☑ **B.** This is a difficult thing to decide and it will surely depend on your situation. The reason why Frame Relay would be considered the best pick in this situation is the fact that cost is an issue and your users will not need to use it all of the time. One of the main benefits of Frame Relay is that it does not cost nearly as much as dedicated circuits because you are only paying for the local loop access instead of the full Point-to-Point link. T1 has much more bandwidth you say? For the most part, that is correct, but remember that Frame Relay is a Layer 2 function and it can run over technologies such as DDS, FT1, or T1. With the use of a CIR you could get a 1.544-Mbps link and set your CIR to 384 Kbps, which would allow your data to transmit at 384 Kbps normally, but burst to wire speed if necessary. It is also much easier and less expensive to set up a meshed WAN with Frame Relay than a dedicated service.

   ☒ **A** is incorrect because most areas do not like to sell BRI service to corporate customers. Notice we said "most" because it is possible but not prevalent. While BRI would allow you to pay only for what you used, a BRI circuit would also strain to support 50 simultaneous users. **C** is incorrect because while T1 does support 1.544 Mbps of traffic, it is also much more expensive. Instead of only paying for local access, you would have to pay for point A–to–point B. This service is also always there and locked in at 1.544 Mbps, whether anyone is using it or not. **D** is incorrect because fractional T1 is also an expensive dedicated circuit. The FT1 does not allow your bandwidth to vary based on need.

3. ☑ **E.** SPID stands for Service Profile Identifier. On a BRI circuit, you generally have two SPIDs assigned to a circuit at the switch. The SPIDs allow you to "synch up" to the switch, and they also identify any special services on your line.

   ☒ **A**, **B**, **C**, and **D** are incorrect because they are not the correct definition of SPID. They are not actual Cisco terms.

4. ☑ **A.** Frame Relay is loosely related to the X.25 packet switching technology. One of the biggest differences between the two technologies is that Frame Relay has error detection, but no error correction. X.25 has both and therefore has more overhead. Another difference is that X.25 is a Layer 3 protocol, but Frame Relay is Layer 2.

   ☒ **B** is incorrect because RS-232 is a serial communications standard, also known as EIA-232. **C** is incorrect because V.42 is actually an error detection method used by modems. **D** is incorrect because X.400 is the format standard for email message layout.

13.02: Point-to-Point Protocol (PPP) Overview

5. ☑ **C.** If you come from the semi-old school of networking, you are accustomed to seeing SLIP defined as Serial Line Interface Protocol. Recently, however, the RFC has been modified and the definition has been changed to Serial Line Internet Protocol. Believe me, it's tougher than you think to relearn things like that.

   ☒ **A** is incorrect because that is the former definition. **B** and **D** are incorrect because they are not valid definitions.

6. ☑ **D.** Using the PPP callback would allow you to verify that the user is at the prescribed location with the correct password. Something to keep in mind about PPP callback is that, while it can help you provide network security, it was intended to be primarily a cost-management feature for the Cisco IOS.

   ☒ **A** is incorrect because if you didn't allow connections from anywhere but the home office, you would effectively cut off your remote users. **B** is incorrect because, while it may work initially, you can't guarantee that it will continue to work in the future. If the passwords were that easy to get the first time, they may be susceptible again. **C** is incorrect because forcing your remote users to get ISDN might speed their connection up, but it would do nothing to aid your security efforts. **E** is incorrect because you can't control how your users take care of their passwords. If someone got ahold of the passwords once, they could probably get ahold of them again.

7. ☑ **C.** There are two components to PPP, which both function at Layer 2. Those components are Link Control Protocol (LCP) and Network Control Protocol (NCP). LCP opens, configures, and terminates the link. NCP opens, configures, and terminates Network layer protocol communication.

☒ **A** is incorrect because TCP and UDP are Transport layer protocols and are not part of the PPP set. **B** is incorrect because IP is a Layer 3 protocol, and Frame Relay is a Layer 2 protocol. Neither IP nor Frame Relay is part of the PPP set. **D** is incorrect because SSAP and DSAP are components of Logical Link Control (LLC) addressing, both LLC1 and LLC2. These addresses are listed as eight-bit hexadecimal values.

8. ☑ **A, B**, and **E** are correct. The improvements over SLIP include authentication (PAP and CHAP), compression, and encryption. SLIP did not incorporate any of these items.

☒ **C** is incorrect because PPP is strictly a Layer 2 function; it does not have any Layer 3 capability or awareness. Remember that Layer 3 protocols are things such as X.25, IP, and IPX. **D** is incorrect because PPP does not incorporate any type of filtering function. Filtering would be something like the access lists on the Cisco routers.

13.03: Configuring Point-to-Point Protocol

9. ☑ **B.** Remember, you need to be in Interface Configuration mode to configure properties of PPP.

☒ **A** is incorrect because this is User EXEC mode, which is very limited in capability and cannot change settings on interfaces. **C** is incorrect because this is Privileged EXEC mode, which also does not have the capability of configuring interface settings. **D** and **E** are incorrect because they are not proper Cisco command modes.

10. ☑ **A.** Multilink is enabled on a PPP interface in the Interface Configuration mode for the intended serial port.

☒ **B** is incorrect because the command must be entered in Interface Configuration mode. **C** is incorrect because the command must be entered in Interface Configuration mode. **D** is incorrect because the command syntax is incorrect. Although multilink is used, it must be preceded by PPP.

11. ☑ **B, C**, and **D** are correct. Selecting Frame Relay allows your WAN network to have inherent redundancy. One of the basic principles of Frame Relay is the ability to compensate for failure by rerouting the packets through a different path. You have set up a PPP link to the Los Angeles office by creating a PPP subinterface on DLCI 300. You have allowed remote users access to your network by setting up the RAS with PPP callback and CHAP authentication.

☒ **A** is incorrect because DDS would have a severely difficult time supporting 300 users. **E** is incorrect because A is not a correct answer.

13.04: Verification of Point-to-Point Protocol

12. ☑ **C.** This is the proper way to show the running-config. This command can also be abbreviated as SHO RUN. SHOW commands will be entered at the Privileged EXEC mode interface. Remember that RAM means running-config (R=R).

☒ **A** and **B** are incorrect because they are not valid Cisco IOS commands. **D** is incorrect because you would use this to see what active Multilink PPP bundles your router has set. **E** is incorrect because this is not a valid Cisco IOS command.

13. ☑ **B.** is the correct command for showing the ISDN status of a specific port. This command can be abbreviated with SHOW ISDN STATUS if you only have one interface that is running ISDN.

☒ **A, C**, and **D** are incorrect because they are not valid Cisco IOS commands.

14. ☑ **D.** RUNNING-CONFIG will tell you, on an interface-by-interface basis, what the configuration is. If you look at the preceding output, you can see that

serial interface 0:23 is set to CHAP authentication. The network requirement calls for PAP authentication.

☒ **A** and **B** are incorrect because they are not valid Cisco IOS commands. **C** is incorrect. While you may think that this would seem logical, merely showing the interface will not give you the authentication method set up on that interface. It will, however, tell you that PPP encapsulation has been set up.

15. ☑ **A.** Showing the Frame Relay map will allow you to see serial subinterfaces, what DLCI it is associated with, and the fact that PPP has been configured.

☒ **B**, **C**, and **D** are incorrect because they are not valid Cisco IOS commands.

13.05: Troubleshooting Point-to-Point Protocol

16. ☑ **E.** DEBUG commands can cause serious performance problems on busy routers. They should only be used if you are certain of the performance issues that will arise and have prepared properly for them.

☒ **A** is incorrect because the router's configuration is stored in the NVRAM and RAM of the router and is not likely to get wiped out by DEBUG commands. **B.** The purpose of DEBUG commands is to allow you to see what is going on inside the router, at a lower level, to find out what the problem is. **C** is incorrect because a DEBUG command is not going to make your router overheat. These commands are designed as packet sniffers, to acquire very detailed information. **D** is incorrect because you can still make configuration changes while debugging is on. It may be bothersome if you can't keep track of your changes, but it can be done.

17. ☑ **A.** This command will list what debugging commands have been activated on the router. This command must be entered at the Privileged EXEC command mode. Here is a sample of its output:

```
Router#show debugging

ARP:

  ARP packet debugging is on
DSX1:
```

```
    DSX1 Signaling debugging is on

    DSX1 Framer debugging is on
CDP:

    CDP packet info debugging is on

    CDP events debugging is on
PPP:

    PPP protocol errors debugging is on

    PPP packet display debugging is on
```

☒   **B** is incorrect because the router is in Global Configuration mode. You must be in Privileged EXEC mode to run this command. **C** is incorrect because this is not a valid Cisco IOS command and it is in the wrong interface. **D** is not correct because it is not the proper command syntax.

LAB ANSWER
Objectives 13.01–13.05

You can verify your configuration answer by using these commands in the order given. The function each command performs immediately follows the command.

1. ```
   AS5300 con0 is now available
        Press RETURN to get started.
   ```
   Function: Press Return for User EXEC access.

2. ```
   AS5300>enable
        Password: ******
        AS5300#
   ```
   Function: Accesses Privileged EXEC mode.

3. ```
   AS5300#configure terminal
   Enters configuration commands, one per line. End with CNTL-Z.
   ```
   Function: Enter Global Configuration mode.

4. ```
   AS5300(config)#interface s1
        AS5300(config-if)#
   ```
   Function: Enters the Interface Configuration mode for Serial 1.

5. ```
   AS5300(config-if)#ip address 172.16.145.18 255.255.255.0
   ```
   Function: Sets the IP information up on serial interface 1.

6. ```
   AS5300(config-if)#encapsulation ppp
   ```
   Function: Sets the encapsulation type to PPP.

7. ```
   AS5300(config-if)#ppp authentication chap pap
   ```
   Function: Sets the authentication type to PAP or CHAP.
   ```

8. `AS5300(config-if)#username Boston password letmein`

Function: Here's the curve ball. Notice that Boston has a username and password. In order for the New York router to know what to expect, this command set must be run. It is case sensitive.

9. `AS5300(config-if)#no shutdown`

Function: Remember to set the interface to NO SHUTDOWN. Otherwise, it is disabled.

10. `AS5300#show running-config`

Function: You can view your configuration information with this command. See the following sample output:

```
!
interface Serial1
 ip address 172.16.145.18 255.255.255.0
 no ip directed-broadcast
 encapsulation ppp
 no fair-queue
 clockrate 2014986
 ppp authentication chap pap
!
Here is our authentication that was set:
Current configuration:
!
version 12.0
service timestamps debug uptime
service timestamps log uptime
no service password-encryption
!
hostname AS5300
!
enable password ccna
!
username async1 password 0 cisco
username Boston password 0 letmein
spe 1/0 1/9
 firmware location system:/ucode/mica_port_firmware
!
```

CISCO CERTIFIED NETWORK ASSOCIATE

14

Configuring Frame Relay Services

TEST YOURSELF OBJECTIVES

T his chapter will test you on the various components of Frame Relay architecture and configuration. Understanding Frame Relay will not only help you on the CCNA exam, it will also prepare you for the workplace. Frame Relay is probably the most common WAN protocol in use today.

Understanding the architecture of Frame Relay enables you to configure your routers in an efficient manner. You should become familiar with the key terms of Frame Relay. The Data-Link Connection Identifier (DLCI) is responsible for end-to-end communication through Frame Relay Network. The LMI settings are responsible for keeping the Frame connection active. You should also know the difference between Permanent Virtual Circuits (PVCs) and Switched Virtual Circuits (SVCs). As a network becomes larger, Frame Relay configurations can become complicated and confusing, so you should have the optimal configuration in order to minimize any chance of errors or the need to reconfigure in the future.

TEST YOURSELF OBJECTIVE 14.01

Frame Relay Architecture

Frame Relay architecture has two main components: the mechanics of the switched fabric owned by the service provider and the terminal equipment that resides at a site. A Frame Relay provider hosts a complex switched environment that is utilized by numerous consumers. The switched environment inside the Frame Relay "cloud," however, is completely transparent to the end users. They are simply provided information for their end-to-end connection via a Permanent Virtual Circuit (PVC) or a Switched Virtual Circuit (SVC).

The Data Communications Equipment (DCE) is responsible for the end connectivity for the circuit. (Usually the DCE is the provider's "demarc" or edge point.) The Data Terminating Equipment (DTE) is usually a router. It is out the router that your network data is encapsulated and prepared to travel across the network to a remote location. Be able to recognize and define the various elements of the Frame Relay fabric for the exam, keeping in mind the dual areas of responsibility between consumer and network provider.

■ Frame Relay provides DTE-to-DTE communication through a DCE (Frame Relay switch).

- Frame Relay is characterized by the use of PVCs and SVCs, which are represented by DLCIs.

- LMI allows the Frame Relay router and switch to communicate status messages.

- Frame Relay supports a variable length payload of up to 4096 bytes.

- Frame Relay is a Layer 2 (Data-Link layer), connection-oriented, packet-switched technology.

- It is a public data network. Frame Relay customers own only the access circuits at either end-point. Phone company responsibility for these circuits ends at the demarc.

- A CSU/DSU is used as an interface between the Frame Relay circuit and the customer's router. It is must be configured for the correct number of channels, line coding, and framing format.

- Traffic is time-division multiplexed onto large public circuits.

- Virtual circuits are kept separate through the use of DLCIs, which are locally significant.

- Frame Relay supports both PVCs and SVCs, though PVCs are most common.

- The switch talks to the router through LMI and keeps it informed of the status of PVCs.

- There are three types of LMI: Cisco (cisco), ITU Q933a (q933a), and ANSI Annex D (ansi).

- Prior to IOS 11.2, LMI defaulted to type Cisco; IOS 11.2 and later uses auto-detection.

- LMI messages are sent every ten seconds by default; these constant messages are known as *keepalives*.

- The command SHOW FRAME-RELAY PVC can be useful in determining the status of PVCs, and where a fault may lie. The three possibilities are Active (no problem), Inactive (problem is likely at the remote side), and Deleted (problem is likely at the near side).

- CIR is the maximum average guaranteed throughput of a Frame Relay circuit or virtual circuit.

- Whenever there is a lull on the physical circuit, your router may burst up to the capacity of the circuit.

■ Congestion conditions are reported through the use of FECNs and BECNs.

■ Discard Eligible (DE) packets may be dropped if congestion occurs.

■ Frame Relay has no congestion avoidance mechanisms.

■ A fully meshed architecture has every node connected to every other node while a partially meshed architecture allows traffic to flow from any node to any node, although a direct connection may not exist.

■ A hub and spoke topology requires that all traffic pass through one common node.

e x a m
ⓦatch
The concepts that you should have down for this section are as follows: the general topologies of Frame Relay design (hub and spoke, partial and full mesh) and the order in which the different pieces fit together.

QUESTIONS

14.01: Frame Relay Architecture

1. What does DLCI stand for?

   A. Data-Layer Computer Interface

   B. Data-Link Control Identifier

   C. Data-Link Connection Identifier

   D. Data-Layer Circuit Input

2. Under what circumstances are Discard Eligible (DE) packets dropped?

   A. When two routers are configured with the same DLCI

   B. When congestion occurs

   C. When LMI is turned up

   D. When you ping a remote host

3. **Current Situation:** Company YYZ is asking you to design a solution for their wide area network. They have fifteen remote offices and one head office location. They are looking for solid connectivity, redundancy, and dependability and

are unsure as what WAN protocol to implement. Using your technological prowess, you attempt to meet the following requirements.

Required Result: Company YYZ requires at least 256-Kbps bandwidth between the head office and each of the remote sites.

Optional Desired Results:

1. Company YYZ requires each remote office to have direct connectivity with each other.

2. The chosen WAN protocol must have a mechanism built in to avoid congestion.

Proposed Solution: You propose that the client should implement a Frame Relay switched solution in a fully meshed topology.

A. The proposed solution meets the required result and all of the optional results.

B. The proposed solution meets the required result and some of the optional results.

C. The proposed solution meets the required result and none of the optional results.

D. The proposed solution does not meet the requirements.

TEST YOURSELF OBJECTIVE 14.02

Configuring Frame Relay

When configuring Frame Relay, there are some commands that are compulsory and some that are optional, depending upon the situation. For example, certain Frame Relay network providers do not require implicit LMI statements in the configuration, and bandwidth statements are not required. Bandwidth statements improve routing decisions in complex environments as well as providing logical reference information within a configuration. It is extremely important that when you are configuring Frame Relay in a production environment, you have all the necessary details from the provider. For the exam, you will be required to recognize the separate components of the Frame Relay configuration and identify how to configure the router correctly.

■ To configure Frame Relay on a physical interface, specify Frame Relay encapsulation.

■ Sometimes the LMI type must be set explicitly.

■ A FRAME-RELAY MAP statement can associate an IP address with a DLCI in legacy Frame Relay configuration.

■ A modern approach to DLCI mapping uses Inverse ARP.

■ The BANDWIDTH statement is used as a metric for routing protocols.

■ An internal CSU/DSU will be configured within the router's IOS. An external CSU/DSU is configured separately.

exam

Watch

As in all exams that test you on configuration, knowing your syntax is the key to success. The exam may require you to recognize an incorrect configuration, or to key in a command, so be prepared to do either. It is not enough to know that the word ENCAPSULATION is used to enable Frame Relay on a Cisco router; you must be able to recognize or reproduce the entire command ENCAPSULATION FRAME-RELAY.

QUESTIONS

14.02: Configuring Frame Relay

4. What is the correct syntax for configuring Frame Relay on an interface?

A. SET FRAME-RELAY ENCAPSULATION

B. FRAME ENCAPSULATION

C. ENCAPSULATION FRAME-RELAY

D. INITIATE FRAME-RELAY ENCAPSULATION

5. Which configuration technique eliminates the problems associated with Frame Relay and split horizon?

A. Setting the LMI Type

B. Configuring subinterfaces

C. Setting the bandwidth

D. Inserting a Frame Relay MAP statement

6. What is wrong with the following configuration? (Choose all that apply.)

```
interface Serial0
    description Connection to San Francisco
    ip address 50.11.10.1 255.255.255.0
    bandwidth 512
    encapsulation frame-relay
    frame-relay lmi-type ansl
    frame-relay interface-dlci broadcast
```

A. There is no such thing as the "ansl" LMI type.

B. The DLCI number is missing from the configuration.

C. The map statement is incorrect.

D. The encapsulation statement is incorrect.

TEST YOURSELF OBJECTIVE 14.03

Configuring Frame Relay Subinterfaces

The configuration of subinterfaces on your router organizes your configuration and prevents the problems associated with split horizon and Frame Relay. Split horizon does not allow packets back out of the interface that it was received on, but the configuration of a logical subinterface alleviates this issue. The traffic may then be redirected out of the subinterface to its destination. It also makes it easier to alter the configuration as new Frame Relay sites are added and subtracted.

- ■ Subinterfaces are configured in a router by referencing them and specifying them as point-to-point or multipoint.

- ■ The router's prompt changes as configuration modes change.

- ■ Each subinterface gets its own Layer 3 (IP, IPX) address.

- ■ The optional IETF parameter may be required when not connecting to Cisco equipment.

exam

⑩atch

When reviewing questions on the exam involving Frame Relay, and specifically subinterfaces, be sure you can recognize why subinterfaces are used on Cisco equipment. Whenever you see a configuration, make sure that the subinterface syntax is correct. For example, the ENCAPSULATION and LMI-TYPE commands should appear in the main interface area, not under one of the subinterfaces.

QUESTIONS

14.03: Configuring Frame Relay Subinterfaces

7. What is wrong with the following configuration? (Choose all that apply.)

```
description Sample config

interface Serial0
   no ip address
   frame-relay lmi-type ansi
   shutdown
interface Serial0.1 point-to-point
   ip address 50.10.11.1 255.255.255.0
   frame-relay interface-dlci 507 broadcast
interface Serial0.2 point-to-point
   ip address 50.10.11.1 255.255.255.0
   frame-relay interface-dlci 509
```

A. The ENCAPSULATION FRAME-RELAY statement is missing.

B. Two subinterfaces have the same IP address.

C. The LMI type is set incorrectly.

D. Interfaces will always be shut down because of the SHUT command.

8. What is the command for configuring a subinterface for the s0 interface?

    A. INTERFACE s0.1

    B. CREATE SUBINTERFACE s0.1

    C. INITIATE SUBINTERFACE s0.1

    D. INTERFACE e0.1

9. **Current Situation:** Company YYZ took a shot at configuring their own router without your assistance. Connectivity has not been established, and they cannot seem to find the problem. They present you with the configuration and ask you to assist in correcting the configuration according to certain criteria. Again, the DLCI for Head Office is 401, the DLCI for Location A is 607, and the DLCI for Location B is 609. Bandwidth at Location A is 512 and it's 256 at Location B. Here is their configuration:

```
description Head Office Config

interface s0

encapsulation frame-relay

frame-relay lmi-type cisco

no shutdown

interface s0.1 point-to-point

ip address 150.98.35.1 255.255.255.0

frame-relay interface-dlci 67 broadcast

interface s0.1 point-to-point

ip address 150.98.35.1 255.255.255.0

frame-relay interface-dlci 69 broadcast
```

Required Result: Your configuration must establish communication between Head Office and remote Location A, and Head Office and remote Location B. Assume that Locations A and B are configured correctly, and fix the configuration problems with HO.

Optional Desired Results:

1. Insert BANDWIDTH statements for HO.

2. Change the LMI type to ANSI.

Proposed Solution: You alter the configuration to read as follows:

```
description Head Office Config

interface s0

encapsulation frame-relay

frame-relay lmi-type ansi

no shutdown

interface s0.2 point-to-point

description Connection to Location A

ip address 150.98.35.1 255.255.255.0

bandwidth 512

frame-relay interface-dlci 67 broadcast

interface s0.2 point-to-point

description Connection to Location B

ip address 150.98.35.2 255.255.255.0

bandwidth 256

frame-relay interface-dlci 69 broadcast
```

What results were met?

A. The proposed solution meets the required result and all of the optional results.

B. The proposed solution meets the required result and some of the optional results.

C. The proposed solution meets the required result and none of the optional results.

D. The proposed solution does not meet the required result.

TEST YOURSELF OBJECTIVE 14.04

Enabling Frame Relay

Enabling Frame Relay in a full implementation requires the network architect to go beyond the configuration of any single device. You must approach the network as a whole, taking into consideration bandwidth, location of users, servers, other network services and workflow. These factors will determine the overall network configuration as you attempt to balance performance, redundancy, and security. The CCNA exam does not spend a lot of time at this higher level, but these concepts are extremely important in real-world implementations.

- The clockrate is set on the DCE and read transparently by the DTE.
- The default state of a serial interface on a Cisco router is in shutdown mode.
- DLCIs do not need to match end to end, though they may if they are connected to different switches.

exam
ⓦatch

Take special care to notice the details within given configurations on the exams. A single configuration alone may look correct but when compared with the other configurations of connecting devices, it may prove faulty. Learn to see how configurations work together to establish connectivity.

QUESTIONS

14.04: Enabling Frame Relay

Questions 10–12   This scenario should be used to answer questions 10, 11, and 12.

Break-a-Leg Insurance Company has expanded and opened offices in six major U.S. cities. Their head office is in New York City. There are six remote locations, which all require connectivity to the head office in New York. They have chosen Frame Relay for their WAN solution and have purchased seven new routers to interconnect the cities.

10. To bring their wide-area network online, in what order should they complete the following steps?

   1.   Test connectivity.

   2.   Design an IP address scheme.

   3.   Obtain physical circuits and frame configurations from a network provider.

   4.   Configure routers and enable Frame Relay.

   A.   1, 2, 3, 4

   B.   2, 1, 4, 3

   C.   2, 3, 4, 1

   D.   3, 4, 1, 2

11. One month into their implementation, Break-a-Leg Insurance Company expands and adds a seventh location. They have designed the solution, ordered the circuits, and deployed the routers, but they are not establishing communications. What are some troubleshooting steps they can take? (Choose all that apply.)

   A.   Check to see if the PVC is in an active or inactive state.

   B.   Check to see if the routers are sending and receiving LMI updates.

   C.   Check IP configuration and subnet mask configuration.

   D.   Check to see if the DLCI information provided by the network service provider is correct.

12. Break-a-Leg Insurance has been experiencing poor network performance between their New York head office and their remote office in Boston. They have a 256-Kbps connection to Boston and a 128-Kbps connection to Detroit. The network is now fully meshed, and after using a protocol/traffic analyzer, they discover all traffic to and from Boston is going through Detroit. What configuration tweak will help the router choose a better path?

   A.   Turn up LMI.

B. Configure the BANDWIDTH option on the Frame Relay configurations in Boston, New York, and Detroit.

C. Increase bandwidth to Detroit to 256 Kbps.

D. Configure subinterfaces.

TEST YOURSELF OBJECTIVE 14.05

Viewing LMI Exchanges

One of the most effective tools for troubleshooting your Frame Relay networks is by viewing the LMI updates between your routers. LMI exchanges take place, by default, every 10 seconds, with a full status update every 60 seconds. LMI exchanges are initiated by the router connected to the circuit. LMI updates contain information about global addressing, virtual-circuit status messages, and multicasting.

The most important things to know for this section are what viewing the LMI exchanges can tell you about the condition of the network, and what are the Cisco IOS commands for viewing the exchanges.

■ You can view LMI exchanges between the router and the switch with the command DEBUG FRAME-RELAY LMI.

■ The sixth LMI exchange is a full status inquiry that includes information on all PVCs.

■ Within a Telnet session, you must issue the TERMINAL MONITOR command to view system messages.

■ Yourseq and myseq are LMI message numbers; if they are incrementing, then LMI is exchanging properly.

exam
ⓦatch

Extreme caution must be used when using DEBUG commands. It is possible to get a deluge of information once you start entering debug mode. If the exam asks you whether or not you will use the command DEBUG ALL to view LMI exchanges, this should send up a red flag because you cannot possibly view all the debug information and pick out on the LMI relevant information. Make sure you look for specific commands.

QUESTIONS

14.05: Viewing LMI Exchanges

13. What is the Cisco IOS command for viewing LMI exchanges?

   A. DEBUG ALL

   B. DEBUG FRAME-RELAY PVC

   C. DEBUG FRAME-RELAY LMI

   D. VIEW FRAME-RELAY LMI

14. While viewing the LMI debug, you notice that the yourseq and myseq values are not rising. What does this mean?

   A. Your connection is stable; these values only change when synchronization is lost.

   B. Your PVC status is active.

   C. Your device is not communicating with the Frame Relay switch within the provider's network.

   D. You have LMI debug turned off.

15. **Current Situation:** Company YYZ has once again asked you to help troubleshoot a connectivity problem within their Frame Relay network. All their technicians are intimidated by Cisco's debug mode and have asked you to assist.

   Required Result: Log on the router and view the debug code in order to troubleshoot the problem.

   Optional Desired Results:

   1. View PVC status and check for discrepancies.

   2. Check the LMI debug information to insure that packets communication is established with the switch fabric.

Proposed Solution: You issue the following commands, and then inform the client that you see nothing wrong.

```
telnet router
<router>show debug frame-relay pvc
<router>show debug frame-relay lmi
```

A. The proposed solution meets the required result and all of the optional results.

B. The proposed solution meets the required result and some of the optional results.

C. The proposed solution meets the required result and none of the optional results.

D. The proposed solution does not meet the required result.

LAB QUESTION

Objectives 14.01–14.05

In this lab, you will build configurations for a Frame Relay implementation from the ground up. Four locations will be configured in a full mesh topology. Each router will, therefore, be required to connect to three locations each. This will require the use of subinterfaces. Assume you are using a routing protocol like EIGRP, which will make intelligent routing decisions based on bandwidth. The Frame Relay LMI type is to be set for "cisco."

The following table lists the IP networks used between each link. Use address "1" and "2" for each endpoint for that subnet. Be sure to use subinterfaces on s0. Draw up four separate configurations to reflect the information given. Do not be concerned with whether or not the routing protocol is configured correctly. Focus on the Frame Relay details. Keep in mind that the bandwidth settings are only localized between the site and the Frame Relay cloud.

City	WAN IP Network	WAN Port	DLCI	Bandwidth
Toronto	10.11.10.0/24—Winnipeg	s0	200 → Winnipeg	256 Kbps
	10.11.11.0/24—Calgary		201 → Calgary	
	10.11.12.0/24—Vancouver		203 → Vancouver	
Winnipeg	10.11.13.0/24—Vancouver	s0	220 → Toronto	128 Kbps
	10.11.15.0/24—Calgary		221 → Vancouver	
	10.11.10.0/24—Toronto		222 → Calgary	
Vancouver	10.11.14.3/24—Calgary	s0	401 → Toronto	128 Kbps
	10.11.13.0/24—Winnipeg		402 → Winnipeg	
	10.11.12.0/24—Toronto		403 → Calgary	
Calgary	10.11.11.0/24—Toronto	s0	301 → Toronto	56 Kbps
	10.11.15.0/24—Winnipeg		302 → Vancouver	
	10.11.14.3/24—Vancouver		303 → Winnipeg	

A QUICK ANSWER KEY

Objective 14.01
1. C
2. B
3. B

Objective 14.02
4. C
5. B
6. A and B

Objective 14.03
7. A, B, and D
8. A
9. D

Objective 14.04
10. C
11. A, B, C, and D
12. B

Objective 14.05
13. C
14. C
15. D

IN-DEPTH ANSWERS

14.01: Frame Relay Architecture

1. ☑ **C.** DLCI stands for Data-Link Connection Identifier.

    ☒ **A, B,** and **D** sound good, but are incorrect definitions.

2. ☑ **B.** Discard Eligible packets are dropped during network congestion.

    ☒ **A** is incorrect. If two routers were configured with the same DLCI, connectivity would be impossible. **C** is incorrect. "Turning up LMI" is a function of the Frame Network Provider when installing a new circuit. **D** is incorrect because a ping per se will not cause DE packets to be dropped. You may lose ICMP packets due to congestion, though.

3. ☑ **B.** Frame Relay will have no problem supporting the 256-Kbps bandwidth requirement, and the client will have flexibility as to providing a little less or more bandwidth where needed. A fully meshed topology will allow all sites to connect directly with other sites in the network without going through a hub connection. The desired requirement of a congestion avoidance mechanism in Frame Relay is not possible.

    ☒ **A** and **C** are incorrect because some of the optional results were not met. **D** is incorrect because the required result was met.

14.02: Configuring Frame Relay

4. ☑ **C.** ENCAPSULATION FRAME-RELAY is the correct answer.

    ☒ **A, B,** and **D** are examples of incorrect syntax.

5. ☑ **B.** Setting subinterfaces eliminates the possibility of split horizon.

    ☒ **A** is incorrect. The LMI type dictates the protocol the routers will use to notify each other of circuit status and reliability. **C** is incorrect because the BANDWIDTH command is used to specify the line speed so the router can determine a route cost. **D** is incorrect because the MAP statements are used for backwards compatibility with older Frame networks.

6. ☑ **A** and **B** are correct. The LMI type is configured incorrectly, and the DLCI number is missing.

    ☒ **C** and **D** are incorrect. The MAP statement and ENCAPSULATION statements are correct. Strictly speaking, a Cisco router can determine the DLCI through the process of Inverse ARP, although this may not work with all routers and traffic types. This question was designed to test the recognition of missing syntax within an implicit DCLI statement.

14.03: Configuring Frame Relay Subinterfaces

7. ☑ **A**, **B**, and **D** are correct. Under interface s0 it should say ENCAPSULATION FRAME-RELAY. Two of the subinterfaces have the same IP address, and the SHUT command should be NO SHUT.

    ☒ **C** is incorrect because the LMI type is set correctly.

8. ☑ **A.** This is the correct syntax.

    ☒ **B** and **C** are incorrect because they are illegal commands, and **D** is incorrect because this will configure subinterfaces for interface e0.

9. ☑ **D.** Even though you have made the correct recommendations for inserting bandwidth commands and repairing the duplicate IP address, you have failed to correct the DLCI configuration, therefore connectivity will not be possible.

    ☒ **A**, **B**, and **C** are incorrect because the required result was not met.

14.04: Enabling Frame Relay

10. ☑ **C.** The first step is always a drawing-board step: sit down and plan your implementation. Second, the physical circuits have to be obtained from a service provider. Third, the routers must be configured. Fourth is testing for connectivity.

    ☒ **A**, **B**, and **D** are incorrect because they are in the wrong order.

11. ☑ **A**, **B**, **C**, and **D** are correct. Each step is relevant to the troubleshooting process when debugging problems with a Frame Relay connection.

12. ☑ **B.** Setting the bandwidth options will help the router choose a better path. (In theory, the routing protocol should be able to make these decisions, but in some cases, with RIP a patch can be chosen over a slower link.)

    ☒ **A** is incorrect because LMI will already be turned on. **C** is incorrect because there is ample bandwidth to Boston as is. There is no need to purchase more; you just have to make sure the router chooses the right path. **D** is incorrect because using subinterfaces will not help the router make a better routing decision.

14.05: Viewing LMI Exchanges

13. ☑ **C.** The correct syntax is shown in C.

    ☒ **A** is incorrect because even though LMI exchanges will be shown with this command, so will all the other router debug information. There is too much information spewing on the screen to make any sense of it. **B** is incorrect. This debug gives PVC-related information. **D** is incorrect syntax.

14. ☑ **C.** If the yourseq and myseq values are not incrementing every ten seconds, communication is not established between the router and the switch.

    ☒ **A** is incorrect because these values should change on a good connection. **B** is incorrect because if your PVC status is active, these numbers will be incrementing. **D** is incorrect because you would not be able to get this information from the router without debug turned on.

15. ☑ **D.** In order to view debug information, you must be in Privileged mode, indicated by a prompt which reads <routername#> (with the pound sign). The commands in the proposed solution would produce no debug information, and your tasks would not be complete.

    ☒ **A**, **B**, and **C** are incorrect because the proposed solution does not meet the required result.

LAB ANSWER
Objectives 14.01–14.05

The proper site configurations that satisfy the question's parameters are shown below.

The Toronto Configuration

```
interface Serial 0
 no shutdown
 no description
 no ip address
 encapsulation frame-relay
 frame-relay lmi-type ansi
!
interface Serial 0.1 point-to-point
 no shutdown
 description connected to Winnipeg
 ip address 10.11.10.1 255.255.255.0
 frame-relay interface-dlci 200
 bandwidth 128
interface Serial 0.2 point-to-point
 no shutdown
 description connected to Calgary
 ip address 10.11.11.1 255.255.255.0
 frame-relay interface-dlci 201
 bandwidth 56
interface Serial 0.3 point-to-point
 no shutdown
```

```
description connected to Vancouver

ip address 10.11.12.1 255.255.255.0

frame-relay interface-dlci 203

bandwidth 128
```

The Winnipeg Configuration

```
interface Serial 0

no shutdown

no description

no ip address

encapsulation frame-relay

frame-relay lmi-type ansi

!

interface Serial 0.1 point-to-point

no shutdown

description connected to Toronto

ip address 10.11.10.2 255.255.255.0

frame-relay interface-dlci 220

bandwidth 256

interface Serial 0.2 point-to-point

no shutdown

description connected to Vancouver

ip address 10.11.13.2 255.255.255.0

frame-relay interface-dlci 221

bandwidth 128

interface Serial 0.3 point-to-point

no shutdown

description connected to Calgary

ip address 10.11.15.2 255.255.255.0

frame-relay interface-dlci 222

bandwidth 56
```

The Calgary Configuration

```
interface Serial 0
 no shutdown
 no description
 no ip address
 encapsulation frame-relay
 frame-relay lmi-type ansi
!
interface Serial 0.1 point-to-point
 no shutdown
 description connected to Toronto
 ip address 10.11.11.2 255.255.255.0
 frame-relay interface-dlci 301
 bandwidth 256
interface Serial 0.2 point-to-point
 no shutdown
 description connected to Vancouver
 ip address 10.11.14.2 255.255.255.0
 frame-relay interface-dlci 302
 bandwidth 128
interface Serial 0.3 point-to-point
 no shutdown
 description connected to Winnipeg
 ip address 10.11.15.1 255.255.255.0
 frame-relay interface-dlci 303
 bandwidth 128
```

The Vancouver Configuration

```
interface Serial 0
 no shutdown
 no description
 no ip address
 encapsulation frame-relay
 frame-relay lmi-type ansi
!
interface Serial 0.1 point-to-point
 no shutdown
 description connected to Toronto
 ip address 10.11.12.2 255.255.255.0
 frame-relay interface-dlci 401
 bandwidth 256
interface Serial 0.2 point-to-point
 no shutdown
 description connected to Winnipeg
 ip address 10.11.13.1 255.255.255.0
 frame-relay interface-dlci 402
 bandwidth 128
interface Serial 0.3 point-to-point
 no shutdown
 description connected to Calgary
 ip address 10.11.14.1 255.255.255.0
 frame-relay interface-dlci 403
 bandwidth 56
```

CISCO CERTIFIED NETWORK ASSOCIATE

Practice Exam

QUESTIONS

1. You want to see what routes are configured on your router. Once you have observed the routes, you find that you have a route to a router (207.79.29.3/24) that is no longer in service. You have three goals:

■ Clear the route from the table.

■ Use an IOS command to view the routing table, before and after removing the route, to ensure proper removal.

■ Back up the configuration to the NVRAM.

What series of commands would you use to accomplish these three goals?

A.
```
Cisco (config)# show ip route
Cisco (config)# no ip route 207.79.29.3 255.255.255.0
Cisco (config)# show ip route
Cisco (config)# copy running-config nvram
```

B.
```
Cisco # show ip route
Cisco # clear ip route 207.79.29.3 255.255.255.0
Cisco # show ip route
Cisco # copy running-config startup-config
```

C.
```
Cisco # show ip route
Cisco # configure
Cisco (config)# clear ip route 207.79.29.3 255.255.255.0
Cisco (config)# show ip route
Cisco (config)# backup running-config
```

D.
```
Cisco # show ip route
Cisco # configure
Cisco (config)# interface serial 0
Cisco (config-if)# no ip route 207.79.29.3 255.255.255.0
Cisco (config-if)# show ip route
Cisco (config-if)# copy running-config startup-config
```

2. Refer to the following illustration to answer the question.

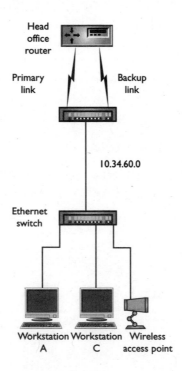

An onsite technical person is at this remote site on Workstation C. He is transferring a new image onto Workstation A using multicasting over the LAN. The remote wireless users (accessing the network through the wireless access point) complain that they have lost network connection. Why have the mobile clients lost network connectivity?

A. The router has detected a broadcast on the 10.34.60.0 network and has prevented its propagation.

B. The multicast frames have to be processed by all workstations on the collision domain, including the wireless access point.

C. The router sees the multicast on its Ethernet interface and is busy processing frames and is unable to forward frames to its primary link interface.

D. The Ethernet switch cannot process the multicast frames coming from Workstation C.

3. A user sends you an email stating that, after the technician left his cubicle, the following output was on his screen. He wanted to make sure it was not important before closing the screen. What is this output?

Protocol	Local Address	Foreign Address	State
TCP	TAMARA1001:1651	hr.employees.toys.com:1807	ESTABLISHED
TCP	TAMARA1001:1655	mail.snap.com:1163	ESTABLISHED
TCP	TAMARA1001:1673	gabriel.toys.com:telnet	ESTABLISHED
TCP	TAMARA1001:1674	chuck.toys.com:telnet	ESTABLISHED
TCP	TAMARA1001:2489	irc.pat.toys.com:6667	ESTABLISHED
TCP	TAMARA1001:3347	taylor:1055	ESTABLISHED
TCP	TAMARA1001:3353	taylor:1068	ESTABLISHED
TCP	TAMARA1001:3360	accounting.toys.com:1070	ESTABLISHED
TCP	TAMARA1001:3361	taylor:1055	ESTABLISHED
TCP	TAMARA1001:4014	taylor:1068	ESTABLISHED
TCP	TAMARA1001:1234	tarzan.irc.toys.com:6666	ESTABLISHED
TCP	TAMARA1001:1238	122.13.236.86:5190	ESTABLISHED
TCP	TAMARA1001:1245	107.8.116.19:5190	ESTABLISHED
TCP	TAMARA1001:1026	localhost:1027	ESTABLISHED
TCP	TAMARA1001:1027	localhost:1026	ESTABLISHED
TCP	TAMARA1001:1033	localhost:1035	ESTABLISHED
TCP	TAMARA1001:1035	localhost:1033	ESTABLISHED

A. A printout of the command HOSTNAME

B. A printout of the command ARP –A.

C. A printout of the command NETSTAT

D. A printout of an FTP listing

4. You have just started your job as the administrator of a medical office. The first assignment that you are given is to design a Frame Relay network with PPP subinterfaces. You are told that the Frame Relay network design must support highest amount of bandwidth possible, and should allow for flexibility. You intend to design a hub-spoke Frame Relay network. Before you begin, you are handed four different versions of the possible WAN configuration, left to you by the former administrator. Which of the following illustrations shows what you could use as your Frame Relay network design?

A.

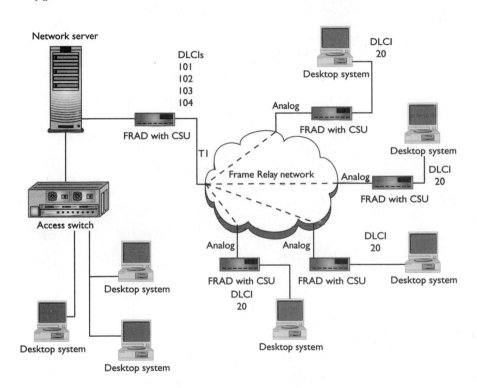

B.

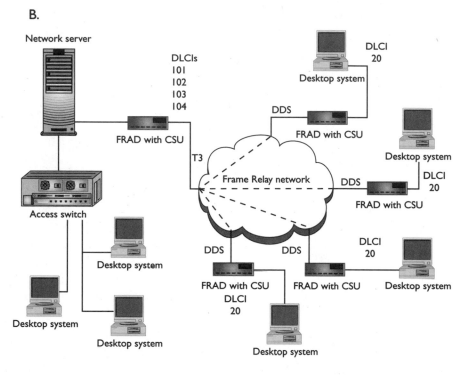

C.

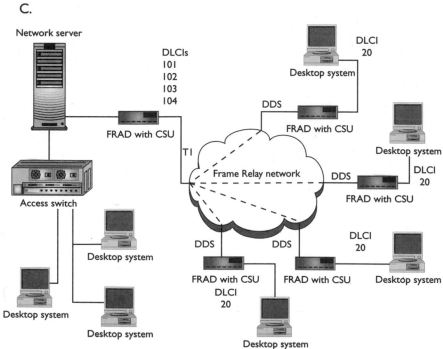

D.

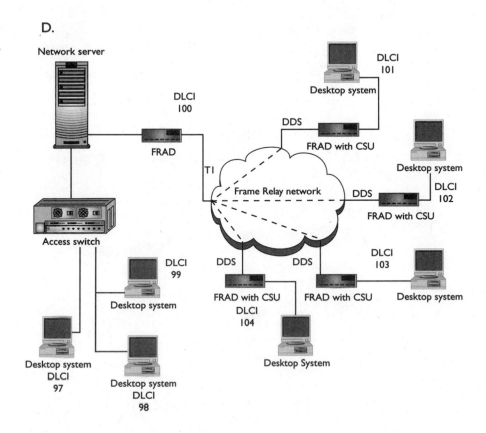

5. Which of the following will display only extended access list 100?

   A. SHOW IP INT

   B. SHOW ACCESS-LISTS

   C. SHOW ACCESS-LIST 100

   D. SHOW INT

6. **Current Situation:** Company X is expanding their network and has asked you to recommend an IP address space.

   Required Result: The IP address space must accommodate at least 20,000 host addresses.

   Optional Desired Results:

   1. The address space should not be subnetted.

   2. The address space should maximize the number of possible networks.

Proposed Solution: You recommend the address space 11.0.0.0 with a subnet mask of 255.0.0.0. What requirements were met?

A. The proposed solution meets the required result and both of the optional results.

B. The proposed solution meets the required result and one of the optional results.

C. The proposed solution meets the required result and none of the optional results.

D. The proposed solution does not meet the required result.

7. Given the following debug on a router's PVCs, what can you determine?

```
DLCI = 16, DLCI USAGE = LOCAL, PVC STATUS = INACTIVE, INTERFACE = Serial0.4
input pkts 0              output pkts 1           in bytes 0
 out bytes 543            dropped pkts 0           in FECN pkts 0
 in BECN pkts 0           out FECN pkts 0          out BECN pkts 0
 in DE pkts 0             out DE pkts 0
 out bcast pkts 1           out bcast bytes 291
pvc create time 2w4d, last time pvc status changed 1w2d
```

A. There are packets coming in on the circuit.

B. This is PVC information for sub-interface serial0.4.

C. The circuit is currently down.

D. The DLCI is set it 16.

8. What is the router mode shown here?

```
Router(config)#
```

A. User EXEC mode

B. Privileged EXEC mode

C. Global Configuration mode

D. Interface Configuration mode

9. Under which condition would an amber port LED indicate normal switch functions?

    A. When the port in question is a VLAN trunk port

    B. When the mode of the switch is set to FDUP, and the port in question is running in full-duplex mode

    C. When the port in question has been blocked by STP

    D. When the mode of the switch is set to UTL, and the port in question is running in full-duplex mode

10. How will the router with the configuration shown here behave when loading an IOS image? (Choose the most correct answer.)

```
boot system tftp 10.1.1.1 c2600-is-mz-113-6.bin
boot system flash c2600-is-mz-113.bin
boot system rom
```

    A. The router will load the IOS image c2600-is-mz-113-6.bin from the TFTP server 10.1.1.1.

    B. The router will load the IOS image c2600-is-mz-113-6.bin from the TFTP server 10.1.1.1; if that image is not available, it will load c2600-is-mz-113.bin from memory; and if that image is not available, it will boot from ROM.

    C. The router will load the IOS image c2600-is-mz-113-6.bin from the TFTP server 10.1.1.1; if that image is not available, it will boot from ROM; and if that image is not available, it will load c2600-is-mz-113.bin from memory.

    D. The router will use the last command entered and boot from ROM.

11. You have just finished setting up your port security, and several company employees have called saying that they cannot do anything on the network. How do you find out what is causing the problem?

    A. Issue the SHOW PORT *mod_num/port_num* command for each user port with network problems.

    B. Use the SHOW INTERFACE *module/port* command for user ports with network problems.

C. Use the SHOW MAC-ADDRESS-TABLE SECURITY [TYPE *module/port*] command for each user port with network problems.

D. Issue the SHOW PORT SECURITY *mod_num/port_num* command for each user port with network problems.

12. In the following illustration, the router for network B goes down. Router D receives an update and marks Router B's network as unreachable in its routing table. Router D passes this information to Router C. Router A receives the information over the slow link that Router B is down. Router B comes back up and Router D receives this information and passes it on to Router C. Router A passes its (now outdated) update to Router C with the information that Router B is down. Router C passes this (inaccurate) information on to Router D. What is the name for the source of this problem?

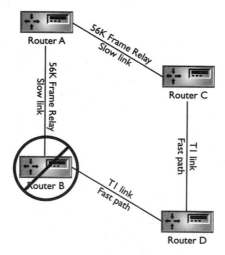

A. Split horizon

B. Slow convergence

C. Desynchronization

D. Poison reverse

13. A router with ISDN interfaces is configured with the call destinations directly associated to the physical interfaces. What type of DDR is the router configured with?

A. Standard DDR

B. Legacy DDR

C. Dialer Profiles

D. Rotary Group DDR

14. In the IPX address 0102.0000.8045.1700, what is the node address?

A. 1700

B. 0102.0000.8045

C. 0102.0000

D. 0000.8045.1700

15. In the following diagram, the Ethernet 0 interface on the router is in VLAN 3, and the Ethernet 1 interface on the router is in VLAN 4. How does traffic get from Workstation A to Workstation C?

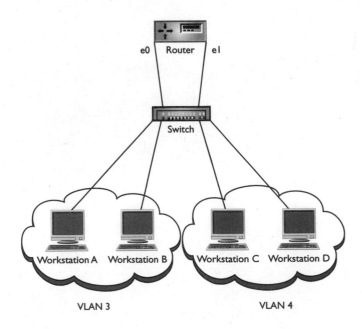

A. Data is sent from Workstation A to the switch, which sends the data to Workstation C.

B. Workstation A broadcasts the traffic to Workstation C.

C. Data is sent from Workstation A to the switch, which then sends the data to the Ethernet 0 port on the router. Ethernet 0 sends the data to Ethernet 1, which then sends the data to the switch. The switch then sends the data to workstation C.

D. Data is sent from Workstation A to the switch, which then sends the data to the Ethernet 1 port on the router. Ethernet 1 sends the data to Ethernet 0, which then sends the data to the switch. The switch then sends the data to workstation C.

16. With reference to the illustration below, everyone in the Engineering Department is on the same broadcast domain and in the same collision domain. In order to have all clients of the engineering department in a separate collision domain and broadcast domain, with what would you replace the bridge?

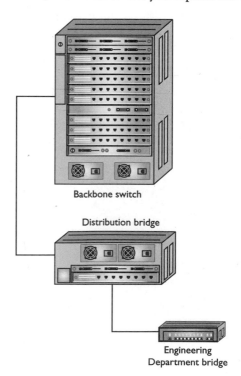

Backbone switch

Distribution bridge

Engineering
Department bridge

A. Router

B. Switch

C. Repeater

D. VLAN

17. After completing the configuration of a serial interface in Interface Configuration mode, what can you do to get back to Privileged EXEC mode?

    A. Press CTRL-A.

    B. Press CTRL-Z or type **exit**.

    C. Type **exit**.

    D. Press CTRL-Z.

18. Which solution would fulfill the following requirements: configure the router to use an IP unnumbered reference address and minimize the possibility of losing remote contact with the router.

    A. Configure the router to use IP unnumbered using the reference address of the loopback vt port 0.

    ```
    cisco (config)# interface serial 1
    cisco (config-if)#ip unnumbered loopback 0
    ```

    B. Configure the router to use IP unnumbered using the reference address of the Ethernet port.

    ```
    cisco (config)# interface serial 1
    cisco (config-if)#ip unnumbered ethernet 0
    ```

    C. Configure the router to use IP unnumbered using the reference address of the serial port.

    ```
    cisco (config)# interface serial 1
    cisco (config-if)#ip unnumbered serial 1
    ```

    D. Configure the router to use IP unnumbered using the reference address of the IDSN port.

    ```
    cisco (config)# interface serial 1
    cisco (config-if)#ip unnumbered bri 1
    ```

19. In the following illustration, there is a router with a BRI interface connecting to a router with a PRI interface, and there is a computer with an analog

modem connecting to the same router with a PRI interface. What hardware is necessary for an analog modem to dial into the router with the PRI interface?

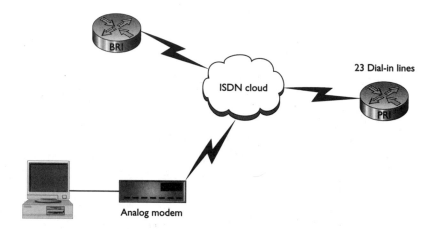

A. TA connected to the analog modem.

B. Digital modem card in the router with the PRI interface.

C. Analog modem card in the router with the PRI interface.

D. No special hardware is required.

20. **Current Situation:** You are the systems administrator of a large network, where you have been adding systems at an alarming rate. Users are complaining that there are extremely slow connection times and a lag on the network, especially when connecting to two nodes: Accounting1 and Accounting2.

You have looked at the network traces and seen that between the router and the host Accounting1, there are a lot of retransmissions. This contrasts with connections between the router and Accounting2. Accounting1 is an older system; Accounting2 is a new, high-powered system.

Required Results: Speed up connections and reduce lag between router and Accounting1.

Optional Desired Results:

1. Reduce packet retransmissions between Accounting1 and the router.

2. Increase packet throughput to Accounting2 in hopes that users will start to use it more.

Proposed Solution: Increase the receiving window size on the router and on Accounting2.

A. The proposed solution produces the required results and both the optional results.

B. The proposed solution produces the required results and only one of the optional results.

C. The proposed solution produces the required results and none of the optional results.

D. The proposed solution does not product the required result.

21. What does the command SHOW PPP MULTILINK do?

A. Shows the active voice calls on the router

B. Shows PPP statistics

C. Shows multilink statistics

D. Shows active multilink bundles

22. You are given the Class C address space 210.10.10.0. Which subnet mask will allow for at least ten networks and ten hosts per network?

A. 255.255.255.240

B. 255.255.0.0

C. 255.255.128.0

D. 255.255.255.224

23. You are currently using a distance vector routing protocol on your network. You are considering switching to the use of a link-state protocol. You desire the following results from the switch:

■ Eliminate periodic broadcast of updates to the routing table.

■ Speed up convergence

■ Decrease the amount of memory and processor utilization by the routers.

Which of these results can you expect to obtain by switching from a distance vector to a link-state protocol?

A. None of the desired results

B. One of the desired results

C. Two of the desired results

D. All of the desired results

24. Your client has made you aware that they would not like print services (SAP service type 7) in network 200 to be available to clients in network 100. With regards to the illustration below, how can this be accomplished?

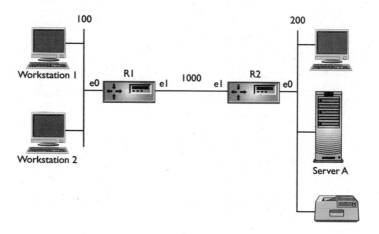

A. `access-list 1001 deny 200 7`
    `access-list 1001 permit -1`
    `applied to the input of R1's e1 interface`

B. `access-list 1001 deny 100 7`
    `access-list 1001 permit -1`
    `applied to the input of R2's e1 interface`

C. `access-list 1001 deny 200 7`
    `access-list 1001 permit -1`
    `applied to the input of R1's e0 interface`

D. `access-list 1001 deny 100 7`
    `access-list 1001 permit -1`
    `applied to the input of R2's e1 interface`

25. Your client has five routers in his corporate office. All are 3640 routers that connect to remote offices via redundant 10MB ATM lines. Your client prefers

to use the latest release of IOS, so he updates his routers frequently. What solution would you suggest for providing IOS images to these five routers?

A. Load all images from Flash.

B. Load all images from a TFTP server.

C. Load all images from Flash; and if no Flash image is available, load from a TFTP server, followed by ROM.

D. Load all images from a TFTP server; and if no TFTP server is available, load from Flash, followed by ROM.

26. How do you recover a forgotten password on a Catalyst 1900 switch?

A. You can't; this requires sending the switch back to Cisco for recovery.

B. By typing the string **ciscopw:recov** at the password prompt.

C. By TFTP downloading a special IOS that the Cisco TAC can send you.

D. By holding down the Mode button while powering up the switch.

27. What kind of topology does the following illustration depict?

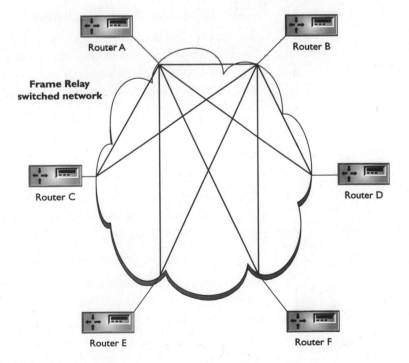

A. Partial mesh

B. Full mesh

C. Hub and spoke

D. Star

28. What command would configure router cisco-1 to use the DNS server at address 207.79.94.25 for its name-to-IP address resolution.

A. ```
Cisco-1 (config)# interface serial 0
Cisco-1 (config-if)# ip domain-lookup
Cisco-1 (config-if)# ip name-server 207.79.94.25
```

B. ```
Cisco-1 (config)# ip domain-lookup
Cisco-1 (config)# ip name-server 207.79.94.25
```

C. ```
Cisco-1 (config)# router
Cisco-1 (config-router)# ip domain-lookup
Cisco-1 (config-router)# ip name-server 207.79.94.25
```

D. ```
Cisco-1 (config)# ip name-server 207.79.94.25
```

29. Your company is based in San Francisco and has international offices in Japan and Europe. You have just been promoted, and now your responsibilities will include providing network services in both Japan and Europe. The offices in these locations have ISDN services, and your new boss wants you to tell him what differences you will have to expect with ISDN outside of North America. What should you tell him?

A. In Japan and Europe, PRI ISDN service is based on the E1 standard and is comprised of 32 channels, using 30 for B channels, one for a D channel, and one reserved for the telephone company.

B. Outside of North America and Japan, PRI ISDN service is based on the E1 standard and is comprised of 32 channels, using 30 for B channels, one for a D channel, and one reserved for the telephone company.

C. The only difference will be the language spoken by the telephone company.

D. Outside of North America and Japan, PRI ISDN service is based on the E1 standard and is comprised of 31 channels, using 30 for B channels and one for a D channel.

30. **Current Situation:** Megan is a network administrator in charge of a single IPX subnet, its attached clients, and their default gateway (router). She wants to upgrade from NetWare 3.11 to 4.12, and she has heard a rumor about Novell switching frame types between these two releases. She's also the only one who can perform this upgrade, and she won't be able to upgrade every client at the same time.

    Required Result: No NetWare client may lose connectivity to any other NetWare client, except for the short time required to perform the upgrade on a particular station.

    Optional Desired Result: The upgrade may be performed over several evenings.

    Proposed Solution: Megan first implements two subinterfaces on her network's default gateway. The first subinterface uses the current IPX network number (0xA) used by the existing clients and uses novell-ether as the encapsulation type. The second subinterface uses a new IPX network number (0xB) and uses SAP as the encapsulation type. Megan upgrades the client stations at her leisure.

    Which of the following results does the proposed solution produce?

    A. The proposed solution produces the required result and the optional result.

    B. The proposed solution produces the required result but not the optional result.

    C. The proposed solution produces neither the required result nor the optional result.

    D. The proposed solution produces the optional result but not the required result.

31. You design and set up a remote site as shown in the illustration that follows. During installation, the on-site technical people are unable to obtain an IP address from the DHCP server when they connect a workstation to the switch port. What is happening, and what would you do to rectify it? (Choose two.)

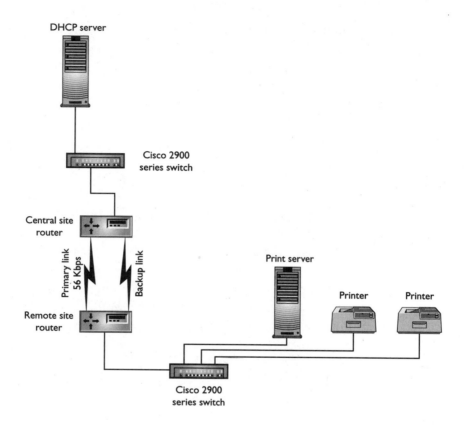

DHCP server

Cisco 2900
series switch

Central site
router

Primary link
56 Kbps

Backup link

Print server

Printer   Printer

Remote site
router

Cisco 2900
series switch

A. There is a problem on the WAN; call the telco and submit a trouble ticket.

B. Re-locate the DHCP server to the remote site.

C. The request for an IP address from the DHCP server has timed out.

D. The problem is due to the Spanning-Tree Protocol. Disable Spanning-Tree.

E. You must configure the associated ports to use Spantree PortFast.

32. Which command should you type at the prompt in Privileged EXEC mode to find all of the available options for the SHOW command?

A. SHOW HELP

B. HELP SHOW

C. SHOW IP ?

D. SHOW ?

33. You have installed a firewall between your Web server and the Internet. You still wish to allow Internet browsers to connect to your server and purchase products via a secured HTTP connection. What port must be opened on your firewall to allow this?

    A. 161

    B. 80

    C. 8080

    D. 443

34. In order to configure VLANs on a Catalyst 1900 VLAN, you need to select the [V] Virtual LAN option from the main menu. Once you select [V], the Virtual LAN Configuration menu is displayed as follows:

```
Catalyst 1900 - Virtual LAN Configuration
-----------------Information----------------
VTP version: 1 Configuration revision: 1
Maximum VLANs supported locally: 1005
Number of existing VLANs: 0
Configuration last modified by: 0.0.0.0 at 07-31-2000
20:04:03


-------------------Settings-----------------
[N] Domain name                    CCNA_VLAN
[V] VTP mode control               Server
[F] VTP pruning mode               Disabled
[O] VTP traps                      Enabled


-------------------Actions------------------
[L] List VLANs              [A] Add VLAN
[M] Modify VLAN             [D] Delete VLAN
[E] VLAN Membership         [S] VLAN Membership Servers
[T] Trunk Configuration     [W] VTP password
[P] VTP Statistics          [X] Exit to Main Menu


Enter Selection:
```

From this menu, how do you create a VLAN and add ports to the VLAN?

A. Select [E] specify VLAN settings, and then add ports to that VLAN.

B. Select [T] and specify VLAN settings. Select [E] to add ports to the VLAN that was just created.

C. Select [A] and specify VLAN settings. Select [E] to add ports to the VLAN that was just created.

D. Select [A] and specify VLAN settings. Select [M] to add ports to the VLAN that was just created.

35. You are setting up a RAS at your location to allow users to connect from home. You want to make sure that the RAS and the users are configured for CHAP. The users have selected CHAP as the authentication method on their PCs, so the only thing left is to configure the RAS. Referencing the following illustration and partial output of your server, what commands still need to be configured?

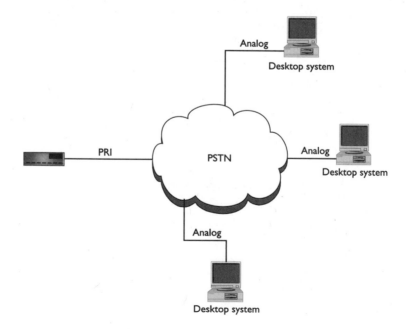

T1 Controller 0

```
controller T1 0
 framing esf
 clock source line primary
 linecode b8zs
 cablelength short 133
 pri-group timeslots 1-24
```

Serial Interface 0:23

```
interface Serial0:23
 no ip address
 no ip directed-broadcast
 no logging event link-status
 dialer-group 1
 isdn switch-type primary-ni
 isdn switch-type primary-ni
 isdn protocol-emulate user
 isdn incoming-voice modem
 fair-queue 64 256 0
```

A. PPP encapsulation on the T1 controller interface

B. PPP encapsulation on serial interface 0:23

C. CHAP authentication on both the T1 controller and the serial interface

D. CHAP authentication on the serial interface 0:23

E. Both A and D

F. Both B and D

G. All of the above

36. **Current Situation:** Your client has asked that you create a set of IP access lists on the network. They would like named IP access lists for better organization and readability. They would like a number of source addresses blocked on the border router Stargate. Furthermore, each of their departmental routers (Cygnus, Alpha-Centuri, and Andromeda) should have a named IP access list that blocks all incoming traffic except for mail, Web, and DNS services.

Required Result: The access lists must block the source addresses requested at the border and allow only mail, Web, and DNS services through each of the interior routers.

Optional Desired Results:

1. Each of the access lists on the interior routers should share the same name.

2. A second access list sharing the same name as the first should be created on the border router Stargate, to block any incoming Telnet traffic from entering the network.

Proposed Solution: You propose to create a standard IP-named access list on the border router Stargate named Blocksome to deal with the source addresses the client wishes to block from entering the network. You also plan to create an extended IP named access list on the border router named Blocksome to deal with the blocking of Telnet traffic into the network. Finally, you plan to create three extended IP named access lists on the interior routers Cygnus, Alpha Centuri and Andromeda to deal with allowing only mail, Web, and DNS traffic into those departments.

A. The proposed solution produces the required result and both of the optional results.

B. The proposed solution produces the required result and only one of the optional results.

C. The proposed solution produces the required result and none of the optional results.

D. The proposed solution doesn't produce the required result.

37. What is wrong with the following configuration?

```
int e0
    ip address 155.89.10.1 255.255.255.255
    no shutdown
int s0
    address 156.11.128.10 255.255.255.0
    no shutdown
```

A. Nothing is wrong with the configuration.

B. The subnet mask on s0 is incorrectly configured.

C. The syntax for assigning an IP address is incorrect on s0.

D. The syntax for assigning an IP address is incorrect on s0, and the mask is invalid for interface e0.

38. In your network, on router cisco2500-1, you execute the command SHOW HOSTS and find a *(perm, ok)* entry in the "flags" column after each of the entries for the hosts you've previously configured. What does this mean?

    A. The entries can never be changed or removed, and the connection is up and running.

    B. The entries have been manually configured, and the connection is up and running.

    C. The entries have been configured manually, and the connection is current with regard to its age expiration.

    D. All connections to this entry are non-virtual connections.

39. You are the new network administrator for your company network, and you wish to view the routing tables on Router A, in order to determine what routes have been entered. You also wish to enter a new default route on Router B. You type the following command at the RouterA# prompt: **ip sh route**. At the RouterB# prompt, you type the following command: **config t**. You then enter the following at the RouterA(config)# prompt: **route ip 0.0.0.0 0.0.0.0 203.21.30.0**. Which of the following results does your proposed solution accomplish?

    A. Show the routing table on Router A.

    B. Allow configuration of Router B from your terminal.

    C. Configure a default route to network 203.21.30.0 for Router B.

    D. The solution accomplishes all desired results.

    E. The solution accomplishes none of the desired results.

40. Choose two ways to retrieve a command that you recently entered into the router via the command-line interface.

    A. CTRL-L and UP ARROW

    B. CTRL-M and UP ARROW

    C. CTRL-N and UP ARROW

    D. CTRL-P and UP ARROW

41. You have arrived at a customer's site because they are having performance issues with their router. The ISDN link at the office was out a few days prior, and a technician from your group assisted with getting everything back online. When you log onto the router, you notice some continual information on the screen:

```
Router#
4d22h: ISDN Se0:23: RX <-  RRp sapi = 0  tei = 0 nr = 0
4d22h: ISDN Se0:23: TX ->  RRf sapi = 0  tei = 0  nr = 0
AS5300#
4d22h: ISDN Se0:23: RX <-  RRp sapi = 0  tei = 0 nr = 0
4d22h: ISDN Se0:23: TX ->  RRf sapi = 0  tei = 0  nr = 0
AS5300#
4d22h: ISDN Se0:23: RX <-  RRp sapi = 0  tei = 0 nr = 0
4d22h: ISDN Se0:23: TX ->  RRf sapi = 0  tei = 0  nr = 0
```

Thinking that you know what the problem is, you seek to turn off the debugging, only you don't know which DEBUG statement is on. How should you turn off all debugging that is currently active on the router?

A. ROUTER#NO DEBUG

B. ROUTER#DEBUG ALL OFF

C. ROUTER#UNDEBUG ALL

D. ROUTER#SYSTEM DEBUG OFF

42. In the following illustration, which protocol belongs in the circle labeled with a question mark?

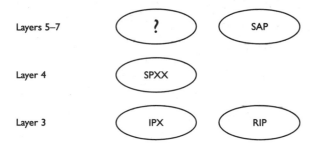

A. DNS

B. DHCP

C. NCP

D. IP/RIP

43. Which of the following are the advantages of segmenting a LAN with a bridge? (Choose all that apply.)

A. Bridges isolate local traffic to one physical segment of the LAN.

B. Bridges isolate non-local and broadcast traffic from local traffic by logically segmenting the LAN.

C. Bridges amplify the electrical signal of the physical media, thereby extending the physical distance of the LAN.

D. Bridges provide security and high-level protocol conversion capabilities.

44. On a Catalyst 5000 series switch, what is the command to set 802.1Q encapsulation on a port belonging to a VLAN?

A. SET TRUNK *mod/port type* 802.1Q

B. SET ENCAPSULATION DOT1Q *vlan identifier*

C. SET TRUNK *mod/port type* DOT1Q

D. ENCAPSULATION DOT1Q *vlan identifier*

45. Which of the following illustrations correctly identifies the reference points in the ISDN circuit?

A.

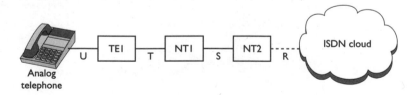

B.

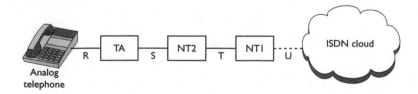

C.

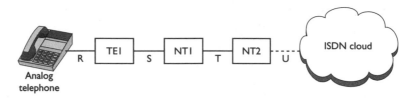

D.

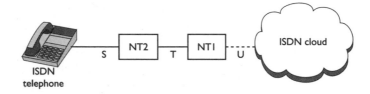

46. The following image shows what kind of screen capture?

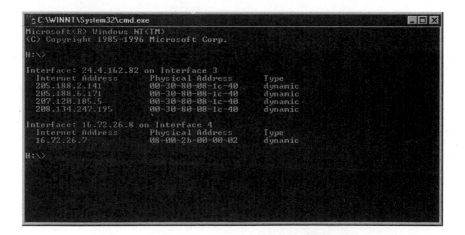

A. Ping output

B. FTP session

C. DNS lookup

D. ARP output

47. While looking at the front panel of your Catalyst 1924 switch, you notice that the LED on port 4 is alternating between green and amber. This switch has been up and running for a few weeks now. What does the alternating color on the LED on port 4 mean?

    A. The switch failed its console port test during the POST.

    B. The switch is blocking that port due to the Spanning-Tree Protocol.

    C. The switch is receiving frame errors on that port.

    D. Port 4 is configured as a VLAN trunk port.

48. Your routing table has routes entered by IGRP, OSPF, and RIP, as well as static routes. What priority will the router use in determining the trustworthiness of routes entered by each, starting with the most trustworthy?

    A. IGRP, RIP, OSPF, Static.

    B. Static, IGRP, RIP, OSPF.

    C. Static, IGRP, OSPF, RIP.

    D. All routes will be considered equally trustworthy.

49. **Current Situation:** Company YYZ has taken your recommendation to install a Frame Relay network, and they wish to contract out the work to you. In order in ensure that their money is well spent, they are going to have Cisco double-check your initial configuration. They are requiring you to submit a sample Frame Relay configuration between their head office and two remote sites. The topology will be hub and spoke, with both remote offices connecting to head office. They require you to submit only the configuration for the Head Office. The contract is yours if you meet all their requirements.

    Required Result: Your configuration must establish communication between the Head Office and remote Location X, and between the Head Office and remote Location Y. The DLCI for Head Office is 401, the DLCI for Location X is 507, and the DLCI for Location Y is 509.

    Optional Desired Results:

    1. The company wants implicit statements for configuring LMI for the cisco type.

    2. They want to establish DLCI mapping through the process called Inverse ARP.

Proposed Solution: You present to Company YYZ the following configuration. Which requirements were met?

```
description Head Office Config

interface Serial0
 no ip address
 encapsulation frame-relay ietf
 frame-relay lmi-type cisco
 no shutdown
interface Serial0.1 point-to-point
 ip address 12.10.10.1 255.255.255.0
 description Connection to Remote Site X
 frame-relay interface-dlci 507 broadcast
interface Serial0.2 point-to-point
 ip address 12.10.10.2 255.255.255.252
 description Connection to Remote Network Y
 frame-relay interface-dlci 509
```

A. The proposed solution meets the required result and both of the optional results.

B. The proposed solution meets the required result and one of the optional results.

C. The proposed solution meets the required result and none of the optional results.

D. The proposed solution does not meet the required result.

50. Which of these lists the three sources for Cisco IOS software?

A. TFTP server, Flash, ROM

B. TFTP server, Flash, RAM

C. TFTP server, RAM, ROM

D. Flash, RAM, ROM

51. Which of the following statements are true about full-duplex Ethernet operation?

    A. Full-duplex is achieved by using point-to-point Ethernet and Fast Ethernet.

    B. Full-duplex transmission between stations is achieved using point-to-multipoint Ethernet and Fast Ethernet.

    C. Full-duplex Ethernet technology requires the transmit circuit wired directly to the receive circuit at the other end.

    D. Hubs can be used to connect users' workstations.

52. **Current Situation:** Kathie is the administrator of a Catalyst 1900 switch. She would like to configure this switch so that only other administrators can make changes to the switch, but also so junior administrators may look at the switch's configuration without being able to make changes to it. She would like to have VLAN support and an IOS-like interface to work with.

    Required Results: Senior administrators must be able to make changes to the switch configuration. Junior administrators should be able just to look at the switch configuration.

    Optional Desired Results:

    1. VLAN support.

    2. An IOS-like interface.

    Proposed Solution: Install Standard Edition firmware on the Catalyst switch.

    A. The proposed solution produces the required result and the optional results.

    B. The proposed solution produces the required result but not the optional results.

    C. The proposed solution produces neither the required result nor the optional results.

    D. The proposed solution produces the optional results, but not the required result.

53. Assume that one of the routers in the following illustration had an IOS image that the network administrator wanted to load on all the other routers of the

same platform. What would be the process, using a TFTP server, to accomplish this task?

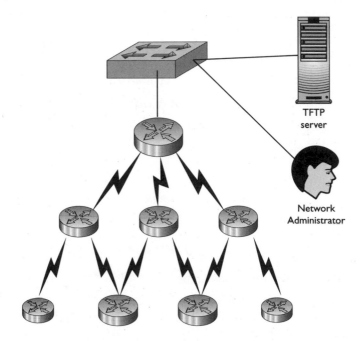

A. Telnet to the router that has the IOS image, type **copy start tftp**, then Telnet to the other routers and type **copy tftp start**.

B. Telnet to the routers that you want the IOS image to be loaded on, and type **copy tftp flash**, followed by the IP address of the router that has the image.

C. Telnet to the router that has the IOS image, type **copy flash tftp**, then Telnet to the other routers and type **copy tftp flash**.

D. Telnet to the TFTP server, and type **get flash**, followed by the IP address of the router that has the image. Then type **send flash** to load the image on the other routers.

54. What is the configuration mode used while setting up a summary route within a RIP-configured router?

A. Global Configuration mode

B. Router Configuration mode

C. Interface Configuration mode

D. User Configuration mode

55. In the following illustration, a network is shown for which you must create an access list. Network A needs to have an access list applied to its router, which allows packets only from Network B. Which would be the correct access list to apply to the incoming interface of the router on Network A?

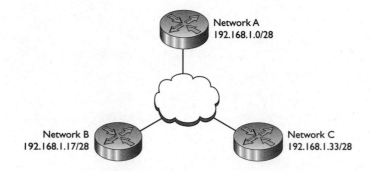

A. ACCESS-LIST 25 PERMIT 192.168.1.16 255.255.255.240

B. ACCESS-LIST 25 PERMIT 192.168.1.16 0.0.0.15

C. ACCESS-LIST 25 DENY 192.168.1.32 255.255.255.240

D. ACCESS-LIST 25 DENY 192.168.1.32 0.0.0.15

56. You are the administrator of a large corporate network, and you have been trying to configure the company's newly acquired T1 circuit from New York to Los Angeles. After configuring your routers, you notice that the T1 controller in your location (NY) is taking code violations. Referring to the following router output, what is the cause of the problem?

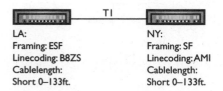

```
Router-NY#show controllers t1
T1 0/0 is down.
   Applique type is Channelized T1
   Cablelength is short 133
   Transmitter is sending remote alarm.
```

```
Receiver has loss of frame.
Version info Firmware: 19990702, FPGA: 6
Framing is SF, Line Code is AMI, Clock Source is Line.
Data in current interval (26 seconds elapsed):
    18594 Line Code Violations, 6234 Path Code Violations
    0 Slip Secs, 10 Fr Loss Secs, 10 Line Err Secs, 1
Degraded Mins
    0 Errored Secs, 0 Bursty Err Secs, 0 Severely Err Secs,
12 Unavail Secs
  Total Data (last 24 hours)
    196686 Line Code Violations, 38755 Path Code Violations,
    1 Slip Secs, 46 Fr Loss Secs, 181 Line Err Secs, 3
Degraded Mins,
    129 Errored Secs, 129 Bursty Err Secs, 0 Severely Err
Secs, 51 Unavail Secs
```

A. The T1 WIC is not installed correctly.

B. You have configured the T1 WIC, but you have not run the command:
   ```
   Router-NY># copy run start
   ```

C. The T1 WIC is receiving an AIS or Blue Alarm. This states that there is a problem upstream from your location in the network cloud.

D. The framing and line-coding scheme does not match. You must have both sides set to SF or ESF, and AMI or B8ZS.

57. Which two commands could you use to display the encapsulation types used on configured interfaces?

A. SHOW IPX INTERFACE

B. SHOW IPX INTERFACE BRIEF

C. SHOW IPX SERVERS

D. SHOW IPX TRAFFIC

58. In the following code examples, which interface is configured with an incorrect subnet mask?

```
interface e0
    ip address 10.1.1.1 255.255.255.0
```

```
interface s0

    ip address 145.45.10.1 255.255.255.0


interface s1

    ip address 205.200.16.65 255.240.0.0


interface s2

    ip address 130.10.11.1 255.255.255.0
```

A. E0

B. S0

C. S1

D. S2

59. You have just taken on a new job as network administrator, and you need to determine whether a specific router (designated as RouterA) has been configured to use the IGRP routing protocol. You enter the proper command and receive the following output:

```
Routing Protocol is igrp 300

Sending updates every 90 seconds, next due in 35 seconds

Invalid after 270 seconds, hold down 280, flushed after 360

Outgoing update filter list for all interfaces is not set

Incoming update filter list for all interfaces is not set

Default networks flagged in outgoing updates

Default networks accepted from incoming updates

IGRP metric weight K1=1, K2=0, K3=1, K5=0

IRGRP maximum hopcount 100

IRGRP maximum metric variance 1

Redistributing IGRP 300

Routing for Networks:

    181.6.0.0

    132.201.0.0
```

```
Routing Information Sources

  Gateway            Distance        Last Update

  132.201.100.1     100              0:00:51

Distance: (default is 100)
```

Which command did you use to determine the routing protocol in use?

A. SH ROUTER PROTOCOL at the RouterA# prompt

B. SH IP PROTOCOL at the RouterA(config)# prompt

C. SHOW PROTOCOL at the RouterA(config)# prompt

D. SHOW IP ROUTE at the RouterA# prompt

60. **Current Situation:** You wish to begin using IGRP within your network on the Ethernet router. Your network has IP subnets 207.79.211.0 and 207.94.12.0. The AS number will be 51.

Required Result: Show a valid series of configuration commands that will be required to set up the internal IGRP configuration to communicate with both networks.

Optional Desired Result: Include a valid configuration to reduce the possibility of routing loops occurring in the network.

Proposed Solution: Use the following configuration commands:

```
cisco (config)# route igrp 51

cisco (config-router)# network 207.79.211.0

cisco (config-router)# network 207.94.12.0

cisco (config-router)# ip split-horizon
```

A. The proposed solution fulfills the required result and the optional result.

B. The proposed solution does not fulfill the required result nor the optional result.

C. The proposed solution fulfills the required result but not the optional result.

D. The proposed solution does not fulfill the required result but does fulfill the optional result.

61. Is the following configuration allowed?

```
Router(config)#line vty 0 4

Router(config-line)#access-group 1 in
```

A. Yes, access lists can be applied to VTY lines.

B. Yes, as long as there is an access-list 1.

C. No, access lists cannot be applied to VTY lines.

D. No, access lists cannot be applied with the ACCESS-GROUP command.

62. Which method of switching has variable latency through the switch?

A. Fragment-free

B. Cut-through

C. Store-and-forward

D. Cut-forward

63. What must be done in order for certain commands to take effect via the Web browser interface?

A. The Refresh button on the browser must be clicked.

B. The Apply button on the Web browser must be clicked.

C. File | Save must be chosen from the browser's menu bar.

D. Nothing; all changes made via the Web browser take effect immediately.

64. What will happen if you unpack a router and install it without configuring the VTY lines, and you later need Telnet access to the router?

A. You will be able to Telnet to the router without entering a password.

B. You will be able to Telnet to the router, and the default password "Cisco" will be required.

C. You will not be able to connect to the router at all because it will not answer on the Telnet port.

D. You will connect the router but will get an error message because no password is configured, and you will not be allowed to attempt to log on.

65. When using TCP, the destination host acknowledges each packet. What triggers a retransmission of a packet from the source host?

   A. A lost packet message from the destination host.

   B. A timer on the source host system.

   C. An SNMP message from a router that the packet is lost.

   D. Packets are not retransmitted because TCP packets will eventually get there.

66. **Current Situation:** Acme, Inc. wishes to acquire a registered IP address that will accommodate their network, with approximately 200 hosts per network. Since all Class A and B networks have been taken, Acme is forced to purchase four contiguous Class C addresses.

   Required Result: Acme must be able to advertise on single network address space to the Internet, not four.

   Optional Desired Results:

   1. Acme also wishes to conserve valuable host addresses on their router-to-router connections.

   2. They wish to ensure that their configuration will not have to be altered as they expand.

   Proposed Solution: You sit down with Acme and show them how they can use Supernetting in order to consolidate their network advertisement to appear as one network. Furthermore, you show them how they can use Variable-Length Subnet Masking to conserve addresses, and you assure them that the configuration will not need to be altered with expansion.

   A. The proposed solution meets the required result and both of the optional results.

   B. The proposed solution meets the required result and one of the optional results.

   C. The proposed solution meets the required result and none of the optional results.

   D. The proposed solution does not meet the required result.

67. You are configuring a static route on a Cisco router using the IP ROUTE command for a network ID 203.23.2.0, subnet mask 255.255.255.0, and next hop router 203.23.11.1. You wish to configure an administrative distance that

indicates the source is extremely trustworthy. Which of the following indicates the highest trustworthiness of the source?

A. IP ROUTE 203.23.2.0 255.255.255.0 203.23.11.1 100

B. IP ROUTE 203.23.2.0 255.255.255.0 203.23.11.1 255

C. IP ROUTE 203.23.2.0 255.255.255.0 203.23.11.1 1

D. IP ROUTE 203.23.2.0 255.255.255.0 203.23.11.1 50

68. What command and syntax could be used to set IGRP route 207.79.15.0/24 to be the preferred path over IGRP route 207.79.12.0/24?

A. ```
   Cisco (config-if)# distance 100 207.79.15.0 0.0.0.255
   Cisco (config-if)# distance 95 207.79.12.0 0.0.0.255
   ```

B. ```
   Cisco (config)# distance 100 207.79.15.0 255.255.255.0
   Cisco (config)# distance 105 207.79.12.0 255.255.255.0
   ```

C. ```
   Cisco (config-if)# distance 100 207.79.15.0 0.0.0.255
   Cisco (config-if)# distance 105 207.79.12.0 0.0.0.255
   ```

D. ```
   Cisco (config)# distance 100 207.79.15.0 0.0.0.255
   Cisco (config)# distance 105 207.79.12.0 0.0.0.255
   ```

69. You have just created VLAN 100 on a Catalyst 5000 and need to assign ports 10 to 20 in module 3 to this VLAN. What CLI command should you use?

A. ASSIGN VLAN 100 3/10-20

B. SET VLAN 100 10-20

C. SET VLAN 100 3/10-20

D. SET VLAN 100 STATIC 3/10-20

70. On your E0 interface on your Cisco router, you have two subinterfaces configured: one running arpa on IPX network 0xA, and another running novell-ether on IPX network 0xB. Your IPX routing table contains 75 entries. How many IPX RIP packets will be sent out the E0 interface at each update interval?

A. 0

B. 1

C. 2

D. 4

ANSWERS

1. ☑ **B.** These commands accomplish all the desired results.

   ☒ **A** is incorrect because these commands allow you to view the routing table but do not accomplish the other results. The configuration context should be global non-configure. The NVRAM parameter does not exist. **C** is incorrect because it starts in global mode but is changed prior to executing the CLEAR IP ROUTE command. The BACKUP command does not exist. **D** is incorrect because viewing the current running configuration is accomplished but the commands shift out of context into the config-if mode and the remaining commands are voided.

2. ☑ **B.** All workstations on the Ethernet switch are in the same collision domain and have to process the frames. The wireless access point is using all its CPU power through processing and deciding that these frames are not for it and that it cannot forward frames from its mobile clients. The correct action would be to do the re-imaging using unicast over a single collision domain.

   ☒ **A** is incorrect because although the router would prevent a broadcast being propagated, it would not prevent clients from using the network. **C** is incorrect. The router has enough CPU power to deal with the multicast and process frames destined for the head office. **D** is incorrect because the Ethernet switch will forward all broadcast frames to each of its ports configured to be in the same collision domain.

3. ☑ **C.** What appears on the screen is a printout of the NETSTAT command. You will notice on the left is the protocol listing, the middle is the local address, followed by the foreign or remote address, and finally by the state of the connection.

   ☒ **A** is incorrect because the HOSTNAME command would only have listed Tamara1001 as the output. **B** is incorrect because the ARP –A command output would include the ARP cache of the local system. **D** is incorrect because an FTP listing is similar to a directory listing, showing file names, size, and other information pertaining to the files.

4. ☑ **C.** All of the images here have a hub-spoke configuration, but only C is correct. Looking at design C, you may think there is a problem with the DLCI

numbering scheme. Remember, Frame Relay DLCIs hold local significance only. The Frame Relay switch at the home office (shown in the following illustration), will be the one to take care of switching the packets from one location to another unless the home office FRAD has that capability.

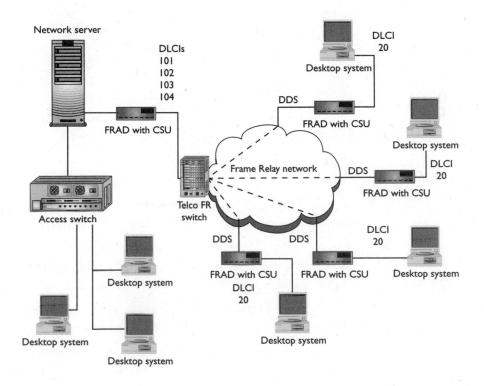

☒   **A** is incorrect. This design cannot be used because the remote office lines are analog. Frame works specifically over dedicated digital circuits. **B** is incorrect. This design cannot be used because of the access line. While the request was for the most available bandwidth, a T1 circuit is the highest access line currently available for Frame Relay. There is a spec for a T3 access line in Frame Relay, but it is not widely used. **D** is incorrect. This design cannot be used because the desktop systems at the home office would not be assigned DLCI numbers.

5.   ☑   **C.** SH ACCESS-LIST 100 will display only the extended access list 100.

☒   **A** is incorrect. Although SH IP INT will show you which access lists are applied to an interface, it does not show the access lists themselves. **B** is incorrect because SH ACCESS-LISTS will show all access lists in the router, not just extended IP access list 100. **D** is incorrect because SH INT shows no access list information.

6. ☑ **B.** The 11.0.0.0 network will accommodate 20,000 hosts easily, as well as meeting the requirement of not subnetting. You cannot, however, maximize the number of networks without subnetting the address.

☒ **A**, **C**, and **D** are incorrect because the required result and one optional result were met.

7. ☑ **B**, **C**, and **D** are correct. The debug indicates the subinterface in the top right and the DCLI in the top left. It also shows that the PVC is currently inactive, therefore the circuit is down.

☒ **A** is incorrect because in pkts=0 indicates that no packets have been received on this circuit.

8. ☑ **C.** Global Configuration mode is the mode shown. The *(config)* portion of the prompt tells you that you are in Global Configuration mode.

☒ **A** is incorrect because the prompt would look like this: Router>. **B** is incorrect because the prompt would look like this: Router#. **D** is incorrect because the prompt would look like this: Router(config-if)#.

9. ☑ **C.** STP will selectively block certain ports that are causing bridging loops, which is its normal function. When this occurs, the port LED will turn amber.

☒ **A** is incorrect because port LEDs give no indication of VLAN configuration. **B** is incorrect because full-duplex ports will have a green LED in FDUP Mode. **D** is incorrect because amber lights are not used in UTL Mode.

10. ☑ **B.** The router will first attempt to boot from the specified TFTP server and image, followed by the specified Flash image, and finally the image in ROM.

☒ **A** is technically correct, but is not the most complete option. **C** lists the proper procedure, but in the incorrect order. **D** is incorrect because the last command entered has no effect on the boot sequence, except that becomes the last option.

11. ☑ **A.** The SHOW PORT command is used to troubleshoot port security problems on a Catalyst 5000 switch.

☒   **B** is not correct because the SHOW INTERFACE command is used on IOS-base switches. **C** is incorrect because the SHOW MAC-ADDRESS-TABLE SECURITY command is used on IOS-base switches. **D** is incorrect because the word SECURITY is not part of the command.

12.   ☑   **B.** Slow convergence is the source of the inaccurate information being propagated through the network.

☒   **A** is incorrect. Split horizon is a means of avoiding routing loops by not sending update information back the same path it came in. **C** is incorrect. Desynchronization is not a term commonly used in routing. **D** is incorrect because poison reverse is a means by which a router can notify neighboring routers that a router is down. It sets the number of hops to the unconnected router to the number that represents infinity. (For example, using RIP with a maximum hop count of 15, infinity is represented by 16.)

13.   ☑   **B.** With Legacy DDR, the call destinations are directly associated with a physical interface.

☒   **A** is incorrect because it is not a valid type of DDR. **C** is not correct because Dialer Profiles separate the dial configuration from the physical interface. **D** is incorrect because it is not a valid type of DDR.

14.   ☑   **D.** The node address is 0000.8045.1700. An IPX address is always written with the network number first, followed by the node address. A socket number is sometimes appended after a colon.

☒   **A** and **C** are incorrect because they are incomplete forms of the node address. **B** is incorrect because it is the network number plus the first four bytes of the IPX host address. An easy way to figure out the IPX host address is to count backward (from right to left) the first 32 bits of the address. Anything that remains is the network address, usually with leading zeroes suppressed.

15.   ☑   **C.** When the traffic leaves Workstation A, it initially goes to the Ethernet 0 port, since the destination is in a different broadcast domain. The router then passes the traffic to Ethernet 1, which then sends it out to VLAN4 to Workstation C.

☒   **A** is incorrect. The traffic can only get from VLAN 3 to VLAN 4 by going through the router. **B** is incorrect because Workstation A and Workstation C are in different broadcast domains and cannot send data directly to each other. It must go through the router first. **D** is incorrect because VLAN 3 cannot send data directly to the Ethernet 1 port. VLAN 3 is connected to the Ethernet 0 port and can only send data to the router via that port.

16. ☑ **B.** In order to have each client of the engineering department on a separate collision domain, you would have to replace the bridge with a switch. However, for all clients to be in separate broadcast domain, you would have to configure the switch so that all the clients are in a separate VLAN.

☒ **A** is incorrect. Although clients in a separate VLAN can only talk to each other through a Layer 3 device, the router itself would not create separate collision and broadcast domains. **C** is incorrect because a repeater would put all clients on the same collision and broadcast domain. **D** is incorrect because VLANs are the technique used on the switch to create separate broadcast domains for the clients.

17. ☑ **D.** Press CTRL-Z. This is one of those tricky questions that require you to pay very close attention. From Interface Configuration mode, only the CTRL-Z keystroke will return you to Privileged EXEC mode.

☒ **A** is incorrect because CTRL-A is the incorrect command. **B** and **C** are also incorrect. Typing **exit** or pressing CTRL-Z from Global Configuration mode will return you to Privileged EXEC mode, but when you are in Interface Configuration mode, typing **exit** returns you to Global Configuration mode.

18. ☑ **A.** Both requirements are met. If an Ethernet reference address goes down, the ability to reach the router remotely is also down. By using a virtual terminal reference address, which will never go down unless the router is turned off, the risk of not being able to communicate with the router eliminated.

☒ **B** and **D** are incorrect. These solutions do configure an IP unnumbered port, but the use of the loopback address is not implemented. In the event that either referenced port goes down, remote communication is lost. **C** is incorrect because this solution fulfills neither requirement.

19. ☑ **B.** In order for an analog modem to dial into a PRI interface, a digital modem card must be installed and configured.

☒ **A**, **C**, and **D** are incorrect because digital modems are required in order for an analog modem to connect to a router via a PRI interface.

20. ☑ **D.** By increasing the receive window size on the router, you are going to be pushing data at a faster rate to Accounting1 and Accounting2 than before.

The problem was that Accounting1 already was unable to handle the speed at which the packets were being sent. Increasing the receive window size on the router will in the end cause even more packet retransmits.

☒   **A, B,** and **C** are incorrect because the required result was not met.

21.   ☑   **D.** This command allows you to see what multilink bundles have been created on the router.

☒   **A** is incorrect because this is what the command SHOW CALL ACTIVE VOICE is used for. **B** is incorrect because there isn't a SHOW PPP STATISTICS command. **C** is incorrect because this is not a valid Cisco IOS command.

22.   ☑   **A.** The 240 mask allows for up to 14 networks and 14 hosts per network.

☒   **B** is incorrect. It is an illegal mask for a Class C address. **C** is incorrect. It is an illegal mask for a Class C address, and the subnetting is being performed in the wrong octet. **D** is incorrect because 224 will only allow for six hosts.

23.   ☑   **C.** By switching from a distance vector to a link-state protocol, you can expect to eliminate the periodic broadcast of updates to the routing table from one router to another, as link-state protocols use event-triggered updates. Convergence is faster with link state protocols because of this. However, link-state protocols generally use more memory and processor time than distance vector protocols, so you can expect to accomplish the first two desired results, but not the last.

☒   **A, B,** and **D** are incorrect. Because two of the desired results are achieved, the other answer are incorrect.

24.   ☑   **A.** This IPX SAP filter list would filter SAP packets from network 200 with a service type of 7. All other packets would be allowed. The filter may be applied to the input of R2's e0, the output of R2's e1, the input of R1's e1, or the output of R1's e0.

☒   **B** is incorrect because print services in network 200 would be contained in SAP packets from network 200. The access list shown here blocks packets from network 100. **C** is incorrect. Although the access list itself is correct, it is being applied to the input of R1's e0. This is in the opposite direction that the packets would be flowing from network 200 to 100. **D** is incorrect because the network we are trying to block print services from is network 200, and the network specified in this access list is 100.

25. ☑ **D.** Loading images from a local TFTP server is a great solution for this customer, because updating each IOS image on each router is much more bothersome than updating the image on the TFTP server.

☒ **B** is not the best answer because it provides no failover way of obtaining an IOS image. The best practice is to update the IOS image on the TFTP server as often as your client requires, and periodically update the IOS image in each router's Flash, so that all critical functions of the router will continue in the event of a TFTP server failure. **C** and **D** are incorrect. ROM is always a last option, and this image will only be loaded if both the TFTP server image and Flash image are unavailable.

26. ☑ **D.** Hold down the Mode button while powering up the switch.

☒ **A** is incorrect because a Catalyst 1900 switch can be recovered if you forget the password. **B** is incorrect because no string typed into the password prompt will recover the switch. **C** is incorrect because you would not be able to download a new file to the switch if you can't get past the password prompt.

27. ☑ **A.** This is a partial mesh topology.

☒ **B** is incorrect because in a full mesh, each node would have a connection to each of the other nodes. **C** is incorrect because a hub-and-spoke topology will have all nodes connecting to one central node. **D** is incorrect because a star topology is the same as hub and spoke in this example.

28. ☑ **B.** The proper mode is the global configuration mode and the syntax for the IP NAME-SERVER command is correct.

☒ **A** is incorrect because it attempts to configure a specific interface for the DNS lookup feature. Subsequent command is in the improper config-if mode. **C** is incorrect because it attempts to configure in a config-router mode for the DNS lookup feature. Subsequent command is in the improper config-router mode. **D** is incorrect. It does not execute the IP DOMAIN-LOOKUP enabling command. It may be that the feature is already on but, without using the SHOW HOST command, you don't know if it is enabled.

29. ☑ **B.** Outside of North America and Japan, PRI ISDN service is based on the E1 standard and is comprised of 32 channels, using 30 for B channels, one for a D channel, and one reserved for the telephone company. Therefore, in Europe you will need to account for these differences, but in Japan ISDN will be virtually the same.

☒ **A** is incorrect because Japan uses the same T1 base ISDN PRI service as North America. **C** is not correct because ISDN in Europe will be based on the E1 standard and have more B channels. Language may be an issue, but it will not be the only difference you have to face. **D** is incorrect because the E1-based PRI service is comprised of 32 channels, not 31. The extra channel is reserved for use by the telephone company.

30. ☑ **A.** By enabling subinterfaces on the IPX network's default gateway, the router can now route between clients using different encapsulation types, even on the same subnet. The NetWare 3.11 clients will be able to communicate among themselves without the router's intervention, and any clients upgraded to 4.12 will communicate among themselves in a similar manner. If a 3.11 client needs to speak with a 4.12 client, it will see that the 4.12 clients are now on a different IPX network and simply send the frames to their default gateway, which performs the data link translation. The 3.11 clients may be upgraded over several nights.

    ☒ **B, C**, and **D** are incorrect. The proposed solution produces the required result and the optional result.

31. ☑ **C** and **E** are correct. Once the PC is connected, the port must go through the four states of the STP (blocking, listening, learning, and forwarding), which takes about 50 seconds. During this time the request for an IP address from the DHCP server has timed out. Spanning-Tree PortFast will allow a port to immediately be forwarding upon startup. This will allow devices to get an IP address because the DHCP request will not have time to timeout. One thing to keep in mind is that PortFast *must* be only used on end devices. It should *never* be used on ports going to other switches or hubs.

    ☒ **B** is incorrect because it would not be practical to locate a DHCP server at every remote site. **A** is incorrect. Although it may have looked as though the WAN links were causing problems, a simple ping would have verified that this was not the case. **D** is incorrect. Although it was Spanning-Tree causing the problem, you must never disable Spanning-Tree. When Spanning-Tree is disabled, you are not protected from the inevitable configuration mistakes that create Layer 2 loops in the network.

32. ☑ **D.** SHOW ?. You can always type as much of a command as you know to find out what options are available.

☒ **A** and **B** are not valid commands, and **C** is incorrect because the command SHOW IP ? will give all of the available arguments for SHOW IP, not for all the SHOW commands.

33. ☑ **D.** Port 443 is the HTTPS port. By opening this port up to traffic, you are allowing users to connect to your server and access the security connection.

☒ **A** is incorrect. Port 161 is used for SNMP. **B** is incorrect. Port 80 is used for standard HTTP traffic, not HTTPS. **C** is incorrect, as Port 8080 is often used for a proxy server, but not HTTPS.

34. ☑ **C.** The [A] Add VLAN option will allow you to specify a new VLAN, and the [E] VLAN Membership option will allow you to add ports to your newly created VLAN.

☒ **A** is incorrect because you need to create a VLAN with the [A] option before you can add members to it. **B** is not correct because the [T] option is not used to create VLANs; it is used for trunk configurations between switches. **D** is incorrect because once the VLAN is created, the [M] option will modify your initial VLAN settings, but will not allow you to add members to the VLAN.

35. ☑ **F.** CHAP authentication is the requirement here, but remember that you must first enable PPP on the interface. You would configure CHAP with the PPP CHAP command.

☒ **A** is incorrect because PPP should be enabled on the serial interface. **C** is incorrect because PPP should be enabled only on the serial interface. **E** is incorrect because A is not a correct answer. **G** is incorrect because not all of these answer options are correct. **B** and **D** are incorrect, as these commands have already been addressed.

36. ☑ **B.** The proposed solution would produce the required result, because a standard IP named access list is all that is needed on the border router to block source addresses. The three extended IP named access lists on the interior routers will be all that is needed to allow only mail, Web, and DNS traffic into those routers. The first optional result is obtained because named IP access lists can share the same name across routers. The second optional result is not possible because only one access list local to a router can have the same name. Even if one access list is extended and one is standard, they still must have unique names.

☒ **A** is incorrect because two lists sharing the same name cannot be created on the border router Stargate. **C** is incorrect because all of the interior routers are able to share the same access list name. **D** is incorrect because the required result is met.

37.   ☑   **D.** 255.255.255.255 is an invalid subnet mask, and the 'ip' portion of the syntax is missing on int s0.

☒   **A** is incorrect because the configuration is wrong. **B** is incorrect because the mask on s0 is configured incorrectly. **C** is incorrect because there are also mistakes on interface e0.

38.   ☑   **C.** The first entry in the "flags" column states the method of obtaining the host entry (perm = manually configured and temp = dynamically learned via DNS). The second entry indicates the aging status of the entry. (OK means that the entry is still valid and being used.)

☒   **A** is incorrect because the entries can be changed via the DNS dynamic method or the manual configuration method. Also, the HOST command pertains to address resolution, not to connection status. **B** is incorrect. The first portion of the answer is correct, but the connection status is not pertinent to the HOST command. **D** is also incorrect. Virtual connections or sessions relate to the VTY status and the SESSION command, not to the HOST command.

39.   ☑   **B.** The command entered at Router B, CONFIG T, will allow you to configure Router B from your terminal.

☒   **A** is incorrect because the command entered at Router A to show the routing table has incorrect syntax. The correct command is SH IP ROUTE. **C** is incorrect because the command entered at Router B, ROUTE IP 0.0.0.0 203.21.30.0, is wrong. The correct syntax is IP ROUTE, and the entry should contain both a network number and subnet mask of 0.0.0.0, thus the correct entry is IP ROUTE 0.0.0.0 0.0.0.0 203.21.30.0. **D** and **E** are incorrect because only B is the correct answer.

40.   ☑   **D.** CTRL-P and UP ARROW will show the last command entered. Repeated pressing of these keys will show the last 10 commands entered at that level of the router. The number of commands can be configured, but 10 is the default.

☒   **A** and **B** are incorrect. CTRL-L and CTRL-M do not have any documented function. **C** is also incorrect. CTRL-N is used to move through the buffer of previous commands in a forward manner, whereas CTRL-P will move backward. It's easy enough to remember these commands: P for Previous, N for Next.

41.   ☑   **C.** This command will allow you to turn off all current debugging on the router. This can also be shortened as ROUTER#UN ALL.

☒ **A**, **B**, and **D** are incorrect because they are not valid Cisco IOS commands.

42. ☑ **C.** NCP, the NetWare Core Protocol, resides at Layer 7 in the OSI reference model.

☒ **A**, **B**, and **D** are incorrect. All the other options are protocols in the TCP/IP suite, and do not apply to IPX.

43. ☑ **A** and **C** are correct. Bridges, like repeaters, amplify the electrical signal between two physical segments, thereby extending the physical media. They also isolate the local traffic on ether side of the bridge.

☒ **B** is incorrect because a bridge does not logically separate LANs, and broadcast traffic is forwarded to all nodes on the logical LAN. **D** is incorrect because bridges do not provide security. However, they can provide protocol conversion between Token Ring and Ethernet LANs.

44. ☑ **C.** The correct command is SET TRUNK *mod/port type* DOT1Q.

☒ **A** is incorrect because the wrong keyword is used for 802.1q encapsulation. The correct keyword is dot1q. **B** is incorrect because SET ENCAPSULATION is not a valid command on the Catalyst 5000 series switch. **D** is incorrect because this is an IOS switching command and would not work on a Catalyst 5000.

45. ☑ **B** and **D** are correct. The reference points are identified correctly in illustrations B and D. The terminal equipment and network termination devices are also in the correct order.

☒ **A** is incorrect because the reference points are backward and the network termination equipment is switched. **C** is incorrect because the analog phone is a TE2 that requires a TA, therefore the TE1 should be a TA. Also, the network termination equipment is switched.

46. ☑ **D.** The figure displayed is of an ARP output.

☒ **A** is incorrect. A ping output would show a single IP address and the time it takes for a reply, if available. **B** is also incorrect because an FTP session is a direct connect session that would display files that may be downloaded. **C** is incorrect because a DNS lookup cannot be done from the command prompt.

47. ☑ **C.** A flashing green and amber LED indicates frame errors on a particular port.

☒ **A** is incorrect. Port 4 might be solid amber if the console port failed during the POST. However, this scenario indicates that the LED is flashing, not solid amber. **B** is incorrect. A solid amber port LED might also indicate that port is being blocked by Spanning-Tree, but in the question scenario, the LED is alternating between green and amber. **D** is incorrect because port LEDs do not give any indication of whether they are trunk ports or not.

48. ☑ **C.** The administrative distance is used to determine the trustworthiness of a routing information source. Each routing protocol or route type is designated a specified administrative distance. The lower the value of the administrative distance, the more trustworthy the source is deemed to be. Static routes are given the default distance of 1, IGRP's default distance is 100, OSPF's default distance 110, and RIP's default distance is 120.

☒ **A** and **B** are not ordered from most to least trustworthy. **D** is incorrect as IGRP, RIP, OSPF and Static are equally trustworthy.

49. ☑ **B.** The configuration is entirely correct, the IP addressing is correct, and all the DLCIs are configured correctly. Implicit statements have been set for the cisco LMI type, but Inverse ARP works only on multipoint connections, not point-to-point.

☒ **A, C,** and **D** are incorrect. The proposed solution meets the required result, but only one of the optional results.

50. ☑ **A.** The three sources for loading the IOS image onto a Cisco router are from a TFTP server, from Flash memory, or from ROM.

☒ **B, C,** and **D** are incorrect. RAM is volatile, meaning that it is erased when the router is turned off, and is therefore not used for storage.

51. ☑ **A** and **C** are correct. You must have point-to-point connections between stations, and transmit circuits must be wired directly to the receive circuits at the other end.

☒ **B** is incorrect because the connection cannot be multipoint. **D** is incorrect because hubs cannot be used for full-duplex operation.

52. ☑ **C.** Installing the Standard Edition software only allows for one login account with Read-Write privileges. VLAN support is not included, and the interface is a menu-driven interface, not an IOS-like CLI.

☒ **A, B,** and **D** are incorrect. The proposed solution produces neither the required result nor the optional result.

53. ☑ **C.** From the router with the image you want to distribute, copy the image to the TFTP server. Then go to the routers on which you would like to load the image and copy the image from the TFTP server.

    ☒ **A** is incorrect because it is the reverse order from what you are trying to accomplish. **B** and **D** are not allowed commands.

54. ☑ **C.** The summary route command line CISCO (CONFIG-IF)# IP SUMMARY ROUTE 121.10.2.0 255.255.255.0 will properly configure the interface to summarize the class B network addresses throughout the third octet of this network.

    ☒ **A** is incorrect because this mode is for more general configuration of the router. **B** is incorrect because this mode is used for the initial configuration of the RIP protocol. **D** is incorrect because no configuration can take place in the User mode. This mode is only for the observing of the router configuration and status.

55. ☑ **B.** 192.168.1.16 is the network address of network B. 0.0.0.15 is the correct wildcard mask for network B. Because all access lists have an implicit DENY ANY at the end of them, all other traffic will be blocked.

    ☒ **A** is incorrect because 255.255.255.240 is not the correct wildcard mask for network B. 255.255.255.240 is the correct netmask, which should not be confused with wildcard mask. **C** is incorrect because a DENY rule, even if written to correctly deny packets from network C, does not allow packets from network B. Furthermore, the wildcard mask shown here is a netmask for network C and not a wildcard mask. **D** is incorrect. Although this rule would correctly block all packets from network C, it would be followed by the implicit DENY ANY rule and block all packets from everywhere else, including network B.

56. ☑ **D.** When configuring a T1 WIC, you must make sure that you have noted what line-coding method to use and what framing is being used on the circuit. Which methods your circuit uses will depend on your provider and what they can support. Some legacy Telco equipment may only support SF (D4)/AMI. Most T1 circuits today are running ESF/B8ZS.

    ☒ **A** is incorrect because you could not configure the controller without it being installed correctly. **B** is incorrect. Although it is recommended that you save your config to the NVRAM, the config in RAM would function properly. **C** is incorrect because the controller is not in AIS.

57. ☑ **A** and **B** are correct. SHOW IPX INTERFACE and SHOW IPX INTERFACE BRIEF will both display the encapsulation types being used on all interfaces currently configured for IPX.

    ☒ **C** is incorrect because SHOW IPX SERVERS will display the router's current SAP database. **D** is incorrect because SHOW IPX TRAFFIC will show a basic IPX traffic analysis.

58. ☑ **C.** Interface S1's Class C address cannot be subnetted in any octet except the last.

    ☒ **A, B**, and **D** have correctly configured subnet masks.

59. ☑ **B.** To display information regarding which protocol is in use and the routing information sources as shown in the output, you use the SH IP PROTOCOL command at the RouterA(config)# prompt. This command displays parameters, filters, and network information about the entire router, and displays the algorithm that is used to calculate the routing metric for IGRP.

    ☒ **A, C**, and **D** are the incorrect commands.

60. ☑ **C.** The AS is configured properly and in the proper mode and so are the networks. However, the split horizon should be configured in a config-if (interface mode), not in a router configuration mode.

    ☒ **B** is incorrect because the required result is met. **A** and **D** are incorrect because the optional result is not met.

61. ☑ **D.** Access lists can be applied to VTY lines, but the ACCESS-CLASS command must be used. In this example, the code listed is not a possible configuration for a Cisco router.

    ☒ **A** and **B** are partially correct in that access lists can be applied to VTY lines but incorrect in saying that the configuration shown would be allowed. **C** is incorrect. There is a way to apply an access list to VTY lines, but the example shown is not the correct method.

62. ☑ **C.** The store-and-forward switching method has variable latency through the switch because Ethernet frames vary in length.

    ☒ **A, B**, and **D** are incorrect because they do not store the entire frame before forwarding.

63. ☑ **B.** The Apply button on the Web browser must be clicked.

☒ **A** is incorrect. Clicking the Refresh button on the browser window would have no effect on the switch accepting any changes you made. **C** is incorrect because choosing File | Save would save a copy of the current HTML file to your PC's hard drive. **D** is also incorrect. Some changes take effect immediately, but others require you to press the Apply button. It's a good habit to click this button whether you need to or not.

64. ☑ **D.** You will be allowed to connect to the router, but a message saying "Password required, but none set" will be displayed.

☒ **A** is incorrect because, for security reasons, a password must be set on VTY lines. **B** is incorrect because there is no default password on VTY lines. **C** is incorrect because the router will respond to calls on the Telnet port with an error message, giving the person attempting to connect a reason why he or she cannot connect to the router through a Telnet session.

65. ☑ **B.** There is a retransmission timer on the source host for each packet that is sent. If the timer reaches zero before an acknowledgment is received, the packet is retransmitted.

☒ **A** is incorrect. Unless the packet is received by the destination host, there is no way for the destination host to know it was to receive the package. **C** is incorrect because the routers have no way of knowing how many packets are being sent; they only look at the protocol and destination address of a packet. **D** is incorrect. Even though TCP is connection oriented and reliable, it still loses packets.

66. ☑ **C.** Only the required result was met. Supernetting will solve Acme's need to advertise under one address. However, if you further subnet their networking using VLSM, then you will not have enough host addresses per network left. Re-configuration will be necessary.

☒ **A**, **B**, and **D** are incorrect. The proposed solution meets the required result, but neither of the optional results.

67. ☑ **C.** The administrative distance indicates trustworthiness of the source as a numeric value from 0 to 255. The higher the number, the lower the trustworthiness, and the lower the number, the higher the degree of trustworthiness.

☒ **A**, **B**, and **D** are incorrect. An administrative distance of 1 (which is the default administrative distance for static routes) indicates a high degree of trustworthiness. Therefore, C is the correct answer.

68. ☑ **D.** Using the smaller Administrative distance value, in global mode, with an inverted mask of 0.0.0.255 (this is a directed broadcast to the network) is the proper command and syntax.

    ☒ **A** is incorrect because it uses an interface mode to configure and because it has the higher value on the preferred route, making it the non-preferred route. **B** is incorrect because it does not use an inverted netmask, which is improper syntax. **C** is incorrect because it still assigns the preferred route in an interface configuration mode.

69. ☑ **C.** The syntax for this command is SET VLAN *vlan_num mod_num/port_num* with *vlan_num* equal to 100, *mod_num* equal to 3, and *port_num* equal to 10–20.

    ☒ **A** is incorrect because ASSIGN is not a valid CLI command for this function. **B** is incorrect because the module number is not specified. **D** is incorrect because STATIC is not a valid parameter for this command.

70. ☑ **D.** RIP and SAP updates must be duplicated for each encapsulation type configured on an interface. Each RIP update may contain a total of 50 routes.

    ☒ To advertise all 75 routes, two IPX RIP packets will be required, per subinterface, for a total of four packets. Consequently, **A**, **B**, and **C** are all incorrect.

Glossary

A TO *Z*

10Base2   Ethernet specification using 50-ohm thin coaxial cable and a signaling rate of 10-Mbps baseband.

10Base5   Ethernet specification using standard (thick) 50-ohm baseband coaxial cable and a signaling rate of 10-Mbps baseband.

10BaseFL   Ethernet specification using fiber-optic cabling and a signaling rate of 10-Mbps baseband, and FOIRL.

10BaseT   Ethernet specification using two pairs of twisted-pair cabling (Category 3, 4, or 5): one pair for transmitting data and the other for receiving data, and a signaling rate of 10-Mbps baseband.

10Broad36   Ethernet specification using broadband coaxial cable and a signaling rate of 10-Mbps baseband.

100BaseFX   Fast Ethernet specification using two strands of multimode fiber-optic cable per link and a signaling rate of 100-Mbps baseband. A 100BaseFXlink cannot exceed 400 meters in length.

100BaseT   Fast Ethernet specification using UTP wiring and a signaling rate of 100-Mbps baseband. 100BaseT sends link pulses out on the wire when there is no data traffic present.

100BaseT4   Fast Ethernet specification using four pairs of Category 3, 4, or 5 UTP wiring and a signaling rate of100-Mbps baseband. The maximum length of a 100BaseT4 segment is 100 meters.

100BaseTX   Fast Ethernet specification using two pairs of UTP or STP wiring and 100-Mbps baseband signaling. One pair of wires is used to receive data; the other is used to transmit. A 100BaseTX segment cannot exceed 100 meters in length.

AAL   *See* Asynchronous Transfer Mode Adaptation Layer.

AARP   *See* AppleTalk Address Resolution Protocol.

access list   A sequential list of statements in a router configuration that identify network traffic for various purposes, including traffic and route filtering.

acknowledgment   Notification sent from one network device to another to acknowledge that a message or group of messages has been received. Sometimes abbreviated ACK. Opposite of NAK.

active hub   A multiport device that repeats and amplifies LAN signals at the Physical layer.

active monitor   A network device on a token ring that is responsible for managing ring operations. The active monitor ensures that tokens are not lost, or that frames do not circulate indefinitely on the ring.

address   A numbering convention used to identify a unique entity or location on a network.

address mapping   Technique that allows different protocols to operate together by associating addresses from one format with those of another.

address mask   A string of bits, which, when combined with an address, describes which portion of an address refers to the network or subnet and which part refers to the host.

address resolution   A technique for resolving differences between computer addressing schemes. Address resolution most often specifies a method for mapping Network layer addresses to Data-Link layer addresses.

Address Resolution Protocol (ARP)   Internet protocol used to map an IP address to a MAC address.

administrative distance   A rating of the preferability of a routing information source. Administrative distance is expressed as a value between 0 and 255. The higher the value, the lower the preference.

advertising   A process in which a router sends routing or service updates at frequent intervals so that other routers on the network can maintain lists of usable routes or services.

algorithm   A specific process for arriving at a solution to a problem.

American National Standards Institute (ANSI)   An organization of representatives of corporate, government, and other entities that coordinates standards-related activities, approves U.S. national standards, and develops positions for the United States in international standards organizations.

ANSI   *See* American National Standards Institute.

AppleTalk   A suite of communications protocols developed by Apple Computer for allowing communication among their devices over a network.

AppleTalk Address Resolution Protocol (AARP)   The protocol that maps a data-link address to an AppleTalk network address.

Application layer   Layer 7 of the OSI reference model. This layer provides services to end-user application processes such as electronic mail, file transfer, and terminal emulation.

ARP   *See* Address Resolution Protocol.

AS   *See* autonomous system.

asynchronous transfer mode (ATM)   An international standard for cell relay suitable for carrying multiple service types (such as voice, video, or data) in fixed-length (53-byte) cells. Fixed-length cells allow cell processing to occur in hardware, thereby reducing latency.

Asynchronous Transfer Mode Adaptation Layer (AAL)   Service-dependent sublayer of the Data-Link layer. The function of the AAL is to accept data from different applications and present it to the ATM layer in 48-byte ATM segments.

Asynchronous Transfer Mode (ATM) Forum   International organization founded in 1991 by Cisco Systems, NET/ADAPTIVE, Northern Telecom, and Sprint to develop and promote standards-based implementation agreements for ATM technology.

asynchronous transmission   Describes digital signals that are transmitted without precise clocking or synchronization.

ATM   *See* asynchronous transfer mode.

attachment unit interface (AUI)   An interface between an MAU and a NIC (network interface card) described in the IEEE 802.3 specification. AUI often refers to the physical port to which an AUI cable attaches.

AUI   *See* attachment unit interface.

autonomous system (AS)   A group of networks under a common administration that share in a common routing strategy.

BackboneFast   BackboneFast is a technology designed as a complementary one to UplinkFast. UplinkFast quickly responds to failures on links directly connected to end-node switches, but it can do nothing if indirect failures in the core of the backbone occur. In such a case BackboneFast will be helpful. BackboneFast can reduce the indirect failover delay from 30 to 50 seconds (with default parameters), but it does not eliminate forwarding delay and provides no assistance in case of a direct failure.

backoff   The retransmission delay used by contention-based MAC protocols such as Ethernet, after a network node determines that the physical medium is already in use.

Backward Explicit Congestion Notification (BECN)   A Frame Relay network facility that allows switches in the network to advise DTE devices of congestion. The BECN bit is set in frames traveling in the opposite direction of frames encountering a congested path.

bandwidth   The difference between the highest and lowest frequencies available for network signals. The term may also describe the throughput capacity of a network link or segment.

baseband   A network technology in which a single carrier frequency is used. Ethernet is a common example of a baseband network technology.

Basic Rate Interface (BRI)   ISDN interface consisting of two B channels and one D channel for circuit-switched communication. ISDN BRI can carry voice, video, and data.

baud   Unit of signaling speed equal to the number of separate signal elements transmitted in one second. Baud is synonymous with bits per second (bps), as long as each signal element represents exactly one bit.

bearer (B) channel   An ISDN term meaning a full-duplex, 64-Kbps channel used to send user data.

BECN   *See* Backward Explicit Congestion Notification.

best-effort delivery   Describes a network system that does not use a system of acknowledgment to guarantee reliable delivery of information.

BGP   *See* Border Gateway Protocol.

BNC *See* British Naval Connector.

Bootstrap Protocol (BOOTP)   Part of the TCP/IP suite of protocols, used by a network node to determine the IP address of its Ethernet interfaces, in order to boot from a network server.

Border Gateway Protocol (BGP)   An interdomain path-vector routing protocol. BGP exchanges reachability information with other BGP systems. It is defined by RFC 1163.

binary   A numbering system in which there are only two digits, ones and zeros.

BPDU *See* Bridge Protocol Data Unit.

BRI *See* Basic Rate Interface.

bridge   Device that connects and forwards packets between two network segments that use the same data-link communications protocol. Bridges operate at the Data-Link layer of the OSI reference model. A bridge will filter, forward, or flood an incoming frame based on the MAC address of the frame.

Bridge Protocol Data Unit   Every few seconds every bridge creates a Bridge Protocol Data Unit (BPDU). BPDU is a special multicast frame that alerts the network to the bridge's presence, its configuration, and any changes to the network that have occurred. All bridges have a unique identifier, which consists of a bridge priority and the MAC address of the bridge. Two different types of BPDUs exist: Configuration BPDUs that are originated by the Root Bridge and radiate away from it; and Topology Change Notification BPDUs (TCN BPDUs) that flow to the Root Bridge to warn it about the topology change.

British Naval Connector (BNC) connector   Standard connector used to connect coaxial cable to an MAU or line card.

broadband   A data transmission system that multiplexes multiple independent signals onto one cable. Also, in telecommunications, any channel with a bandwidth greater than 4KHz. In LAN terminology, a coaxial cable using analog signaling.

broadcast   Data packet addressed to all nodes on a network. Broadcasts are identified by a broadcast address that matches all addresses on the network.

broadcast address   Special address reserved for sending a message to all stations. At the Data-Link layer, a broadcast address is a MAC destination address of all ones.

broadcast domain   The group of all devices that will receive the same broadcast frame originating from any device within the group. Because routers do not forward broadcast frames, broadcast domains are typically bounded by routers.

broadcast frames   One network device sends out information packets to all the devices on a segment. This traffic is ineffective, as every device needs time to analyze the received packet, generating increased CPU utilization on every device and reducing network performance. Unfortunately, this type of traffic is necessary for some network applications. Address Resolution Protocol (ARP), Routing Information Protocol (RIP), version 1, and Microsoft Windows Logon Request are examples of broadcast traffic.

broadcast storms   A broadcast storm is an incorrect packet flow or an excessive transmission of broadcast traffic. It happens when a broadcast across a network causes most hosts to respond all at once with each response resulting in even more responses. If network traffic reaches near 100 percent of the available bandwidth, all network traffic can be blocked.

buffer   A memory storage area used for handling data in transit. Buffers are used in internetworking to compensate for differences in processing speed between network devices or signaling rates of segments. Bursts of packets can be stored in buffers until they can be handled by slower devices.

bus   Common physical path composed of wires or other media, across which signals are sent from one part of a computer to another.

byte   A series of consecutive binary digits that are operated upon as a unit, usually eight bits.

cable   Transmission medium of copper wire or optical fiber wrapped in a protective cover.

cable range   A range of network numbers on an extended AppleTalk network. The cable range value can be a single network number or a contiguous sequence of several network numbers. Nodes assign addresses within the cable range values provided.

carrier   Electromagnetic wave or alternating current of a single frequency, suitable for modulation by another, data-bearing signal.

Carrier Detect (CD)   Signal that indicates whether an interface is active.

Category 5 cabling   One of five grades of UTP cabling described in the EIA/TIA-586 standard. Category 5 cabling can transmit data at speeds up to 100 Mbps.

CCITT   *See* Consultative Committee for International Telegraphy and Telephony.

CD   *See* Carrier Detect.

CDP   *See* Cisco Discovery Protocol.

cell   The basic data unit for ATM switching and multiplexing. A cell consists of a five-byte header and 48 bytes of payload. Cells contain fields in their headers that identify the data stream to which they belong.

CGMP   *See* Cisco Group Management Protocol.

Channel Service Unit (CSU)   Digital interface device that connects end-user equipment to the local digital telephone loop. Often referred to together with DSU, as CSU/DSU.

checksum   Method for checking the integrity of transmitted data. A checksum is an integer value computed from a sequence of octets taken through a series of arithmetic operations. The value is recomputed at the receiving end and compared for verification.

CIDR   *See* Classless Interdomain Routing.

CIR   *See* Committed Information Rate.

circuit switching   A system in which a dedicated physical path must exist between sender and receiver for the entire duration of a call. Used heavily in telephone networks.

Cisco Discovery Protocol (CDP)   CDP was developed by Cisco as a tool for all Cisco products (routers and switches) to communicate with each other to gain detailed network topology information. Switches that are running CDP communicate with each other to learn and understand the network topology. CDP is built into the IOS software and is available on the Catalyst 1900 switch, even though it does not run IOS. CDP is available on the Catalyst 1900 series switches starting with software release version 5.

Cisco Group Management Protocol (CGMP)   CGMP was developed to prevent flooding of multicast packets to all ports in a VLAN. The 1900 uses CGMP to communicate with Cisco routers to identify clients that are receiving multicast packets. The routers gather this Layer 3 information via the Internet Group Management Protocol (IGMP) from other routers in the network. With this information, the switch uses the forwarding engine to send these multicast packets only to the ports to which the destination clients are connected. CGMP allows for close communication between Catalysts and Cisco routers to handle the needs of Layer 3 and multicast information. This is a feature not found on other vendors' routers and switches.

Classless Interdomain Routing (CIDR)   Technique supported by BGP4 and based on route aggregation. CIDR allows routers to group routes together in order to cut down on the quantity of routing information carried by the core routers. With CIDR, several IP networks appear to networks outside the group as a single, larger entity. With CIDR, IP addresses and their subnet masks are written as four octets, separated by periods, followed by a forward slash and a two-digit number that represents the subnet mask.

client   Node or software program or front-end device that requests services from a server.

collision   In an ethernet, the result of two nodes transmitting simultaneously. The frames from each device cause an increase in voltage when they meet on the physical media, and are damaged.

Committed Information Rate (CIR)   The rate at which a Frame Relay network agrees to transfer information under normal conditions, averaged over a minimum increment of time. CIR, measured in bits per second, is one of the key negotiated tariff metrics.

congestion   Traffic in excess of network capacity.

connectionless   Term used to describe data transfer without the prior existence of a circuit.

console   A DTE device, usually consisting of a keyboard and display unit, through which users interact with a host.

Consultative Committee for International Telegraphy and Telephony (CCITT) International organization responsible for the development of communications standards. Now called the ITU-T.

contention Access method in which network devices compete for permission to access the physical medium. Compare with circuit switching and token passing.

cost A value, typically based on media bandwidth or other measures, that is assigned by a network administrator and used by routing protocols to compare various paths through an internetwork environment. Cost values are used to determine the most favorable path to a particular destination—the lower the cost, the better the path.

count to infinity A condition in which routers continuously increment the hop count to particular networks. Often occurs in routing algorithms that are slow to converge. Usually, some arbitrary hop count ceiling is imposed to limit the extent of this problem.

CPE *See* customer premises equipment.

CRC *See* cyclic redundancy check.

CSU *See* Channel Service Unit.

customer premises equipment (CPE) Terminating equipment, such as terminals, telephones, and modems, installed at customer sites and connected to the telephone company network.

cut-through switching Cut-through switching mode starts the forwarding process as soon as the destination address is received. It reduces the latency to 4.8 microseconds in 10-Mbps networks, the time needed to receive the six octets destination address. This mode cannot detect errored frames before the whole frame is forwarded. In this case, errored frames are discarded later by a receiving device.

cyclic redundancy check (CRC) An error-checking technique in which the receiving device performs a calculation on the frame contents and compares the calculated number to a value stored in the frame by the sending node.

data (D) channel Full-duplex, 16-Kbps (BRI) or 64-Kbps (PRI) ISDN channel.

data circuit-terminating equipment (DCE) The devices and connections of a communications network that represent the network end of the user-to-network interface. The DCE provides a physical connection to the network and provides a clocking signal used to synchronize transmission between DCE and DTE devices. Modems and interface cards are examples of DCE devices.

Data Network Identification Code (DNIC)   Part of an X.121 address. DNICs are divided into two parts: the first specifying the country in which the addressed PSN is located and the second specifying the PSN itself.

Data Terminal Equipment (DTE)   Device at the user end of a user-network interface that serves as a data source, destination, or both. DTE connects to a data network through a DCE device (for example, a modem) and typically uses clocking signals generated by the DCE. DTE includes such devices as computers, routers and multiplexers.

datagram   Logical unit of information sent as a Network layer unit over a transmission medium without prior establishment of a circuit.

Data-Link Connection Identifier (DLCI)   A value that specifies a virtual circuit in a Frame Relay network.

Data-Link layer   Layer 2 of the OSI reference model. This layer provides reliable transit of data across a physical link. The Data-Link layer is concerned with physical addressing, network topology, access to the network medium, error detection, sequential delivery of frames, and flow control. The Data-Link layer is divided into two sublayers: the MAC sublayer and the LLC sublayer.

DCE   *See* data circuit-terminating equipment.

DDR   *See* dial-on-demand routing.

de facto standard   A standard that exists because of its widespread use.

de jure standard   Standard that exists because of its development or approval by an official standards body.

DECnet   Group of communications products (including a protocol suite) developed and supported by Digital Equipment Corporation. DECnet/OSI (also called DECnet Phase V) is the most recent iteration and supports both OSI protocols and proprietary Digital protocols. Phase IV Prime supports inherent MAC addresses that allow DECnet nodes to coexist with systems running other protocols that have MAC address restrictions.

dedicated line   Communications line that is indefinitely reserved for transmissions, rather than switched as transmission is required.

default route   A routing table entry that is used to direct packets when there is no explicit route present in the routing table.

delay   The time between the initiation of a transaction by a sender and the first response received by the sender. Also, the time required to move a packet from source to destination over a network path.

demarc   The demarcation point between telephone carrier equipment and CPE.

demultiplexing   The separating of multiple streams of data that have been multiplexed into a common physical signal for transmission, back into multiple output streams. Opposite of multiplexing.

destination address   Address of a network device to receive data.

DHCP   *See* Dynamic Host Configuration Protocol.

dial-on-demand routing (DDR)   Technique whereby a router can automatically initiate and close a circuit-switched session as transmitting stations demand. The router spoofs keepalives so that end stations treat the session as active. DDR permits routing over ISDN or telephone lines using an external ISDN terminal adapter or modem.

Discovery mode   Method by which an AppleTalk router acquires information about an attached network from an operational router and then uses this information to configure its own addressing information.

distance vector routing algorithm   Class of routing algorithms that use the number of hops in a route to find a shortest path to a destination network. Distance vector routing algorithms call for each router to send its entire routing table in each update to each of its neighbors. Also called Bellman-Ford routing algorithm.

DLCI   *See* Data-Link Connection Identifier.

DNIC   *See* Data Network Identification Code.

DNS   *See* Domain Name System.

Domain Name System (DNS)   System used in the Internet for translating names of network nodes into addresses.

DTE   *See* Data Terminal Equipment.

Dynamic Host Configuration Protocol (DHCP)   Provides a mechanism for allocating IP addresses dynamically so that addresses can be reassigned instead of belonging to only one host.

dynamic routing   Routing that automatically adjusts to changes in network topology or traffic patterns.

E1   Wide-area digital transmission scheme used in Europe that carries data at a rate of 2.048 Mbps.

Electronics Industries Association/Telecommunications Industry Association 232 (EIA/TIA-232)   Common Physical layer interface standard, developed by EIA and TIA, that supports unbalanced circuits at signal speeds of up to 64 Kbps. Formerly known as RS-232.

encapsulation   The process of attaching a particular protocol header to a unit of data prior to transmission on the network. For example, a frame of Ethernet data is given a specific Ethernet header before network transit.

end point   Device at which a virtual circuit or virtual path begins or ends.

Enterprise network   A privately maintained network connecting most major points in a company or other organization. Usually spans a large geographic area and supports multiple protocols and services.

entity   Generally, an individual, manageable network device. Sometimes called an alias.

error control   Technique for detecting and correcting errors in data transmissions.

EtherChannel   EtherChannel makes combinations of a few physical links into one logical link possible. EtherChannel enables you to establish advancing speed links without incorporating another technology. It gives you some link speed scaling options by effectively merging or bundling the Fast Ethernet or Gigabit Ethernet links and making a switch or a router use the merged ports as a single port.

Ethernet   Baseband LAN specification invented by Xerox Corporation and developed jointly by Xerox, Intel, and Digital Equipment Corporation. Ethernet networks use the CSMA/CD method of media access control and run over a variety of cable types at 10 Mbps. Ethernet is similar to the IEEE 802.3 series of standards.

EtherTalk   Apple Computer's data-link product that allows an AppleTalk network to be connected by Ethernet cable.

Explorer packet   Generated by an end station trying to find its way through a SRB network. Gathers a hop-by-hop description of a path through the network by being marked (updated) by each bridge that it traverses, thereby creating a complete topological map.

Fast Ethernet   Any of a number of 100-Mbps Ethernet specifications. Fast Ethernet offers a speed increase ten times that of the 10BaseT Ethernet specification, while preserving such qualities as frame format, MAC mechanisms, and MTU. Such similarities allow the use of existing 10BaseT applications and network management tools on Fast Ethernet networks. Based on an extension to the IEEE 802.3 specification.

FDDI   *See* Fiber-Distributed Data Interface.

FECN   *See* Forward Explicit Congestion Notification.

Fiber-Distributed Data Interface (FDDI)   LAN standard, defined by ANSI X3T9.5, specifying a 100-Mbps token-passing network using fiber-optic cable, with transmission distances of up to 2 km. FDDI uses a dual-ring architecture to provide redundancy.

file transfer   Category of popular network applications that features movement of files from one network device to another.

File Transfer Protocol (FTP)   An application protocol, part of the TCP/IP protocol stack, used for transferring files between hosts on a network.

filter   Generally, a process or device that screens network traffic for certain characteristics, such as source address, destination address, or protocol, and determines whether to forward or discard that traffic or routes based on the established criteria.

firewall   Router or other computer designated as a buffer between public networks and a private network. A firewall router uses access lists and other methods to ensure the security of the private network.

Flash memory   Non-volatile storage that can be electrically erased and reprogrammed as necessary.

Flash update   Routing update sent asynchronously when a change in the network topology occurs.

flat addressing   A system of addressing that does not incorporate a hierarchy to determine location.

flooding   Traffic-passing technique used by switches and bridges in which traffic received on an interface is sent out all of the interfaces of that device except the interface on which the information was originally received.

flow control   Technique for ensuring that a transmitting device, such as a modem, does not overwhelm a receiving device with data. When the buffers on the receiving device are full, a message is sent to the sending device to suspend transmission until it has processed the data in the buffers.

Forward Explicit Congestion Notification (FECN)   A facility in a Frame Relay network to inform DTE receiving the frame that congestion was experienced in the path from source to destination. DTE receiving frames with the FECN bit set can request that higher-level protocols take flow-control action as appropriate.

forwarding   The process of sending a frame or packet toward its destination.

fragment   Piece of a larger packet that has been broken down to smaller units.

fragment-free switching   Fragment-free switching mode combines some of the best qualities of cut-through and store-and-forward switching. Like the cut-through, it does not wait until the entire frame is received to start forwarding it; instead, it forwards a frame after the first 64 octets of the frame received. Analyzing the first 64 octets of a packet received, it is almost always possible to tell whether the whole packet is errored or not. So, the advantages of fragment-free switching mode are low latency and good possibility to detect errored packet in a short period of time.

fragmentation   Process of breaking a packet into smaller units when transmitting over a network medium that is unable to support a transmission unit the original size of the packet.

frame   Logical grouping of information sent as a Data-Link layer unit over a transmission medium. Sometimes refers to the header and trailer, used for synchronization and error control, which surround the user data contained in the unit. The terms cell, datagram, message, packet, and segment are also used to describe logical information groupings at various layers of the OSI reference model and in various technology circles.

Frame Filtering   Frame Filtering occurs when the source and destination reside on the same interface or occurs when a network designer manually creates a filtering table on the switch. A filtering table usually contains so-called filtering information that operates on many fields inside the data frame.

Frame Relay   Industry-standard, switched Data-Link layer protocol that handles multiple virtual circuits over a single physical interface. Frame Relay is more efficient than X.25, for which it is generally considered a replacement.

frequency   Number of cycles, measured in hertz, of an alternating current signal per unit of time.

FTP   *See* File Transfer Protocol.

full duplex   Capability for simultaneous data transmission and receipt of data between two devices.

full mesh   A network topology in which each network node has either a physical circuit or a virtual circuit connecting it to every other network node.

gateway   In the IP community, an older term referring to a routing device. Today, the term router is used to describe devices that perform this function, and gateway refers to a special-purpose device that performs an Application layer conversion of information from one protocol stack to another.

Get Nearest Server (GNS)   Request packet sent by a client on an IPX network to locate the nearest active server of a particular type. An IPX network client issues a GNS request to solicit either a direct response from a connected server or a response from a router that tells it where on the internetwork the service can be located. GNS is part of the IPX SAP.

GNS *See* Get Nearest Server.

half duplex Capability for data transmission in only one direction at a time between a sending station and a receiving station.

handshake Sequence of messages exchanged between two or more network devices to ensure transmission synchronization.

HDLC *See* High-level Data-Link Control.

header Control information placed before data when encapsulating that data for network transmission.

Hello packet Multicast packet that is used by routers for neighbor discovery and recovery. Hello packets also indicate that a client is still operating on the network.

Hello protocol Protocol used by OSPF and other routing protocols for establishing and maintaining neighbor relationships.

hierarchical addressing A scheme of addressing that uses a logical hierarchy to determine location. For example, IP addresses consist of network numbers, subnet numbers, and host numbers, which IP routing algorithms use to route the packet to the appropriate location.

High-level Data-Link Control (HDLC) Bit-oriented synchronous Data-Link layer protocol developed by ISO and derived from SDLC. HDLC specifies a data encapsulation method for synchronous serial links and includes frame characters and checksums in its headers.

holddown State of a routing table entry in which routers will neither advertise the route nor accept advertisements about the route for a specific length of time (known as the holddown period).

hop Term describing the passage of a data packet between two network nodes (for example, between two routers).

hop count Routing metric used to measure the distance between a source and a destination. RIP uses hop count as its metric.

host   A computer system on a network—similar to the term node except that host usually implies a computer system, whereas node can refer to any networked system, including routers.

host number   Part of an IP address that designates which node is being addressed. Also called a host address.

hub   A term used to describe a device that serves as the center of a star topology network; or an Ethernet multiport repeater, sometimes referred to as a concentrator.

ICMP   *See* Internet Control Message Protocol.

IEEE   *See* Institute of Electrical and Electronics Engineers.

Institute of Electrical and Electronics Engineers (IEEE)   A professional organization among whose activities are the development of communications and networking standards. IEEE LAN standards are the most common LAN standards today.

Integrated Services Digital Network (ISDN)   Communication protocol, offered by telephone companies, that permits telephone networks to carry data, voice, and other source traffic.

interface   A connection between two systems or devices; or in routing terminology, a network connection.

Interior Gateway Protocol (IGP)   A generic term for an Internet routing protocol used to exchange routing information within an autonomous system. Examples of common Internet IGPs include IGRP, OSPF, and RIP.

Internet   Term used to refer to the global internetwork that evolved from the ARPANET, that now connects tens of thousands of networks worldwide.

Internet Control Message Protocol (ICMP)   A Network layer Internet protocol that provides reports of errors and other information about IP packet processing. ICMP is documented in RFC 792.

Internet Protocol (IP)   Any protocol that is part of the TCP/IP protocol stack. It is also a Network layer protocol in the TCP/IP stack offering a connectionless datagram service. IP provides features for addressing, type-of-service specification, fragmentation and reassembly, and security. Documented in RFC 791.

Internet Protocol (IP) address   A 32-bit address assigned to hosts using the TCP/IP suite of protocols. An IP address is written as four octets separated by dots (dotted decimal format). Each address consists of a network number, an optional subnetwork number, and a host number. The network and subnetwork numbers together are used for routing, while the host number is used to address an individual host within the network or subnetwork. A subnet mask is often used with the address to extract network and subnetwork information from the IP address.

Internetwork Packet Exchange (IPX)   NetWare Network layer (Layer 3) protocol used for transferring data from servers to workstations. IPX is similar to IP in that it is a connectionless datagram service.

Internet Packet Exchange Control Protocol (IPXCP)   The protocol that establishes and configures IPX over PPP.

Internet Packet Exchange Wide Area Network (IPXWAN)   A protocol that negotiates end-to-end options for new links on startup. When a link comes up, the first IPX packets sent across are IPXWAN packets negotiating the options for the link. When the IPXWAN options have been successfully determined, normal IPX transmission begins, and no more IPXWAN packets are sent. Defined by RFC 1362.

internetwork   Collection of networks interconnected by routers and other devices that functions (generally) as a single network.

internetworking   General term used to refer to the industry that has arisen around the problem of connecting networks together. The term may be used to refer to products, procedures, and technologies.

Inverse Address Resolution Protocol (Inverse ARP)   Method of building dynamic address mappings in a Frame Relay network. Allows a device to discover the network address of a device associated with a virtual circuit.

IP   *See* Internet Protocol.

IPX   *See* Internet Packet Exchange.

IPXCP   *See* Internet Packet Exchange Control Protocol.

IPXWAN   *See* Internet Packet Exchange Wide Area Network.

ISDN   *See* Integrated Services Data Network.

keepalive interval   Period of time between keepalive messages sent by a network device.

keepalive message   Message sent by one network device to inform another network device that it is still active.

LAN   *See* local area network.

LANE   *See* local area network emulation.

LAPB   *See* Link Access Procedure, Balanced.

LAPD   *See* Link Access Procedure on the D channel.

latency   The amount of time elapsed between the time a device requests access to a network and the time it is allowed to transmit; or, amount of time between the point at which a device receives a frame and the time that frame is forwarded out the destination port.

leased line   Transmission line reserved by a communications carrier for the private use of a customer. A leased line is a type of dedicated line.

link   Network communications channel consisting of a circuit or transmission path and all related equipment between a sender and a receiver. Most often used to refer to a WAN connection. Sometimes called a line or a transmission link.

Link Access Procedure, Balanced (LAPB)   The Data-Link layer protocol in the X.25 protocol stack. LAPB is a bit-oriented protocol derived from HDLC.

Link Access Procedure on the D (LAPD) channel   ISDN Data-Link layer protocol for the D channel. LAPD was derived from the LAPB protocol and is designed to satisfy the signaling requirements of ISDN basic access. Defined by ITU-T Recommendations Q.920 and Q.921.

link-state routing algorithm   Routing algorithm in which each router broadcasts or multicasts information regarding the cost of reaching each of its neighbors to all nodes in the internetwork. Link state algorithms require that routers maintain a consistent view of the network and are therefore not prone to routing loops.

LLC   *See* Logical Link Control.

local area network (LAN)   High-speed, low-error data network covering a relatively small geographic area. LANs connect workstations, peripherals, terminals, and other devices in a single building or other geographically limited area. LAN standards specify cabling and signaling at the physical and Data-Link layers of the OSI model. Ethernet, FDDI, and token ring are the most widely used LAN technologies.

Local Area Network Emulation (LANE)   Technology that allows an ATM network to function as a LAN backbone. In this situation LANE provides multicast and broadcast support, address mapping (MAC-to-ATM), and virtual circuit management.

Logical Link Control (LLC)   Higher of two Data-Link layer sublayers defined by the IEEE. The LLC sublayer handles error control, flow control, framing, and MAC-sublayer addressing. The most common LLC protocol is IEEE 802.2, which includes both connectionless and connection-oriented types.

Local Management Interface (LMI)   A set of enhancements to the basic Frame Relay specification. LMI includes support for keepalives, a multicast mechanism; global addressing, and a status mechanism.

load balancing   In routing, the ability of a router to distribute traffic over all its network ports that are the same distance from the destination address. Load balancing increases the utilization of network segments, thus increasing total effective network bandwidth.

local loop   A line from the premises of a telephone subscriber to the telephone company central office.

LocalTalk   Apple Computer's proprietary baseband protocol that operates at the data-link and Physical layers of the OSI reference model. LocalTalk uses CSMA/CA and supports transmissions at speeds of 230.4 Kbps.

loop   A situation in which packets never reach their destination, but are forwarded in a cycle repeatedly through a group of network nodes.

MAC   *See* Media Access Control.

LAN   *See* local area network.

MAN *See* metropolitan area network.

media The various physical environments through which transmission signals pass. Common network media include cable (twisted-pair, coaxial, and fiber optic) and the atmosphere (through which microwave, laser, and infrared transmission occurs). Sometimes referred to as physical media.

Media Access Control (MAC) Lower of the two sublayers of the Data-Link layer defined by the IEEE. The MAC sublayer handles access to shared media.

Media Access Control (MAC) address Standardized Data-Link layer address that is required for every port or device that connects to a LAN. Other devices in the network use these addresses to locate specific ports in the network and to create and update routing tables and data structures. MAC addresses are 48 bits long and are controlled by the IEEE. Also known as a hardware address, a MAC-layer address, or a physical address.

mesh Network topology in which devices are organized in a segmented manner with redundant interconnections strategically placed between network nodes.

message Application layer logical grouping of information, often composed of a number of lower-layer logical groupings such as packets.

metropolitan area network (MAN) A network that spans a metropolitan area. Generally, a MAN spans a larger geographic area than a LAN, but a smaller geographic area than a WAN.

modified cut-through switching Modified cut-through switching, "stores" the first 64 bytes, then forwards the packet to the destination port. Ethernet collisions cause runt frames (frames that are less than 64 bytes in length) to exist on the wire. If the arriving frame is at least 64 bytes, then it cannot be a runt. Although a proper error check cannot be performed until the Frame Check Sequence (FCS) arrives with the end of the frame, the frame is forwarded with very little additional latency.

MSAU *See* Multistation Access Unit.

Multistation Access Unit (MSAU) A wiring concentrator to which all end stations in a token ring network connect. Sometimes abbreviated MAU.

multiaccess network   A network that allows multiple devices to connect and communicate by sharing the same medium, such as a LAN.

multicast   A single packet copied by the network and sent to a specific subset of network addresses. These addresses are specified in the Destination Address field.

multicast address   A single address that refers to multiple network devices. Sometimes called a group address.

multicast frames   Sometimes it happens that one network device has to communicate with a subset of all the network devices. An example of this kind of situation is a real audio data stream that occurs when a number of people on a LAN listen to the same radio station on the Internet. Therefore, one network device communicates with a number of other network devices, which falls into a so-called multicast group. As in the case of broadcast traffic, one device communicates with a number of other devices, but here the communication is processed only among the select devices that really need to be part of this communication. Real Audio and Real Video applications are the examples of this type of traffic.

multiplexing   A technique that allows multiple logical signals to be transmitted simultaneously across a single physical channel.

mux   A multiplexing device. A mux combines multiple input signals for transmission over a single line. The signals are demultiplexed, or separated, before they are used at the receiving end.

NAK   *See* Negative Acknowledgment.

Name Binding Protocol (NBP)   AppleTalk Transport level protocol that translates a character string name into the DDP address of the corresponding socket client.

name resolution   The process of associating a symbolic name with a network location or address.

NAT   *See* Network Address Translation.

NBMA   *See* Nonbroadcast Multiaccess.

NBP   *See* Name Binding Protocol.

Negative Acknowledgment (NAK)　A response sent from a receiving device to a sending device indicating that the information received contained errors.

Network Address Translation (NAT)　A technique for reducing the need for globally unique IP addresses. NAT allows an organization with addresses may conflict with others in the IP address space, to connect to the Internet by translating those addresses into unique ones within the globally routable address space.

Network Basic Input/Output System (NetBIOS)　An application programming interface used by applications on an IBM LAN to request services from lower-level network processes such as session establishment and termination, and information transfer.

NetWare　A network operating system developed by Novell, Inc. Provides remote file access, print services, and numerous other distributed network services.

network　Collection of computers, printers, routers, switches, and other devices that are able to communicate with each other over some transmission medium.

network interface　Border between a carrier network and a privately-owned installation.

Network layer　Layer 3 of the OSI reference model. This layer provides connectivity and path selection between two end systems. The Network layer is the layer at which routing takes place.

NetWare Link Services Protocol (NLSP)　Link-state routing protocol for IPX based on IS-IS.

NLSP　*See* NetWare Link Services Protocol.

node　Endpoint of a network connection or a junction common to two or more lines in a network. Nodes can be processors, controllers, or workstations. Nodes, which vary in their functional capabilities, can be interconnected by links, and serve as control points in the network.

Nonbroadcast Multiaccess (NBMA)　Term describing a multiaccess network that either does not support broadcasting (such as X.25) or in which broadcasting is not feasible.

non-volatile RAM (NVRAM)   RAM that retains its contents when a device is powered off.

NVRAM   *See* non-volatile RAM.

Open System Interconnection (OSI) reference model   A network architectural framework developed by ISO and ITU-T. The model describes seven layers, each of which specifies a particular network. The lowest layer, called the Physical layer, is closest to the media technology. The highest layer, the Application layer, is closest to the user. The OSI reference model is widely used as a way of understanding network functionality.

OSI   *See* Open System Interconnection.

out-of-band signaling   Transmission using frequencies or channels outside the frequencies or channels used for transfer of normal data. Out-of-band signaling is often used for error reporting when normal channels are unusable for communicating with network devices.

packet   Logical grouping of information that includes a header containing control information and (usually) user data. Packets are most often used to refer to Network layer units of data. The terms datagram, frame, message, and segment are also used to describe logical information groupings at various layers of the OSI reference model, and in various technology circles.

partial mesh   Term describing a network in which devices are organized in a mesh topology, with some network nodes organized in a full mesh, but with others that are only connected to one or two other nodes in the network. A partial mesh does not provide the level of redundancy of a full mesh topology, but is less expensive to implement. Partial mesh topologies are generally used in the peripheral networks that connect to a fully meshed backbone.

packet Internet groper (PING)   ICMP echo message and its reply. Often used in IP networks to test the reachability of a network device.

PING   *See* packer Internet groper.

poison reverse updates   Routing updates that explicitly indicate that a network or subnet is unreachable, rather than implying that a network is unreachable by not including it in updates. Poison reverse updates are sent to defeat large routing loops.

port   Interface on an internetworking device (such as a router). In IP terminology, an upper-layer process that receives information from lower layers. Ports are numbered, and each numbered port is associated with a specific process. For example, SMTP is associated with port 25. A port number is also known as a well-known address. To rewrite software or microcode so that it will run on a different hardware platform or in a different software environment than that for which it was originally designed.

Point-to-Point Protocol (PPP)   A successor to SLIP that provides router-to-router and host-to-network connections over synchronous and asynchronous circuits. Whereas SLIP was designed to work with IP, PPP was designed to work with several Network layer protocols, such as IP, IPX, and ARA. PPP also has built-in security mechanisms, such as CHAP and PAP. PPP relies on two protocols: LCP and NCP.

PortFast   PortFast is a technique specially created to optimize operation of switch ports connected to end-station devices such as workstations, notebooks, printers, and servers. Use of PortFast allows these devices to get instant access to the Layer 2 network. PortFast works by making a simple change in the STP process. Instead of starting out at the bottom of the blocking-to-forwarding hierarchy of states as normal STP, PortFast starts right at the top. A switch spends only two seconds in listening and learning modes, and then the port is placed in the forwarding state. If a switch detects a loop later, the device makes all of the root and designated port calculations. If a loop is found, the port is put into the blocking state.

POST   *See* power on self test.

power on self test (POST)   The POST is a series of 13 tests that check on the status of the components of the switch. It is important to understand the results of these tests, as they will indicate if your switch is functional or not.

PPP   *See* Point-to-Point Protocol.

Presentation layer   Layer 6 of the OSI reference model. This layer ensures that information sent by the Application layer of one system will be readable by the Application layer of another. The Presentation layer is also concerned with the data structures used by programs and therefore negotiates data transfer syntax for the Application layer.

PRI   *See* Primary Rate Interface.

Primary Rate Interface (PRI)   ISDN interface to primary rate access. Primary rate access consists of a single 64-Kbps D channel plus 23 (T1) or 30 (E1) B channels for voice or data.

protocol   Formal description of a set of rules and conventions that govern how devices on a network exchange information.

protocol stack   Set of related communications protocols that operate together and, as a group, address communication at some or all of the seven layers of the OSI reference model. Not every protocol stack covers each layer of the model, and often a single protocol in the stack will address a number of layers at once. TCP/IP is a typical protocol stack.

Proxy Address Resolution Protocol (Proxy ARP)   Variation of the ARP protocol in which an intermediate device (for example, a router) sends an ARP response on behalf of an end node to the requesting host. Proxy ARP can lessen bandwidth use on slow-speed WAN links.

query   Message used to inquire about the value of some variable or set of variables.

queue   A backlog of packets stored in buffers which are waiting to be forwarded over a router interface.

RAM   *See* random access memory.

random access memory (RAM)   Volatile memory that can be read and written by a computer.

read-only memory (ROM)   Non-volatile memory that can be read, but not written, by the computer.

reassembly   The putting back together of an IP datagram at the destination after it has been fragmented either at the source or at an intermediate node.

reload   The event of a Cisco router rebooting, or the command that causes the router to reboot.

Request for Comments (RFC)   Document series used as the primary means for communicating information about the Internet. Some RFCs are designated by the IAB as Internet standards.

RFC   *See* Request for Comments.

ring   Connection of two or more stations in a logically circular topology. Information is passed sequentially between active stations. Token ring, FDDI, and CDDI are based on this topology.

ring topology   Network topology that consists of a series of repeaters connected to one another by unidirectional transmission links to form a single closed loop. Each station on the network connects to the network at a repeater.

RIP   *See* Routing Information Protocol.

ROM   *See* read-only memory.

routed protocol   Protocol that carries user data so it can be routed by a router. A router must be able to interpret the logical internetwork as specified by that routed protocol. Examples of routed protocols include AppleTalk, DECnet, and IP.

router   Network layer device that uses one or more metrics to determine the optimal path along which network traffic should be forwarded. Routers forward packets from one network to another based on Network layer information.

routing   Process of finding a path to a destination host.

Routing Information Protocol (RIP)   A routing protocol for TCP/IP networks. The most common routing protocol in the Internet. RIP uses hop count as a routing metric.

routing metric   Method by which a routing algorithm determines preferability of one route over another. This information is stored in routing tables. Metrics include bandwidth, communication cost, delay, hop count, load, MTU, path cost, and reliability. Sometimes referred to simply as a metric.

routing protocol   Protocol that accomplishes routing through the implementation of a specific routing algorithm. Examples of routing protocols include IGRP, OSPF, and RIP.

routing table   Table stored in a router or some other internetworking device that keeps track of routes to particular network destinations and, in some cases, metrics associated with those routes.

routing update   Message sent from a router to indicate network reachability and associated cost information. Routing updates are typically sent at regular intervals and after a change in network topology. Compare with flash update.

SAP   *See* Service Access Point; Service Advertising Protocol.

segment   Section of a network that is bounded by bridges, routers, or switches.

In a LAN using a bus topology, a segment is a continuous electrical circuit that is often connected to other such segments with repeaters.

Term used in the TCP specification to describe a single Transport layer unit of information.

Sequenced Packet Exchange (SPX)   Reliable, connection-oriented protocol at the Transport layer that supplements the datagram service provided by IPX.

serial transmission   Method of data transmission in which the bits of a data character are transmitted sequentially over a single channel. Compare with parallel transmission.

Service Access Point (SAP)   Field defined by the IEEE 802.2 specification that is part of an address specification. Thus, the destination plus the DSAP define the recipient of a packet. The same applies to the SSAP.

Service Advertising Protocol (SAP)   IPX protocol that provides a means of informing network routers and servers of the location of available network resources and services.

session   Related set of communications transactions between two or more network devices. In SNA, a logical connection that enables two NAUs to communicate.

Session layer   Layer 5 of the OSI reference model. This layer establishes, manages, and terminates sessions between applications and manages data exchange between Presentation layer entities. Corresponds to the data flow control layer of the SNA model.

Shortest Path First (SPF) algorithm   Routing algorithm that sorts routes by length of path to determine a shortest-path spanning tree. Commonly used in link-state routing algorithms. Sometimes called Dijkstra's algorithm.

Simple Network Management Protocol (SNMP)   Network management protocol used almost exclusively in TCP/IP networks. SNMP provides a means to monitor and control network devices, and to manage configurations, statistics collection, performance, and security.

sliding window flow control   Method of flow control in which a receiver gives a transmitter permission to transmit data until a window is full. When the window is full, the transmitter must stop transmitting until the receiver acknowledges some of the data, or advertises a larger window. TCP, other transport protocols, and several Data-Link layer protocols use this method of flow control.

SNAP   *See* Subnetwork Access Protocol.

SNMP   *See* Simple Network Management Protocol.

socket   Software structure operating as a communications end point within a network device.

SONET   *See* Synchronous Optical Network.

source address   An address of a network device that is sending data.

Spanning-Tree   Loop-free subset of a network topology.

Spanning-Tree Protocol (STP)   Developed to eliminate loops in the network. The STP ensures a loop-free path by placing one of the bridge ports in "blocking mode," preventing the forwarding of packets.

SPF   *See* Shortest Path First.

split horizon updates   Routing technique in which information about routes is prevented from being advertised out the router interface through which that information was received. Split-horizon updates are used to prevent routing loops.

SPX   *See* Sequenced Packet Exchange.

standard   Set of rules or procedures that are either widely used or officially specified.

star topology   LAN topology in which end points on a network are connected to a common central switch by point-to-point links. A ring topology that is organized as a star implements a unidirectional closed-loop star, instead of point-to-point links.

static route   Route that is explicitly configured and entered into the routing table. Static routes take precedence over routes chosen by dynamic routing protocols.

store-and-forward switching   Store-and-forward switching mode receives the complete frame first, and only after that starts the switching process. When the entire frame is received the switch detects its source and destination addresses and applies specially created filters to modify the default forwarding. If any errors are detected, the frame is discarded. This mode prevents errored frames from slowing down the network. The store-and-forward switching can be the best choice for a network experiencing a high rate of frame alignment or FCS errors. However, this mode is only a temporary solution here. The real solution will be to fix the cause of errors.

STP   *See* Spanning-Tree Protocol.

subinterface   A virtual interface defined as a logical subdivision of a physical interface.

subnet address   Portion of an IP address that is specified as the subnetwork by the subnet mask.

subnet mask   32-bit address mask used in IP to indicate the bits of an IP address that are being used for the subnet address. Sometimes referred to simply as mask. *See* also address mask and IP address.

subnetwork   In IP networks, a network sharing a particular subnet address.

Subnetworks are networks arbitrarily segmented by a network administrator in order to provide a multilevel, hierarchical routing structure while shielding the subnetwork from the addressing complexity of attached networks. Sometimes called a subnet.

Subnetwork Access Protocol (SNAP)   Internet protocol that operates between a network entity in the subnetwork and a network entity in the end system. SNAP specifies a standard method of encapsulating IP datagrams and ARP messages on IEEE networks.

switch   Network device that filters, forwards, and floods frames based on the destination address of each frame. The switch operates at the Data-Link layer of the OSI model.

General term applied to an electronic or mechanical device that allows a connection to be established as necessary and terminated when there is no longer a session to support.

Synchronous Optical Network (SONET)   High-speed synchronous network specification developed by Bellcore and designed to run on optical fiber.

T1   Digital WAN carrier facility. T1 transmits DS-1-formatted data at 1.544 Mbps through the telephone-switching network, using AMI or B8ZS coding.

TCP   *See* Transmission Control Protocol.

TCP/IP   *See* Transmission Control Protocol/Internet Protocol.

throughput   Rate of information arriving at, and possibly passing through, a particular point in a network system.

timeout   Event that occurs when one network device expects to hear from another network device within a specified period of time, but does not. A timeout usually results in a retransmission of information or the termination of the session between the two devices.

token   Frame that contains only control information. Possession of the token allows a network device to transmit data onto the network.

Token Ring   Token-passing LAN developed and supported by IBM. Token Ring runs at 4 or 16 Mbps over a ring topology. Similar to IEEE 802.5.

TokenTalk   Apple Computer's data-link product that allows an AppleTalk network to be connected by Token Ring cables.

Transmission Control Protocol (TCP)   Connection-oriented Transport layer protocol that provides reliable full-duplex data transmission. TCP is part of the TCP/IP protocol stack.

Transmission Control Protocol/Internet Protocol (TCP/IP)   Common name for the suite of protocols developed by the U.S. DoD in the 1970s to support the construction of worldwide internetworks. TCP and IP are the two best-known protocols in the suite.

Transport layer   Layer 4 of the OSI reference model. This layer is responsible for reliable network communication between end nodes. The Transport layer provides mechanisms for the establishment, maintenance, and termination of virtual circuits, transport fault detection and recovery, and information flow control.

twisted pair   Relatively low-speed transmission medium consisting of two insulated wires arranged in a regular spiral pattern. The wires can be shielded or unshielded. Twisted-pair is common in telephony applications and is increasingly common in data networks.

UDP   *See* User Datagram Protocol.

unicast frames   This type of traffic occurs when one network device communicates with another network device. It is the most commonly used type of traffic with FTP, Web, and Telnet being examples of this.

User Datagram Protocol (UDP)   Connectionless Transport layer protocol in the TCP/IP protocol stack. UDP is a simple protocol that exchanges datagrams without acknowledgments or guaranteed delivery, requiring that error processing and retransmission be handled by other protocols. UDP is defined in RFC 768.

Unshielded Twisted Pair (UTP)   Four-pair wire medium used in a variety of networks. UTP does not require the fixed spacing between connections that is necessary with coaxial-type connections.

UplinkFast   UplinkFast is a proprietary Cisco feature that allows wiring closet switches to converge in two to three seconds. UplinkFast is designed to operate only on switches that are end-nodes. If enabled in the core of a network, it generally leads to unexpected traffic flows. UplinkFast is a useful and effective feature. It provides much faster convergence than any of the timer tuning techniques and is much safer. When used only on end-node switches, it increases the possibility of maintaining the safety of STP, while improving failover times in most situations.

UTP   *See* unshielded twisted pair.

variable-length subnet masking (VLSM)   Ability to specify a different length subnet mask for the same network number at different locations in the network. VLSM can help optimize available address space.

virtual circuit   Logical circuit created to ensure reliable communication between two network devices. A virtual circuit is defined by a VPI/VCI pair, and can be either permanent or switched. Virtual circuits are used in Frame Relay and X.25. In ATM, a virtual circuit is called a virtual channel. Sometimes abbreviated VC.

virtual local area network (VLAN)   Group of devices on one or more LANs that are configured (using management software) so that they can communicate as if they were attached to the same wire, when in fact they are located on a number of different LAN segments. Because VLANs are based on logical instead of physical connections, they are extremely flexible.

VLAN   *See* virtual local area network.

VLSM   *See* variable-length subnet masking.

WAN   *See* wide area network.

wide area network (WAN)   Data communications network that serves users across a broad geographic area and often uses transmission devices provided by common carriers. Frame Relay, SMDS, and X.25 are examples of WANs. Compare with LAN and MAN.

wildcard mask   32-bit quantity used in conjunction with an IP address to determine which bits in an IP address should be matched and ignored when comparing that address with another IP address. A wildcard mask is specified when defining access list statements.

X.21   ITU-T standard for serial communications over synchronous digital lines. The X.21 protocol is used primarily in Europe and Japan.

X.25   ITU-T standard that defines how connections between DTE and DCE are maintained for remote terminal access and computer communications in public data networks. X.25 specifies LAPB, a Data-Link layer protocol, and PLP, a Network layer protocol. Frame Relay has to some degree superseded X.25.

X.121   ITU-T standard describing an addressing scheme used in X.25 networks. X.121 addresses are sometimes called IDNs (International Data Numbers).

zone   In AppleTalk, a logical group of network devices.